The Development of the Right to Property in the European Convention on Human Rights

Interdisciplinary Studies on the Council of Europe and Its Conventions

VOLUME 1

The titles published in this series are listed at *brill.com/isce*

The Development of the Right to Property in the European Convention on Human Rights

By

Henrik Jorem

BRILL | NIJHOFF

LEIDEN | BOSTON

Library of Congress Cataloging-in-Publication Data

Names: Jorem, Henrik, author.
Title: The development of the right to property in the European Convention on Human Rights / Henrik Jorem.
Description: Leiden ; Boston : Brill Academic Publishers, Inc., 2025. | Series: ISCE, 2950-3612 ; 1 | Includes bibliographical references and index. |
Identifiers: LCCN 2025024539 | ISBN 9789004710153 (hardback) | ISBN 9789004735088 (pdf)
Subjects: LCSH: Right of property–European UNion countries. | Convention for the Protection of Human Rights and Fundamental Freedoms (1950 November 5)
Classification: LCC KJE1261 .J67 2025 | DDC 346.2404/32–dc23/eng/20250522
LC record available at https://lccn.loc.gov/2025024539

Typeface for the Latin, Greek, and Cyrillic scripts: "Brill". See and download: brill.com/brill-typeface.

ISSN 2950-3612
ISBN 978-90-04-71015-3 (hardback)
ISBN 978-90-04-73508-8 (e-book)
DOI 10.1163/9789004735088

This book is printed on acid-free paper and produced in a sustainable manner.

[T]hese rights arose as a reaction to devastation and dictatorship. The generation to which I belong knows this situation and has personal experience of it. But the Convention has become more than a reaction… As it began to make its presence felt in our everyday life, it became a yardstick for our civilisation. As long as we are capable of preserving freedom, we ought not to shrink from fleshing out the Convention with positive life in all its aspects.

JUDGE HERMAN MOSLER

The Fifth ECHR Colloquy, Frankfurt 1980

Contents

PART 3

Series Editors' Preface

'The Development of the Right to Property in the European Convention on Human Rights' by Henrik Jorem is the first monograph in the new book series 'Interdisciplinary Studies on the Council of Europe and Its Conventions'. The aim of this series is to provide rigorous and innovative scholarly contributions on the principles, values, conventions of the Council of Europe from various perspectives: legal, historical, philosophical, sociological.

Unsurprisingly, the inaugural volume examines the legal framework of perhaps the most celebrated and extensively researched Council of Europe treaty – the European Convention on Human Rights. However, when the Convention was drafted the right to property was deemed to be too controversial to be included in the main text and was instead incorporated into its first Additional Protocol.

The history of last seventy years in Europe has clearly shown the fundamental role played by the right to property in the construction of an effective space for the protection of human rights within European countries, their democracies and rule of law, and in the social and economic development of the continent. This has been true both with regard to the Western European countries characterised by a free economy since the end of World War II and the Eastern European countries that embraced it after the fall of the Berlin Wall.

This monograph explores the development of the European Court of Human Rights' (ECtHR or the Court) case law on the right to property. The author begins with the premise that the Court has expanded the initial scope of this provision and undertakes a meticulous analysis of this claim. The author does this by clearly setting the background of the Court's approach to interpretation of the Convention including such fundamental concepts as the principle of effectiveness, autonomous interpretation of the Convention and others.

The monograph then examines the elements of the right to property and how the ECtHR has developed its jurisprudence on various aspects of Article 1 of Protocol 1 over the years. This analysis explores the types of property covered by the provision, potential limitations, and the justifications available for such restrictions. Offering a detailed examination of the Court's approach, this monograph serves as a comprehensive study of the right to property under the European Convention on Human Rights.

While the descriptive part of the monograph clarifies the nature of the right to property, its key analytical contribution lies in exploring the evolution of the Court's approach to the rights enshrined in the European Convention on Human Rights. The right to property serves as a particularly useful case study in this regard. Given its nature, the right to property allows for a relatively broad margin of discretion for states, meaning much of the Court's jurisprudential development could be perceived as an unjustified intervention in the sovereign domain of the Convention's Contracting Parties. The author examines this tension by analysing a wide array of judgments delivered by the Court over the years.

In sum, the book is a valuable contribution to the legal scholarship examining the Court's approach to the right to property. It will be of great utility to the researchers dealing with property rights but equally it will be useful to lawyers who are applying the law of the European Convention on Human Rights in their legal practice.

Kanstantsin Dzehtsiarou and Michele Nicoletti

Acknowledgements

This book is based on my PhD dissertation, which I submitted to the Faculty of Law at the University of Bergen, Norway, on 30 June 2023, and which I defended in public on 27 October 2023. I have sought to take account of relevant case law and literature available as of the date of publication.

In many ways, my education came full circle with the completion of my PhD. It began with studies in Russian language and culture in the Norwegian armed forces. As a student of international relations and history at the London School of Economics, I was introduced to the political institutions set up in Europe after the Second World War. An elective course in public international law inspired me to study law in Norway, and my subsequent work as a lawyer in private practice made me curious about the protection of the right to property in international human rights law.

The years I spent writing have witnessed the first signs of an unravelling of the post-Cold War international order. In March 2022, Russia was expelled from the Council of Europe after its invasion of Ukraine. This historic development makes it all the more important to understand the values and ideals that the European Convention on Human Rights exists to promote.

Many deserve thanks for helping me through the writing process. My supervisors Jørgen Aall and Marius Emberland encouraged me for many years to pursue a PhD, and continued to do so during the long haul of rewriting and editing. I received valuable assistance from colleagues and students at the Faculty of Law in Bergen, including Emilie Hestnes and Eline Fosse. Hallvard Sund and Peter Hatlebakk, whose questions and insights always paved the way for new understanding, also deserve special mention. I am also grateful to Clement Endresen, Bjarte Thorson, and Eirik Bjørge for comments on the manuscript, and to Arnfinn Bårdsen for his hospitality and stimulating company during my visits to Strasbourg.

Finally, I should thank my family for their support. Pursuing a PhD in law is no ordinary job. Questions and answers kept turning up when least expected – in the car, while running or while playing with my children. If that is an occupational hazard, it surely did not help that the subject of my research is something as immanent as the right to property, one that even a two-year-old can have a relatively firm grasp of.

Turning the dissertation into a book has required further rewriting and re-reading of material. I want to thank the editors at Brill, and in particular associate editor Akiko Hakuno, for patiently allowing me to finalise the manuscript. All remaining mistakes are entirely my own.

PART 1

CHAPTER 1

Introduction

1 Jurisprudential Developments in the Right to the Peaceful Enjoyment of Property

The European Convention on Human Rights ('the ECHR' or 'the Convention') has undergone a remarkable development at the hands of the European Court of Human Rights ('the Court') during the seven decades of its existence.[1] This book concerns the right to the peaceful enjoyment of property in Article 1 of Protocol No. 1 ('Protocol 1 Article 1') to the Convention.[2] Jurisprudential developments in this area of Strasbourg law have been observed in the literature[3] as well as in the case law.[4]

What are these jurisprudential developments and how can they be explained in the context of the ECHR? These are the questions this book sets out to answer.

The Strasbourg Court's adjudicatory role in the area of property rights is controversial because it brings the Court into the realm of the domestic politics of the Member States.[5] It is worthwhile to consider how the Court has responded to the controversial issues posed by the right to property in the

1 Formally 'The Convention for the Protection of Human Rights and Fundamental Freedoms' (European Treaty Series No. 005). The ECHR was opened for signature in Rome on 4 November 1950 and came into force in 1953.

2 Protocol to the Convention for the Protection of Human Rights and Fundamental Freedoms (European Treaty Series No. 009).

3 See e.g. B Rainey, P McCormick and C Ovey, *Jacobs, White and Ovey: The European Convention on Human Rights* (8th edn, Oxford University Press 2020) 590.

4 See e.g. *Lindheim and Others v. Norway* (13221/08; 2139/10) judgment 12 June 2012, para. 135. A note on citations of case law from the Convention institutions is in order: In this book, all judgments and decisions are rendered with the names of the parties in italics – the first time in full, thereafter usually with the name of only the parties; the application number in parentheses; either 'judgment' (by the Court's chamber unless followed by [GC] to denote the Grand Chamber) or 'decision' (by the Court unless followed by [EComHR] to denote the former European Commission of Human Rights); and the date of the judgment or decision. References to the hard-copy publications (reports) have not been included for judgments and decisions which are accessible in the HUDOC database (http://hudoc.echr.coe.int). Internal references have been omitted whenever quotations from the Court's judgments or decisions are rendered in the text.

5 See e.g. J Sumption, *Trials of the State: Law and the Decline of Politics* (Profile Books 2019).

 | DOI:10.1163/9789004735088_002

context of the ECHR and justified legal protection of property rights at the international level.

Jurisprudential developments are understood here as changes in the Court's interpretation and application of the terms of Protocol 1 Article 1.[6] This working definition calls for an immediate qualification. Obviously, not every interpretative change can be accounted for. Observers of the Court agree that jurisprudential developments in ECHR law are largely driven by its teleological method of interpretation, which leads the Court to adopt the interpretation which it deems most appropriate to give effect to the object and purpose of the Convention.[7]

The Court's teleology has different aspects, which offer different explanations for the developments taking place in ECHR law. One important aspect is the principle of effective protection – that the Convention must be interpreted in a manner which ensures that rights are practical and effective, and not theoretical or illusory. The principle of effective protection generally mandates a broad interpretation of Convention's rights and freedoms on one hand, and a narrow interpretation of permissible restrictions on the other.[8]

The notion of securing effective rights is a central principle whenever Convention rights are in issue.[9] At the same time, the Court must always be mindful of the institutional setting in which it operates. When interpreting and applying the Convention, it must pay due respect to the sovereignty of the Member States, in particular in areas of law where it encroaches on internal political questions. Clearly, there are limits to how far the Court can go in the service of securing effective rights protection.

In a broader sense, the Convention's object and purpose may also be understood as the ideals and values that it exists to promote. One might say that the ECHR reflects a certain ideology which guides the Court in its interpretation of the rights and freedoms. There is a general tendency that the fundamental values underpinning the ECHR have an increasing normative impact on the Court's case law, but it is far from obvious which of these

6 As Gardiner has pointed out, in most situations the processes of interpretation and application are intertwined to the extent that it is not possible to distinguish clearly between them, see A Gardiner, *Treaty Interpretation* (2nd edn, Oxford University Press 2015) 27.

7 See e.g. F Matscher, 'Methods of Interpretation of the Convention' in R St J Macdonald et al. (eds), *The European System for the Protection of Human Rights* (Martinus Nijhoff Publishers 1993) 65.

8 R Bernhardt, 'Evolutive Treaty Interpretation, Especially of the European Convention of Human Rights' (1999) *German Yearbook of International Law* 14.

9 B Rainey, P McCormick and C Ovey (n 3) 75.

values can most aptly explain developments in the protection of property under Protocol 1 Article 1.

As already noted, the Court's teleological method of interpretation does not account for every change in the jurisprudence. As Mahoney and Mowbray have both observed, the policy of the Court is generally to make incremental changes, alongside breakthroughs in single, landmark cases.[10] The incremental developments taking place in the Court's day-to-day work are a part of this picture as well, but the premise here is that the most important developments in the case law concerning Protocol 1 Article 1 can be explained by reference to the Court's teleological method of interpretation.

2 Structure and Outline

The main objective of this book is to account for developments in the Court's case law concerning Protocol 1 Article 1 and explain these developments in light of the teleological method of interpretation introduced above. Various approaches are conceivable for achieving this objective. In legal doctrine, a distinction is drawn between two basic elements of human rights, which can provide different perspectives on how the right to property has evolved.[11]

The first element concerns the scope of rights, which determines whether the Court has jurisdiction to examine the applicant's complaint, and whether the State must advance a justification for interfering with those rights. The scope of Protocol 1 Article 1 is defined by how far the terms 'property' and 'possessions' extend, whose property rights are protected, and what characterises interference in the right to property.

The second structural element concerns the Court's justification assessment, which determines whether the right in question has been violated. As the case is with other qualified rights in the ECHR, the requirements for

---

10 P Mahoney, 'Judicial Activism and Judicial Self-Restraint in the European Court of Human Rights: Two Sides of the Same Coin' (1990) 11 *Human Rights Law Journal* 57, and A Mowbray 'The Creativity of the European Court of Human Rights' (2005) 5 *Human Rights Law Review* 61.

11 See generally J Gerards and H Senden, 'The Structure of Fundamental Rights and the European Court of Human Rights' (2009) 7 *International Journal of Constitutional Law* 619–653. The analysis pertains to the qualified rights in the Convention – understood here as articles containing limitation clauses, notably Articles 8–11, Protocol 1 Article 1, Protocol 4 Article 2 and Protocol 7 Article 2 – and not to absolute rights from which derogation is not possible, such as Article 3.

justified interference in the right to property under Protocol 1 Article 1 are normally framed as three questions: Whether the interference has been carried out in accordance with law, whether it pursues a legitimate aim and whether the State has struck a 'fair balance' between the demands of the general interest of the community and the requirements for the protection of the individual's fundamental rights.

Modelled on this two-fold structure of human rights, the book is divided into four parts. Part 1 (Chapters 1–3) provides the background, first by means of the present chapter. Chapter 2 revisits the birth of the Convention in an effort to identify the intention behind Protocol 1 Article 1. The issues which emerged during the drafting provide an important backdrop for the discussions of the developments in the Court's case law. Chapter 3 gives a more detailed presentation of the different aspects of the Court's teleological method to set the scene for the analysis in the two main parts.

Part 2 (Chapters 4–6) examines developments in Protocol 1 Article 1's scope of applicability. Chapter 4 analyses the ECHR's autonomous concept of 'possessions', which is key to the material scope. Chapter 5 deals with the article's personal scope – in other words, whose property rights are protected by the Convention. Chapter 6 discusses the characteristics of interference in the right to property and the merits of the Court's 'three rules' approach.

Protocol 1 Article 1 is one of the most frequently invoked rights in the ECHR.[12] That fact alone makes it important to understand the dynamics of the Court's justification assessment. Part 3 (Chapters 7–10) is devoted to this topic.

Chapter 7 argues that the Court must take three fundamental considerations when determining whether Protocol 1 Article 1 has been violated: it must ensure that the right to property is practical and effective (the substantive dimension), respect the sovereignty of the Member States (the institutional dimension) and safeguard the rule of law (the procedural dimension). At the justification stage, there have been developments within these three dimensions as well as in the interaction between them.

Chapter 8 accounts for developments in the substantive dimension. Recent case law reflects a heightened level of scrutiny on the part of the Court with respect to the material relationship between the interference and the

12 ECHR statistics show that violations of Protocol 1 Article 1 historically rank fourth after violations of Article 6 (length of proceedings and right to a fair trial) and Article 5 (right to liberty and security), see <https://www.echr.coe.int/Documents/Stats_violation_1959_2022_ENG.pdf> accessed 30 May 2025.

aim pursued. Chapter 9 analyses changes in the institutional dimension. The nature and intensity of the Court's review derives from the basic notion that the Court's responsibility for securing the Convention's rights and freedoms is subsidiary to that of the Contracting States. Chapter 10 discusses the emergence of a procedural dimension in the justification assessment, which is concerned with the function of Protocol 1 Article 1 as a safeguard against arbitrary interference in property rights.

Part 4 (Chapters 11 and 12) offers a few reflections. Chapter 11 summarises how the Convention's object and purpose, in particular the rule of law, has contributed to the development of the protection of property in the ECHR. Chapter 12 provides historical context for this development and reflects on the role of the rule of law in Strasbourg jurisprudence more generally.

3 Selection of Materials

There is an abundance of case law from Strasbourg concerning Protocol 1 Article 1, and a selection of materials is needed to provide for a fruitful analysis.[13] The materials chosen must be suited for documenting the developments that have taken place in the jurisprudence, and to this end, a basic understanding of the Court's interpretative method and the case law as a source of law is required.

The Court does not consider it desirable to elaborate a general theory or doctrine concerning the extent of the Convention guarantees.[14] Rather, it prefers to rely on specific formulas – essentially, interpretative statements reflecting its understanding of the legal principles – as a basis for discussing the relevant issues.[15]

In the case law concerning Protocol 1 Article 1, these 'formulas' have originated in a handful of landmark judgments, which have provided the framework within which the case law has developed. Most of the Court's landmark judgments are recognised as such in the literature, and these judgments will provide refence points for the analysis in the book. Even

13 As of 30 May 2025, the Convention organs had rendered more than 25,000 judgments and decisions in response to Protocol 1 Article 1 complaints, according to the HUDOC database.

14 See e.g. *VgT Verein gegen Tierfabriken v. Switzerland* (24699/94) judgment 28 June 2001, para. 46.

15 See A Nussberger, *The European Court of Human Rights* (Oxford University Press 2020) 73.

though some of the cases are old, the fact that they are still cited by the Court testifies to their continued relevance.

Other cases have been consulted to establish the state of the law in the time before and after the landmark judgments were handed down.[16] The analysis generally relies on judgments from the Court, either sitting as a Chamber or the Grand Chamber. Admissibility decisions as well as decisions by the former European Commission of Human Rights ('the Commission') have been included insofar as they contribute to the Court's prevailing interpretation of Protocol 1 Article 1.[17]

That said, the selection of case law is not exhaustive in the sense that every judgment and decision regarding Protocol 1 Article 1 has been reviewed. Christoffersen pointed out more than a decade ago that no claim of exhaustiveness can be made if an even remotely thorough analysis of case law is to be conducted. An adequate selection of relevant practice is sufficient.[18] Given the incessant growth in the Court's caseload, this is even more true today. Again, the objective is not to account for every change in the Court's understanding of the right to property. The aim has been to identify a sufficient number of judgments and decisions to gain a proper understanding of the most significant developments in the case law concerning Protocol 1 Article 1.

To illustrate the findings, comparisons are sometimes drawn between the Convention and other legal instruments protecting the right to property. This is done only for illustration purposes and the book is not intended to be a comparative study. In addition, the discussions draw upon mostly English-language literature about ECHR law in general and Protocol 1 Article 1 in particular.[19]

16 The landmark judgments mentioned above have been used as reference for searches in the HUDOC database.

17 As Pellonpää has pointed out, the Commission was in some ways more articulate in its dealings with the right to property than the Court, see M Pellonpää, 'The Commission's Case Law on Article 1 of Protocol No. 1' in M de Salvia and M Villiger (eds), *The Birth of European Human Rights Law: Liber Amicorum Carl Aage Nørgaard* (Nomos 1998) 165.

18 J Christoffersen, *Fair Balance: Proportionality, Subsidiarity and Primarity in the European Convention on Human Rights* (Martinus Nijhoff Publishers 2009) 29.

19 Notable contributions to the study of property rights in ECHR law include T R G van Banning, *The Human Right to Property* (Intersentia 2002), A R Çoban, *Protection of Private Property Rights Within the European Convention of Human Rights* (Ashgate 2004), T Allen, *Property and the Human Rights Act 1998* (Oxford University Press 2005), H Vandenberghe et al. (eds), *Propriété et Droits de l'Homme / Property and Human Rights* (Bruylant 2006), D Popović, *Protecting Property in European Human Rights Law*

The right to property is one of the cornerstones of national legal orders in Europe, and the theory and philosophy of property rights fill countless volumes. The scope of this book does not allow for a detailed account of the right to property as a legal concept, or its moral and philosophical justification, nor does its purported objective require it. It takes the prevailing regimes of property as given, and seeks to analyse how the right has developed in the specific context of the ECHR.

(Eleven International Publishing 2009), and D Maxwell, 'The Human Right to Property: A Practical Approach to Article 1 of Protocol No. 1 to the ECHR' (Hart Publishing 2022). A few works shed light on certain aspects of the right to property, such as A C Buyse, *Post-Conflict Housing Restitution: The European Human Rights Perspective, With a Case Study on Bosnia and Herzegovina* (Intersentia 2008) and M Sigron, *Legitimate Expectations under Article 1 of Protocol No. 1 to the European Convention on Human Rights* (Intersentia 2014). The studies mentioned will be discussed in Parts 2–4 where they are relevant.

CHAPTER 2

The Genesis of Protocol 1 Article 1

1 The Convention

For observers of the Strasbourg Court, the dynamism in the case law is so pronounced that it is easy to forget why the Convention text is written the way it is. This chapter will therefore provide a brief account of how Protocol 1 Article 1 came into being.[1] The drafting history shows that the drafters were unable to agree on a number of difficult issues, which they left to the Court to resolve. As such, the genesis of Protocol 1 Article 1 provides an important backdrop for the subsequent discussions of developments in the case law.

In May 1948, leading politicians, government representatives and members of civil society assembled in the Hague for the Congress of Europe. They resolved to draft a Charter of Human Rights, and to set up a Court of Justice supervising the implementation of the Charter. The Statute of the Council of Europe was signed on 5 May 1949 and established the new organisation's primary organs: The Committee of Ministers, which would have the power to make all important decisions, and the Consultative Assembly consisting of parliamentarians from the Member States, which would discuss matters and make recommendations to the Committee of Ministers.[2]

On 12 July 1949, the European Movement submitted a draft convention with a list of civil and political rights and freedoms to the Committee of

1 Accounts of the drafting history of Protocol 1 Article 1 are given in e.g. T Allen, *Property and the Human Rights Act 1998* (Oxford University Press 2005) 17–28, and Y Haeck, 'The Genesis of the Property Clause under Article 1 of the First Protocol to the European Convention on Human Rights', in H Vandenberghe et al. (eds), *Propriété et Droits de l'Homme / Property and Human Rights* (Bruylant 2006) 163–194, and the present chapter builds to some extent on these accounts. The birth of the European Convention on Human Rights is otherwise documented in the general literature, see in particular A W B Simpson, *Human Rights and the End of Empire* (Oxford University Press 2001) and E Bates, *The Evolution of the European Convention on Human Rights: From Its Inception to the Creation of a Permanent Court of Human Rights* (Oxford University Press 2010).

2 See Articles 15 and 22, respectively, of the Statutes of the Council of Europe (European Treaty Series 001).

 | DOI:10.1163/9789004735088_003

Ministers.[3] The list included the '[f]reedom from arbitrary deprivation of property'.[4] In August, the Consultative Assembly began work on a European Convention on Human Rights on the basis of the draft convention. The Assembly set up a Legal Affairs Committee and tasked it with formulating the rights and freedoms. The Committee's French rapporteur, Pierre-Henri Teitgen, proposed to include the right to own property 'in accordance with Article 17 of the United Nations Declaration', which reads:

> Everyone has the right to own property alone as well as in association with others.
> No one shall be arbitrarily deprived of his property.[5]

The minutes from the debates in the Consultative Assembly reveal some of the arguments that were initially advanced for and against including the right to property in the ECHR.

Those who most forcefully supported its inclusion regarded the right to own property as a God-given natural right, which guarantees the independence of the individual and the family and secures political freedom and participation. Some delegates pointed to the fact that confiscation of property was an instrument used by totalitarian States to enforce their will and to suppress their political opponents.[6]

Those who argued against including a right to property in the Convention emphasised the difficulties in agreeing on permissible restrictions. In their view, property rights were essentially a matter for domestic legislation and jurisdiction. Pointing to the fact that political opinions about property rights and their limits vary significantly with each country's economic policies, these delegates voiced concern that differences of opinion might be a

3 A platform for the coordination of the organisations created in the wake of the Second World War, the European Movement was a precursor to the Council of Europe and to the European Economic Community.

4 Council of Europe, *Collected Edition of the 'Travaux Préparatoires' of the European Convention on Human Rights / Recueil des Travaux Préparatoires de la Convention Européenne des Droits de l'Homme* (Martinus Nijhoff 1975–85) (*'Travaux Préparatoires'*) vol I Appendix, 296.

5 'Report of the Legal Committee to the Consultative Assembly' 5 September 1949. *Travaux Préparatoires* vol I, 216–235. Neither the International Covenant on Civil and Political Rights nor the International Covenant on Economic, Social and Cultural Rights, which made the Universal Declaration legally binding, make any reference to property.

6 See e.g. remarks by Arthur Sundt (Norway) in the Consultative Assembly's session on 8 September 1949. Ibid., vol II, 70.

stumbling block to getting States to ratify the Convention.[7] Delegates from socialist parties maintained that it would be unsatisfactory to include the right to property in the proposed Convention while excluding social rights such as the rights to work, to rest, and to decent living standards.[8]

Some delegates advocated for including a limited right to property in the Convention. Because property is an extension of the owner's personality, they argued, international legal protection should be restricted to possessions for the owner's personal use.[9] In the same vein, delegates from socialist parties maintained that the right to property should not extend to ownership over the means of production.[10] The majority appears to have found it difficult to formulate a general definition of property and divorce the personal aspects from the economic aspects.[11] At the same time, they acknowledged that property has a social function and that limitations in the interests of the community are necessary.

By a narrow margin – 43 votes in favour and 40 votes against – the Consultative Assembly resolved to refer the right to property back to the Legal Affairs Committee. Apart from this referral, Teitgen's proposals were adopted with almost no changes. On 9 September 1949, the Consultative Assembly submitted a recommendation to the Committee of Ministers along with a draft Convention, without a clause on the right to property.

The Committee of Ministers proceeded to set up its own *ad hoc* drafting organ – a Committee of Legal Experts consisting of academics, senior magistrates and public servants from the Council of Europe's Member States. In its report dated 16 March 1950, the Legal Experts recommended including the right to property in the Convention 'in order to counteract the tendency of totalitarian regimes to interfere with the right to own property as a means of exercising illegitimate pressure on its nationals'.[12]

---

7 See e.g. remarks by Lord Layton (United Kingdom) in the Consultative Assembly's session on 8 September 1949. Ibid., vol II, 50–56.

8 See e.g. remarks by Paul Reynaud (France) in the Consultative Assembly's session on 8 September 1949. Ibid., vol II, 92, 94.

9 See e.g. remarks by André Philip (France) in the Consultative Assembly's session on 8 September 1949. Ibid., vol II, 72.

10 See e.g. remarks by Will Nally (United Kingdom) in the Consultative Assembly's session on 8 September 1949. Ibid., vol II, 76, 78.

11 See e.g. remarks by Lynn Ungoed-Thomas (United Kingdom) and by Paul Reynaud (France) in the Consultative Assembly's session on 8 September 1949. Ibid., vol II, 60–62, 92–94, respectively.

12 'Report of the Committee of Experts to the Committee of Ministers' 16 March 1950, in Council of Europe, *Collected Edition of the Travaux Préparatoires* Doc H(61)4 ('*Collected Edition*'), vol II, 409.

By the time the Consultative Assembly reconvened for its second session in August 1950, the Legal Affairs Committee had submitted a new draft text:

> All individuals and corporate bodies are entitled to respect for their property.
>
> Such property shall not be liable to arbitrary confiscation. This shall not, however, in any way prejudice the right of the different States to enact such laws as may be necessary to ensure the use of this property for the public good.[13]

The Legal Affairs Committee explained that this draft 'represents an attempt to define the right as requested by the Assembly … and endeavours to make the distinction between arbitrary confiscation and the social conception of property which allows it to be used by regulation legislation for the public good'.[14] As a French delegate explained, the proposed article reaffirmed 'that [property] should be protected from arbitrary confiscation, that is to say, from those high-handed administrative or private measures of which all the totalitarian regimes furnished such sinister examples. On the other hand we expressly reserved to each State the right to safeguard the social purpose of the property by appropriate legislative [enactments]'.[15]

The new text still raised concerns in the Consultative Assembly. Some members objected that the term 'arbitrary' has no clear meaning and might make the laws adopted by democratically elected legislatures subject to international scrutiny. Others opposed that idea out of national interest. Delegates from the United Kingdom, for example, were concerned that laws relating to taxes or the nationalisation of industry would come under the scrutiny of the future Court. They demanded assurances that the article would not interfere with the States' existing power to carry out social policies, whether by nationalisation, regulating the use of property, or imposing taxes or other contributions.[16] Supporters argued that it should be left to

13 'Supplementary Report of the Committee to the Consultative Assembly' 8 August 1950, *Collected Edition*, vol IV, 822.

14 'Report of the Legal Committee to the Consultative Assembly' 24 August 1950. Ibid., vol IV, 903–906.

15 See remarks by Paul Bastid (France) in the Consultative Assembly's session on 25 August 1950, *Travaux Préparatoires*, vol VI, 116–118.

16 See e.g. remarks by Alice Bacon (United Kingdom) in the Consultative Assembly's session on 25 August 1950. Ibid., vol VI, 138.

the future Court to distinguish between arbitrary and legitimate acts of the States.[17]

Despite these reservations, on 25 August 1950, the Consultative Assembly adopted the following draft article with a 97 to 0 vote and 11 abstentions:

> Every natural or legal person is entitled to the peaceful enjoyment of his possessions. Such possessions cannot be subjected to arbitrary confiscation. The present measures shall not however be considered as infringing, in any way, the right of a State to pass necessary legislation to ensure that the said possessions are utilised in accordance with the general interest.[18]

The Committee of Ministers assembled in Rome on 3–4 November 1950 to consider the recommendations from the Consultative Assembly. Seemingly without any substantive discussion, and on the recognition that further attempts to reach agreement would delay signature of the Convention, the Ministers decided that the right to property should be referred back to the Committee of Legal Experts for inclusion in a separate protocol. On 4 November 1950, the European Convention on Human Rights and Fundamental Freedoms was opened for signature, without a clause relating to the right to property.[19]

2 The First Additional Protocol

After the decision had been made to include the right to property in a separate protocol, attention turned back to the drafting. The Committee of Legal Experts saw it as necessary 'to define as accurately as possible what is meant by the right of property, what is meant by "arbitrary confiscation" and what exceptions are to be permitted in the general interest to the individual rights of enjoyment of one's possessions'.[20] When the Committee

17 See e.g. remarks by Georges Pernot (France) in the Consultative Assembly's session on 25 August 1950. Ibid., vol VI, 106.

18 'Recommendation no. 24' 25 August 1950. *Collected Edition*, vol IV, 946.

19 'Meeting of the Committee of Ministers on 3 November 1950 in Rome'. *Ibid*, vol IV, 1020.

20 'Note on the amendments to the Convention on Human Rights proposed by the Consultative Assembly about which the Committee of Ministers were not able to reach unanimous agreement' prepared by the Secretariat General 14 November 1950. Ibid., vol V, 1051–1052.

reconvened in February 1951, it had agreed on the wording of the first sentence: 'Every natural or legal person is entitled to the peaceful enjoyment of his possessions'.[21]

No agreement could be reached on the remaining text, however. There was still considerable dispute about whether the article should guarantee compensation in the event of expropriation. The majority of Legal Experts believed that a right to compensation should be expressly laid down and made binding on national legislatures. The delegations from France and the United Kingdom were unable to support this position: formulating a right to property comprising the principle of compensation in all situations of State acquisition was simply not possible, in their view.[22] In its second meeting, in April 1951, the Committee of Legal Experts adopted the following draft:

> Every natural or legal person is entitled to the peaceful enjoyment of his possessions. No one shall be deprived of his possessions except in the public interest, in such cases and by such procedure as are established by law and subject to such compensation as shall be determined in accordance with the conditions provided for by law.
>
> The present measures shall not however infringe, in any way, the right of a State to pass legislation to control the use of property in accordance with the general interest or to impose taxes or other contributions.[23]

At this point, the words 'arbitrary confiscation' had been taken out. A later report from the Secretariat General explained that these terms were thought to be too imprecise in a legal text as they are capable of varying interpretations. They were ultimately replaced by the phrase 'subject to the conditions provided for by law', which was believed to cover adequately the object in mind, as some right to compensation would normally be provided for in domestic legislation concerning nationalisation or expropriation of property.[24]

21 *Travaux Préparatoires*, vol VII, 206.

22 'Report of the Committee of Experts to the Committee of Ministers' 24 February 1951. *Collected Edition*, vol V, 1090–1091.

23 'Draft Report and Report of the Committee of Experts to the Committee of Ministers' 19 April 1951. Ibid., vol V, 1110–1111.

24 'Commentary by the Secretariat General on the draft Protocol' 18 September 1951. *Travaux Préparatoires*, vol VIII, 8–10.

Furthermore, the phrase 'subject to the conditions provided for … by the general principles of international law' was later included to secure compensation to foreigners even where such compensation is not owed to nationals.[25] Finally, the draft article's second paragraph was expanded in order to make clear that the right to property 'does not prevent the state from collecting taxes, or applying other regulatory measures to the whole of property of individuals in question'.[26]

In its final meetings on 5 and 6 June 1951, the Committee of Legal Experts agreed on the following text:

> Every natural or legal person is entitled to the peaceful enjoyment of his possessions. No one shall be deprived of his possessions except in the public interest and subject to the conditions provided for by law and by the general principles of international law.
>
> The present measures shall not however infringe in any way the right of a State to pass legislation to control the use of property in accordance with the general interest or to secure the payment of taxes or other contributions.

On 3 August 1951, the Committee of Ministers unanimously approved the draft Protocol. The Consultative Assembly made no amendments and adopted the text on 8 December 1951 with 75 votes in favour, none against and 23 abstentions. The First Additional Protocol to the Convention for the Protection of Human Rights and Fundamental Freedoms was signed in Paris on 20 March 1952. It entered into force on 18 May 1954, following ratification by the first 10 Member States. It is currently ratified by 44 of the 46 Council of Europe Member States.[27]

Protocol 1 Article 1 reads in English:

> Article 1 Protection of property

---

25 Ibid. The Committee of Ministers subsequently, on 19 March 1952, adopted a resolution according to which the '"general principles of international law" shall be taken to mean the obligation to pay compensation to non-nationals in cases of expropriation'.

26 'Commentary by the Secretariat General on the draft Protocol' 18 September 1951. Ibid., vol VIII, 10.

27 At the time of writing, Switzerland and Monaco have not ratified the First Additional Protocol.

> Every natural or legal person is entitled to the peaceful enjoyment of his possessions. No one shall be deprived of his possessions except in the public interest and subject to the conditions provided for by law and by the general principles of international law.
>
> The preceding provisions shall not, however, in any way impair the right of a State to enforce such laws as it deems necessary to control the use of property in accordance with the general interest or to secure the payment of taxes or other contributions or penalties.

The French version reads:

> Article 1 Protection de la propriété
>
> Toute personne physique ou morale a droit au respect de ses biens. Nul ne peut être privé de sa propriété que pour cause d'utilité publique et dans les conditions prévues par la loi et les principes généraux du droit international.
>
> Les dispositions précédentes ne portent pas atteinte au droit que possèdent les États de mettre en vigueur les lois qu'ils jugent nécessaires pour réglementer l'usage des biens conformément à l'intérêt général ou pour assurer le paiement des impôts ou d'autres contributions ou des amendes.

3 Conclusion

The right to the peaceful enjoyment of property proved to be one of the most controversial topics during the drafting of the European Convention of Human Rights. As this brief account of the history of Protocol 1 Article 1 has shown, disagreement among the drafters revolved around three main issues.

The first issue was whether a right of property should be included in the Convention at all. The majority of delegates in the Consultative Assembly appear to have been in favour of including a right to property because they regarded it as a fundamental right and a prerequisite for political and social freedom. Opponents were concerned about the limitations which a human right to property might impose on their governments' economic and social policies, and some argued that the right to property should not be included in the Convention unless other economic and social rights were included as well.

While a narrow majority in the Consultative Assembly decided that the Convention should include a right to property, it proved difficult to reach agreement on the content of such a right. This brings us to a second contentious issue. The drafters were acutely aware that the very notion of property posed significant problems of definition and interpretation. One point of view advanced in the Consultative Assembly was that the right to property should be limited to property for personal use. Because of the practical difficulty in separating personal and economic interests in property, however, the majority appears to have been in favour of a wide concept.

The third point of disagreement revolved around permissible State restrictions on the right to property. No member of the Consultative Assembly advocated for the right of property as an absolute and inviolable right. On the contrary, it was widely accepted that property has a social function and that the use of property must be restricted for the common good. In line with Article 17 of the United Nations Declaration, Protocol 1 Article 1 was initially conceived as a safeguard of freedom from arbitrary confiscation, but the term 'arbitrary' was ultimately deemed too vague and replaced with a requirement of lawfulness.

Throughout the negotiations, the drafters thus recognised the social function of property and the inherently political nature of property regulation. This explains the inclusion of the second sentence of Protocol 1 Article 1, which explicitly grants States wide powers to 'control' the use of property. The drafters also acknowledged that it would ultimately be up to the future Court to distinguish between legitimate and illegitimate State interference with property rights.

Many drafters were reluctant to accept that an international tribunal should have the power to review decisions made by competent national authorities regarding private property. For some delegates, such as those from the United Kingdom, opposition was a matter of safeguarding interests and economic policies at home. Others objected to the very idea that national economic and social legislation could be struck down by an international court. They asked whether a law passed by a national parliament duly elected under democratic rules can ever be 'arbitrary'.[28] Clearly, the drafters envisioned some degree of international judicial review of the substance of

28 See e.g. remarks by Pierre-Henri Teitgen (France) in the Consultative Assembly's session on 8 September 1949, *Travaux Préparatoires* Vol II, 128.

domestic legislation, but the parameters for determining which situations justify judicial intervention remained a matter of disagreement.

The final text was the result of historical circumstances and formidable efforts at political compromise, rather than legal drafting in the traditional sense. In the words of the United Kingdom's delegate Sir David Maxwell-Fyfe, it represented an effort 'to reconcile the social conception of property with the prohibition of arbitrary confiscation'.[29] The outcome was probably the maximal measure of agreement given the mounting pressure to have the Convention and Protocol adopted, which made the delegates disposed to 'accept more or less any text upon which agreement could be reached'.[30]

The brief and broadly formulated text encompasses two opposing notions: On one hand, that the right to property is a fundamental right; on the other hand, that State regulation of property is necessary for society to function. It leaves important issues unresolved, such as the scope of the right to property, which exceptions to the right are permissible in the general interest and whether the owner is entitled to compensation in the event of expropriation. It has been the task of the European Court of Human Rights to find ways of resolving these questions.

---

29 See remarks in the Consultative Assembly's session on 25 August 1950. *Collected Edition*, vol IV, 913.

30 A W B Simpson, *Human Rights and the End of Empire: Britain and the Genesis of the European Convention* (Oxford University Press 2001) 788–789.

CHAPTER 3

Aspects of the Court's Teleology

1 Introduction

Much has been written about the interpretative method of the Strasbourg Court, and it is not possible to account for every aspect within the confines of this book.[1] Since it is concerned with jurisprudential developments in the protection of the right to property specifically, the present chapter will focus on the aspects which can explain how those developments have taken place. The characteristics of the Court's method will also become apparent from the discussions in Parts 2 and 3.

The European Convention on Human Rights is formally a treaty of international law. Its provisions must therefore be construed in accordance with established principles of treaty interpretation set out in the Vienna Convention on the Law of Treaties.[2] Accordingly, the ECHR is to be interpreted 'in good faith in accordance with the ordinary meaning to be given to its terms in their context and in the light of its object and purpose'.[3] The text of Protocol 1 Article 1 is the natural starting point for the interpretative exercise, and the meaning of the text will be discussed at relevant points in later chapters.

Observers agree that while the Strasbourg Court generally adheres to the principles laid down in the Vienna Convention, it has developed its own

---

1 See, in particular, F Matscher, 'Methods of Interpretation of the Convention' in R St J Macdonald et al. (eds), *The European System for the Protection of Human Rights* (Martinus Nijhoff Publishers 1993) 63–82, and D J Harris et al., *Law of the European Convention on Human Rights* (4th edn, Oxford University Press 2018) 6–24. The Court occasionally seizes the opportunity to elaborate on its interpretative method, see e.g. *Magyar Helsinki Bizottság v. Hungary* (18030/11) judgment [GC] 8 November 2016, paras. 118–122 and 125. For a normative perspective on the interpretation of the ECHR, see G Letsas, *A Theory of the Interpretation of the European Convention on Human Rights* (Oxford University Press 2007).

2 Vienna Convention on the Law of Treaties (1969) 1155 United Nations Treaties Series 331 ('the VCLT' or 'the Vienna Convention'). The VCLT is not directly applicable to the Convention, as not all the Member States have ratified it. Its principles of treaty interpretation are nonetheless recognised as customary international law, and the Court has referred to these principles on several occasions, see e.g. *Golder v. the United Kingdom* (4451/70) judgment 21 February 1975, para. 29.

3 See Article 31 para. 1 VCLT.

 | DOI:10.1163/9789004735088_004

interpretative method with particular emphasis on the Convention's object and purpose.[4] Put differently, the Court generally seeks to interpret the Convention text in a manner which ensures that the object and purpose of the ECHR are realised as far as possible. To that end, it applies a set of distinctive methodological principles.[5] These principles or aspects of the Court's teleological method have no precise content, and they interact and overlap in various ways. Nonetheless, they offer different explanations for the developments that have taken place in Court's case law under Protocol 1 Article 1 and they will therefore be presented in some detail in this chapter.

Section 2 begins by discussing the principle of effective protection, by which the Court seeks to ensure that rights are interpreted and applied in a manner which make them practical and effective. Section 3 then describes the notion of evolutive interpretation, through which the Court seeks to make the Convention rights effective in the light of present-day conditions. In a broader sense, the Convention's object and purpose may also be understood as the fundamental values that the Convention exists to promote. These are discussed in Section 4.

2 The Principle of Effectiveness

Throughout its history, it has been something of an article of faith for the Court to ensure that the Convention guarantees rights are practical and effective, not theoretical or illusory.[6] In a substantive sense, effective protection implies that the articles in the Convention must be interpreted in a

4 See e.g. D J Harris et al. (n 1) 6, and G Letsas (n 1) 59. See also H Waldock, 'The Evolution of Human Rights Concepts and the Application of the European Convention on Human Rights' in *Mélanges offerts à Paul Reuter: le droit international, unité et diversité* (Pedone 1981), and S Greer, *The European Convention on Human Rights – Achievements, Problems and Prospects* (Cambridge University Press 2006) 193–230.

5 See B Rainey, P McCormick and C Ovey, *Jacobs, White and Ovey: The European Convention on Human Rights* (8th edn, Oxford University Press 2020) 82. Other interpretative principles, such as the principles of proportionality, margin of appreciation and subsidiarity, are contemplated in the literature, see e.g. F Matscher (n 1) 147. In Part 3 the function of these principles is discussed generally and specifically in the context of Protocol 1 Article 1.

6 See *Case 'Relating to Certain Aspects of the Laws on the Use of Languages in Education in Belgium' v. Belgium* (the '*Belgian Linguistic case*') (1474/62 et al.) judgment 23 July 1968, para. 5, where the Court observed that the ECHR's overriding ambition is to create an effective instrument for the protection of human rights. See also *Airey v. Ireland* Series (6289/73) judgment 9 October 1979, para. 24, *Artico v. Italy* (6694/74) judgment

manner that ensures that their purpose and nature are realised as far as possible. The effectiveness principle mandates a broad interpretation of the scope of the Convention's rights and freedoms on one hand, and a narrow interpretation of permissible restrictions on the other. Such an interpretation generally implies a strengthening of the rights and freedoms enjoyed by the individuals and a corresponding extension of the obligations of the Member States.[7] The notion of effective rights is a natural extension of the teleological method, since a restrictive interpretation of the Convention would endanger respect for the individual rights and freedoms enshrined in the Convention.

Whether the protection offered by the Court's interpretation and application is effective or ineffective depends, of course, on what the Court perceives to be the nature and purpose of the right at issue. This question may be relatively straightforward with respect to absolute rights such as the prohibition of torture and inhuman or degrading treatment or punishment in Article 3, the principal purpose of which is to ensure respect for human dignity.[8] It is more difficult to define the purpose served by the qualified rights in the Convention, which expressly provide for exceptions. Jurisprudential developments driven by the principle of effectiveness thus raise the question of what, in the Court's view, is the purpose of the right to property in the Convention. Possible answers to this question will emerge in the analysis in Parts 2 and 3 below.[9]

At this juncture, three important manifestations of the principle of effectiveness should be highlighted because they are of particular importance to the later discussions. Firstly, the notion that the ECHR's terms are autonomous means that its terms are not defined or limited by the domestic laws of any of the Member States. This principle governs the interpretation of

---

13 May 1980, para. 33, and *Sakhnovskiy v. Russia* (21272/03) judgment [GC] 2 November 2010, para. 95.

7 See e.g. *Stoll v. Switzerland* (69698/01) judgment [GC] 10 December 2007, para. 61, where the Court stated that 'clauses which allow interference with Convention rights must be interpreted restrictively'. See also *Wemhoff v. Germany* (2122/64) judgment 27 June 1968, para. 8, where the Court held that '[g]iven that it is a law-making treaty, it is also necessary to seek the interpretation that is most appropriate in order to realise the aim and achieve the object of the treaty, not that which would restrict to the greatest possible degree the obligations undertaken by the Parties'.

8 See e.g. *Bouyid v. Belgium* (23380/09) judgment [GC] 28 September 2015, para. 81.

9 See e.g. T Allen, 'Liberalism, Social Democracy and the Value of Property under the European Convention on Human Rights' (2010) 59(4) *International and Comparative Law Quarterly* 1078, who notes the absence of 'a close examination by the Court of the purpose and nature of [Protocol 1 Article 1]'.

concepts such as 'civil rights' and 'criminal charge' in Article 6, 'law' in Articles 8–11, and 'possessions' and 'property' in Protocol 1 Article 1.[10] The underlying rationale is that the Convention applies to a large and increasing number of States with no unifying law or set of legal norms. To leave it to each individual State to define core concepts in the Convention would undermine the principle of legal certainty and the coherence in the ECHR system. To the extent possible, therefore, their meaning should reflect common legal standards among the Member States.[11] Furthermore, adhering to the domestic classification of concepts which have bearing on the interpretation of the Convention's rights may lead to results which are at odds with its object and purpose.[12]

Secondly, in order for the rights and freedoms in the Convention to be effective, States must be obligated to do more than merely refrain from interfering with them. They may also have to implement positive measures to ensure that individuals can take advantage of their rights under the Convention.[13] Protocol 1 Article 1's introductory reference to the right to the 'peaceful enjoyment of [one's] possessions' has been understood to imply positive obligations for the States.

Thirdly, the principle of effective protection applies not just when the Court establishes the scope of a given right, but also when it assesses the State's justification for interfering with that right. It commits the Court to carrying out a genuine review of the respondent State's acts and omissions, and to subject the reasons for interfering to close and careful scrutiny.[14] The effectiveness principle has provided the normative basis for the 'fair balance' test – the most significant requirement for justified interference in Protocol 1 Article 1.[15]

10 See Chapter 4.

11 The preamble to the statutes of the Council of Europe refers to the aim of achieving 'greater unity between its members' through the realisation of human rights and fundamental freedoms.

12 See e.g. *Engel and Others v. the Netherlands* (5100/71 et al.) judgment 8 June 1976, para. 81, and *Chassagnou and Others v. France* (25088/94; 28331/95; 28443/95) judgment [GC] 29 April 1999, para. 100. See also R Bernhardt, 'The Convention and Domestic Law' in R St J Macdonald et al. (eds), *The European System for the Protection of Human Rights* (Martinus Nijhoff Publishers 1993) 34.

13 *Marckx v. Belgium* (6833/74) judgment 13 June 1979, para. 31. See also A Mowbray, 'The Creativity of the European Court of Human Rights' (2005) 5 *Human Rights Law Review* 72–78.

14 See, in relation to Article 10, *Stoll v. Switzerland* (69698/01) judgment [GC] 10 December 2007, para. 128.

15 See Part 3 below.

3 Evolutive Interpretation

In order for rights to be effectively protected over time, the Convention must take account of the changing norms and values in European societies.[16] Unlike a national supreme or constitutional court, the Strasbourg Court cannot leave the task of developing norms to the legislator. Leaving legislative action to the States is equally uncertain, as they are notoriously inhibited by political considerations. Instead, the Court has chosen to regard the Convention's terms as standards whose content may evolve over time. As it stated in *Tyrer v. the United Kingdom*, in the interpretation of the Convention the Court 'cannot but be influenced by the developments and commonly accepted standards in the ... member States of the Council of Europe'.[17]

Evolutive interpretation in ECHR law is premised on the existence of a European consensus with regard to particular human rights norms.[18] If there is evidence of a common approach among the Member States towards a certain problem or phenomenon, the Court may rely on a strict interpretation of the right in question. Conversely, if no actual or emerging consensus is deemed to exist, the States generally have a broader margin of appreciation when interpreting the extent of their obligations. Some of the Court's most famous decisions have reflected changed social attitudes towards, for example, homosexuals or children born out of wedlock.[19]

One argument advanced to justify an evolutive interpretation is that the Convention contains an inherent evolutionary element – in other words, that the drafters intended for the meaning of its terms to change over

16 The principle of evolutive interpretation has been called the 'temporal dimension' of the principle of effective protection, see D Rietiker, 'The Principle of "Effectiveness" in the Recent Jurisprudence of the European Court of Human Rights: Its Different Dimensions and Its Consistency with Public International Law – No Need for the Concept of Treaty *Sui Generis*' (2010) 79 *Nordic Journal of International Law* 260. See also A Mowbray (n 13) 72–79, and P Mahoney, 'Judicial Activism and Judicial Self-Restraint in the European Court of Human Rights: Two Sides of the Same Coin' (1990) 11 *Human Rights Law Journal* 64.

17 *Tyrer v. the United Kingdom* (5856/72) judgment 25 April 1978, para. 31.

18 It is normally not a condition that the evolution in question has occurred in all the States; common ground among the great majority of the democratic systems will in principle provide a basis for adaptation of the Convention, see K Dzehtsiarou, *European Consensus and the Legitimacy of the European Court of Human Rights* (Cambridge University Press 2015) 38.

19 See e.g. *Marckx v. Belgium* (6833/74) judgment 13 June 1979.

time.[20] A degree of evolution is certainly foreseen in the Preamble to the Convention, which refers to the 'further realisation of Human Rights and Fundamental Freedoms' in the third recital.[21] Furthermore, the purpose of the Convention is not to lay down rights and obligations in pursuance of national interests, as the case is for most treaties in international law, but to realise the aims and ideals of the Council of Europe. In this view, evolving human rights standards should not only be permissible, but should even be seen as crucial to the effectiveness of the ECHR system.[22]

Still, the 'living instrument' doctrine has been controversial because it has been used to expand the Convention guarantees beyond what the States could reasonably have foreseen when they acceded to the Convention. Rietiker has held that the main achievement of the doctrine has been to allow the Court to enlarge the scope of the Convention's substantive provisions.[23] The evolutive approach has thus left the Court open to the criticism that it has, by way of interpretation, introduced obligations that were not included in the Convention. Such objections have emanated from within the Court as well as from without.[24]

This book is not the place for addressing the legitimacy of the 'living instrument' doctrine in general.[25] What is worth noting here is that when the Court has invoked the 'living instrument' as a basis for developing the rights in the Convention, it has done so on the basis of – and often with express reference to – changing norms and values in European societies. Otherwise,

20 E Bjørge, *Evolutionary Interpretation of Treaties* (Oxford University Press 2014) 5.

21 The Preamble is a recognised part of a treaty's text pursuant to Article 31 para. 2 VCLT.

22 See e.g. *Bayatyan v. Armenia* (23459/03) judgment [GC] 7 July 2011, para. 102, where the Court noted that '[s]ince it is first and foremost a system for the protection of human rights, the Court must have regard to the changing conditions in Contracting States and respond, for example, to any emerging consensus as to the standards to be achieved'.

23 See D Rietiker (n 16) 263.

24 See e.g. *Golder v. the United Kingdom* (n 2), separate opinion of Judge Fitzmaurice, and *Mamatkulov and Askarov v. Turkey* (46827/99; 46951/99) judgment [GC] 4 February 2005, joint partly dissenting opinion of Judges Caflisch, Türmen and Kovler. For perspectives from outside the Court, see e.g. P Mahoney (n 16) 87–88, A Mowbray (n 13) 57–79, and S C Prebensen, 'Evolutive Interpretation of the European Convention on Human Rights' in P Mahoney et al. (eds), *Protecting Human Rights: The European Perspective. Studies in Memory of Rolv Ryssdal* (Heymann 2000) 1123–1124.

25 See e.g. G Letsas, 'The ECHR as a Living Instrument: Its Meaning and Legitimacy' in A Føllesdal, B Peters and G Ulfstein (eds), *Constituting Europe: The European Court of Human Rights in a National, European and Global Context* (Cambridge University Press 2013) 106–141, and A Nussberger, *The European Court of Human Rights* (Oxford University Press 2020) 76–88.

it has generally relied on the need to ensure that the rights in the ECHR are interpreted and applied in a manner which make them practical and effective.

4 The Convention's Fundamental Values

So far, we have looked at the methodological principles used by the Court to ensure the effective protection of human rights. In a wider sense, the Convention's 'object and purpose' can also be understood as the ideals and values that it exists to promote.[26]

As a legal instrument, the ECHR is inevitably shaped by the time and place of its inception. Moved by the horrors of the Second World War and the spectre of Communist expansion, the drafters wished to pledge their commitment to a system of liberal ideals and values. The values underpinning the Convention can be discerned between the lines of the treaty text and are sometimes spelled out in the Court's judgments. They are also articulated in the Preamble, which the Court has described as a 'very useful tool' for determining the ECHR's object and purpose.[27]

The values enshrined in the Convention have been understood in different ways, but for the purposes of the present discussion, they will be defined as human dignity, democracy and political freedom, and the rule of law.[28] Clearly, these values are interdependent and mutually reinforcing. But even though there is a degree of overlap between them, it can be assumed that they are imbued with substantive content which can be objectively determined. The remainder of this chapter will discuss briefly their role in the context of the ECHR and their *prima facie* relevance to the interpretation of Protocol 1 Article 1.

4.1 *Human Dignity*

The Preamble opens with a reference to the Universal Declaration of Human Rights, whose first recital proclaims the 'inherent dignity and …

---

26 The statutes of the Council of Europe refer to 'ideals and principles' which are the 'common heritage' of the Member States, see the Statute of the Council of Europe (European Treaty Series 1/6/7/8/11) Article 1 b).

27 See e.g. *Golder v. the United Kingdom* (n 2), para. 34.

28 See by comparison A Nussberger (n 25) 38, who identifies democracy, human rights, and the rule of law as the Convention's fundamental values, and M Emberland, *The Human Rights of Companies – Exploring the Structure of ECHR Protection* (Oxford University Press 2006) 40, who sees economic liberalism as an additional value underlying the ECHR.

equal and inalienable rights of all members of the human family'. The Convention's endorsement of the Universal Declaration strongly suggests that human dignity belongs to the ECHR's fundamental values. Indeed, the Court has affirmed that respect for human dignity is the 'very essence' of the Convention.[29]

Property has always been viewed as crucial for the security of the individual and the preservation of human dignity. In one view, the purpose of protecting private property rights in the legal system is to ensure the fulfilment of individual needs and the enhancement of human well-being.[30] As discussed in Chapter 2, some of the drafters advanced such arguments as a rationale for including the right to property in the Convention.

In this vein, Schermers has argued that the core purpose of the right to property as a human right is the protection of possessions which are necessary to facilitate private life.[31] Yet human dignity cannot explain why legal protection of property should extend to pure economic or commercial assets.[32] Nor can it justify protecting the property rights of legal persons, which are explicitly covered by Protocol 1 Article 1.[33] As Emberland has observed, human dignity only indirectly supports the protection of artificial persons, in the sense that their activity ultimately derives from human activity.[34] The rationale for Protocol 1 Article 1's wide scope of application must therefore be sought elsewhere.

4.2 *Democracy and Political Freedom*

Democracy is a fundamental value which has found direct expression in the Convention's Preamble. The fourth recital refers to 'an effective political democracy' as a precondition for the enjoyment of the Convention's rights and freedoms, and the fifth recital makes clear that the signatories to the Convention are 'like-minded and have a common heritage of political traditions [and] ideals'.

---

29 See e.g. *Pretty v. the United Kingdom* (2346/02) judgment 29 April 2002, para. 65, and *Vinter and Others v. the United Kingdom* (66069/09; 130/10; 3896/10) judgment [GC] 9 July 2013, para. 113.

30 See e.g. T R G van Banning, *The Human Right to Property* (Intersentia 2002).

31 H G Schermers, 'The International Protection of the Right to Property' in F Matscher and H Petzold (eds), *Protecting Human Rights: The European Dimension. Studies in Honour of Gérard J Wiarda* (Heymann 1988) 572–573. See also the American Declaration on the Rights and Duties of Man (1946), which limits protection to property which 'meets the essential needs of decent living'.

32 See Chapter 4 below.

33 See Chapter 5 below.

34 M Emberland (n 28) 39.

The notion of democracy features prominently in the Convention text. For example, Articles 8–11 provide that interference in the rights must be 'necessary in a democratic society' to be legitimate, and Protocol 1 Article 3 guarantees the right to vote and stand for election. There is little doubt that the Court's interpretation of the rights and freedoms in the Convention has been guided by the general spirit of the Convention as an instrument designed to maintain and promote the ideals and values of a democratic society.[35] Still, democracy remains an elusive concept in ECHR law.

In the context of Protocol 1 Article 1, the Court has recognised, at least implicitly, that the protection of property belonging to privately owned media is instrumental for securing pluralism in political discourse.[36] In line with this, some scholars argue that private ownership is vital for democracy because it provides an essential basis for any opposition to form a political platform against those in power.[37] On the other hand, the right to property is not strictly speaking required for democracy to function in the same way as, for example, freedom of expression.

In a broader sense, the Convention is a treaty not only for the protection of human rights but also for 'fundamental freedoms'. The Preamble proclaims that those freedoms are 'the foundation of justice and peace in the world'. The drafters saw democracy primarily as a bulwark against totalitarian rule, and freedom in the sense of absence of arbitrary public encroachment of the private sphere is a requisite for the Convention's conception of democracy.[38]

In this view, property ownership provides the basis for freedom from governmental coercion and abuse of power. Legal protection of property secures the ability of legal subjects to act independently and maintain a degree of autonomy and privacy from the power of the State.[39] Put differently, the right to property supports and enhances the enjoyment of other human rights.[40] In line with these ideas, Frowein has argued that freedom

35 See e.g. *Soering v. the United Kingdom* (14038/88) judgment 7 July 1989, para. 87.

36 See e.g. *Centro Europa 7 S.R.L. and Di Stefano v. Italy* (38433/09) judgment [GC] 7 June 2012, paras. 129–135.

37 See e.g. J Waldron, *The Right to Private Property* (Clarendon Press 1988) 230–317.

38 S Marks, 'The European Convention on Human Rights and its "Democratic Society"' (1996) 66 *British Yearbook of International Law* 212.

39 T R G van Banning, *The Human Right to Property* (Intersentia 2002) 182.

40 See in particular J W Ely Jr, *The Guardian of Every Other Right: A Constitutional History of Property Rights* (3rd edn, Oxford University Press 2008).

as enshrined in the Convention cannot be upheld if State organs are entitled to interfere with private property in an arbitrary manner.[41]

4.3 *The Rule of Law*

This brings us to a third Convention value, namely the rule of law. The Preamble's fifth recital refers to the rule of law as part of the 'common heritage' of the Member States, and the Court has long regarded observance of the rule of law as integral to the ECHR's object and purpose, and therefore generally a relevant source of interpretation.[42] It has described the rule of law as '[o]ne of the fundamental principles of a democratic society', a concept which is 'inherent in all the Articles of the Convention' and 'belong[s] to the core values imbuing the Convention' – indeed, the very principle 'from which the whole Convention draws its inspiration'.[43]

In ordinary usage, the rule of law refers to the notion that the exercise of public power must be subjected to formal constraints in order to avoid arbitrary outcomes.[44] The rule of law is a contested concept outside the Convention, and this book is not the place for reiterating the various renderings of it or for elaborating on its role in the legal system or society in general. Rather, it is concerned with the impact of the rule of law on the Court's interpretation of the Convention in general and Protocol 1 Article 1 in particular.

There appears to be consensus that the rule of law has an autonomous meaning within the ECHR system, which broadly reflects the conceptions

41 J Frowein, 'The Protection of Property' in R St J Macdonald et al. (eds), *The European System for the Protection of Human Rights* (Martinus Nijhoff Publishers 1993) 515.

42 *Golder v. the United Kingdom* (n 2), para. 29. The Statute of the Council of Europe refers to the rule of law in the Preamble, where the signatory States affirm their 'devotion' to this principle, and in Article 3, which provides that 'every Member of the Council of Europe must accept the principle of the rule of law'.

43 See, respectively, *Klass and Others v. Germany* (5029/71) judgment 6 September 1978, para. 55, *Béláné Nagy v. Hungary* (53080/13) judgment [GC] 13 December 2016, paras. 112 and 89, and *Rozhkov v. Russia (No. 2)* (38898/04) judgment 31 January 2017, para. 76.

44 In the words of Waldron, the rule of law is a 'multi-faceted ideal ... Most conceptions of this ideal ... give central place to a requirement that people in positions of authority should exercise their power within a constraining framework of public norms, rather than on the basis of their own preferences, their own ideology, or their own individual sense of right and wrong', see J Waldron, 'The Concept and the Rule of Law' in L May and P Morrow (eds), *Procedural Justice* (Routledge 2012) 204. See generally B Z Tamanaha, *On the Rule of Law: History, Politics, Theory* (Cambridge University Press 2004) and P Gowder, *The Rule of Law in the Real World* (Cambridge University Press 2016).

emanating from various European legal traditions.[45] While no abstract definition of the rule of law can be found in the Court's jurisprudence, observers of the Court have derived a set of principles from it, which are closely interrelated and can be grouped into broad categories of legality and due process.[46] These principles will be explored further in later chapters.

At this juncture, an important distinction should be made between formal and substantive conceptions of the rule of law.[47] In a formal understanding, the rule of law simply refers to the notion that laws – whatever their substantive content – must be precisely formulated and provide adequate safeguards against arbitrary interference. A legal system based on the denial of human rights may conform to these requirements of the rule of law better than any of the legal systems in one of the Western democracies. It may be an immeasurably worse legal system, but it will excel in its conformity to the rule of law.[48]

In a substantive conception, the rule of law also sets limits on the substantive contents of domestic law which interfere with the rights and freedoms of individuals. In the words of Lord Bingham, it is a good start for public authorities to observe the letter of the law, but not enough if the law does not protect what are regarded as basic entitlements.[49]

Even though the Court does not normally refer to the rule of law in a substantive sense, its general attitude appears to be that the rule of law does

---

45 See e.g. G Lautenbach *The Concept of the Rule of Law and the European Court of Human Rights* (Oxford University Press 2013) 10, and M Emberland (n 28) 44.

46 See in particular G Lautenbach (n 45) 211, who concludes that the existence of judicial safeguards and the requirements concerning the quality of law form the core contents of the rule of law concept in the ECHR. See also J G Merrills, *The Development of International Law by the European Court of Human Rights* (2nd ed, Manchester University Press 1993) 128, who defines the rule of law in the context of the ECHR as '[t]he principle that the individual's dealing with the State and his fellow citizen should be regulated by a framework of legal rules, whose interpretation and application is in the hands of independent courts'.

47 These aspects are also referred to as 'thin' and 'thick' versions of the rule of law, respectively. See generally P Craig, 'Formal and Substantive Conceptions of the Rule of Law: An Analytical Framework' (1997) *Public Law* 467.

48 J Raz, 'The Rule of Law and Its Virtue' in J Raz, *The Authority of Law: Essays on Law and Morality* (Oxford University Press 1979) 211. See also *Shaughnessy v. Mezei*, 345 US 206, S. 224, dissenting opinion of Justices Frankfurter and Jackson, who famously believed that it would be preferable 'to live under Soviet substantive law applied in good faith by our common-law procedures than under our substantive law enforced by Soviet procedural practices'.

49 T Bingham, *The Rule of Law* (Allen Lane 2010) 84.

require the core contents of basic human rights to be respected.[50] Parts 2 and 3 will show how the rule of law has manifested itself in the case law related to Protocol 1 Article 1.

50 See e.g. *Soering v. the United Kingdom* (n 35), para. 88. See also G Lautenbach (n 45) 62, who notes that the rule of law must be understood to require a minimum degree of protection of the most basic rights.

PART 2

CHAPTER 4

The Autonomous Property Concept

1 Introduction

The aim of Part 2 is to account for the development of Protocol 1 Article 1's scope of application. Chapters 5 and 6 discuss, respectively, whose property rights are protected by the Convention and the notion of interference in the right to property. The topic of this chapter is the article's material scope – the extent of the term 'property' or 'possessions'.[1]

Section 2 offers a conceptual analysis, which can serve as a framework for the study of the developments in the case law. In essence, the Court understands property both as the rights held by the applicant under domestic law, and the asset to which those rights are attached. The evolution of the material scope of Protocol 1 Article 1 can be mapped along these two 'axes'.

Section 3 explores developments along the 'rights axis', beginning with the attributes of ownership and proceeding to limited rights in property. Section 4 explores developments along the 'assets axis'. For an asset to qualify as a 'possession' within the meaning of Protocol 1 Article 1 it must, as a rule, have economic value, a criterion which sometimes gives rise to practical difficulties. Case law related to intangible assets will be used to demonstrate how the Court has sought to draw the line between protected and unprotected possessions.

The primary function of Protocol 1 Article 1 is to protect rights which already exist under domestic law. However, the Court has applied the doctrine of autonomous interpretation to extend Convention protection to legal positions without a clear basis in domestic law, founded on 'legitimate expectations'. Section 5 explains how the Court has justified this notable expansion of the article's material scope.

1 As part of its applicability assessment, the Court must determine whether the interests of the applicant are protected as 'property' or 'possessions' within the meaning of Protocol 1 Article 1. If the applicant fails to demonstrate an interest which falls within the scope of application of Protocol 1 Article 1, the application is rejected as incompatible *ratione materiae* with the provisions of the Convention, see Article 35 para. 3 cf para. 4.

 | DOI:10.1163/9789004735088_005

2 Conceptual Analysis – Property as Rights and Assets

2.1 *A Substantive Guarantee of the Right to Property*

The right to property does not figure as such in the operative parts of Protocol 1 Article 1.[2] In its first judgments, the Court interpreted the text to contain a substantive guarantee of the right to property.[3] In *Marckx v. Belgium*, it explained this interpretation in the following way:

> [b]y recognising that everyone has the right to the peaceful enjoyment of his possessions, Article 1 (P1–1) is in substance guaranteeing the right of property. This is the clear impression left by the words 'possessions' and 'use of property' (in French: 'biens', 'propriété', 'usage des biens'); the 'travaux préparatoires', for their part, confirm this unequivocally: the drafters continually spoke of 'right of property' or 'right to property' to describe the subject-matter of the successive drafts which were the forerunners of the present Article 1 (P1–1).[4]

Given that Protocol 1 Article 1 is to be understood as a substantive guarantee of the right to property, it is necessary to define the scope of that right.

In the legal literature, Protocol 1 Article 1's scope of protection is often defined through enumerations of the various proprietary interests which the Court has deemed to constitute 'possessions' in the past.[5] A conceptual framework is needed to articulate the principles governing the interpretation of that key term, and to illustrate the developments that have taken place.[6]

The concept of property in the European Convention on Human Rights is a considerable topic in its own right, raising, as it does, questions about the relationship between the right to property in ECHR law on one hand and doctrines of property in civil law jurisdictions and the common law on the other.[7] This book will generally leave these questions for other studies, and

2 The heading refers to the '[p]rotection of property' in English and '[p]rotection de la propriété' in French.

3 *Handyside v. the United Kingdom* (5493/72) judgment 7 December 1976, para. 62.

4 *Marckx v. Belgium* (6833/74) judgment 13 June 1979, para. 63.

5 See e.g. D J Harris et al., *Law of the European Convention on Human Rights* (4th edn, Oxford University Press 2018) 850–851.

6 The need for a conceptual analysis of this notion was pointed out by Judge Koskolo in her separate opinion in *Kurban v. Turkey* (75414/10) judgment 24 November 2020.

7 For studies of the relationship between the right to property in ECHR law and the common law, see in particular D Rook, *Property Law and Human Rights* (Blackstone 2001),

focus instead on the conceptual elements of the right to property that can be derived from the Court's case law.

First, a point of linguistic clarification is in order. Protocol 1 Article 1 uses the terms 'possessions' and 'property' in English, and 'biens' and 'propriété' in French. The two pairs are not applied consistently, however: In the first paragraph, the English version uses the term 'possessions' while the French version uses both 'biens' and 'propriété'. In the second paragraph, 'property' is used synonymously with 'biens', while the heading uses the terms 'property' and 'propriété' in English and French, respectively.[8]

In light of these inconsistencies, it is unlikely that the terms 'property' and 'possessions' were intended to convey different legal meanings. On the contrary, the *travaux préparatoires* intimate that the drafters were unable to agree on a precise definition of the property concept and left the task of imbuing it with content to the Court. As the above-cited passage from *Marckx* shows, the Court resolved early on to interpret Protocol 1 Article 1 as guaranteeing in substance the right to property, and in so doing, it essentially stripped any differences between the English and French texts of significance.

It may be that the terms 'possessions' and 'biens' convey a different, somewhat wider meaning than the terms 'property' and 'propriété' do in ordinary usage. The Court generally takes the former pair as the nominal vantage point for its interpretative exercise. This book will mainly refer to 'possessions' as the operative English term, but with the understanding that it has the same material content as the term 'property'.

2.2 *The Two 'Axes' of the Property Concept*

The word 'possession' has more than one connotation in everyday language. It is understood as both the act of owning or controlling something, and the

---

T Allen, *Property and the Human Rights Act 1998* (Oxford University Press 2005), and D Maxwell, 'The Human Right to Property: A Practical Approach to Article 1 of Protocol No. 1 to the ECHR' (Hart Publishing 2022).

8 As Judge Fitzmaurice pointed out in his separate opinion in *Marckx*, the apparent interchangeability of these terms in different contexts and without evident reason is confusing. Fitzmaurice also objected to the drafters' choice of words: The French word 'biens' is best translated into English by 'assets' not 'possessions', but the best French rendering of the English word 'assets' is 'avoirs'. In addition, there is no satisfactory French equivalent of 'possessions' as such, and in the plural. Fitzmaurice dismissed the drafting of Protocol 1 Article 1 as 'obviously poor ... both in the English and French versions', see *Marckx v. Belgium* (n 4), dissenting opinion of Judge Fitzmaurice.

object which is owned or controlled.[9] In *Gasus Dosier- und Fördertechnik GmbH v. the Netherlands*, the Court analysed the term in the following way:

> … the notion 'possessions' (in French: biens) in Article 1 of Protocol No. 1 (P1–1) has an autonomous meaning which is certainly not limited to ownership of physical goods: certain other rights and interests constituting assets can also be regarded as 'property rights', and thus as 'possessions', for the purposes of this provision (P1–1).[10]

Gasus is one of the landmark judgments in the Court's case law regarding Protocol 1 Article 1, owing in particular to the 'formula' just cited. It inspires three important observations about the ECHR's property concept.

Firstly, the Court recognised the distinction between rights on one hand and assets on the other, which also characterises the term in ordinary usage. Rights are the privileges or powers in law held by the legal subject, and assets are the objects to which those privileges or powers are attached.[11]

Secondly, and extending the first point, the Court made clear that the notion of 'possessions' in Protocol 1 Article 1 is 'not limited to ownership of physical goods: certain other rights and interests constituting assets can also be regarded as … "possessions"'. In other words, legal rights that do not amount to ownership, and assets other than physical goods, can qualify as 'possessions' and obtain protected status under the Convention. The Court did not specify which other rights and assets it had in mind, but the cited passage imparts that 'possessions' should be interpreted broadly.

Thirdly, the Court in *Gasus* declared that the notion of 'possessions' has an autonomous meaning. In fact, this point proved decisive for the outcome: The case concerned a security right in a concrete mixer, which the Court deemed to be a 'possession' within the meaning of Protocol 1 Article 1, even though security rights were not recognised as property rights under Dutch law. Before exploring the developments in the case law with respect to which rights and assets qualify for protection under Protocol 1 Article 1,

9 See e.g. 'possession', (Merriam-Webster Online Dictionary) <www.merriam-webster.com/dictionary/possession> accessed 30 May 2025.

10 *Gasus Dosier- und Fördertechnik GmbH v. the Netherlands* (15375/89) judgment 23 February 1995, para. 53.

11 This conceptualisation generally corresponds to the 'rights-thing' understanding of property acknowledged in international law, see J G Sprankling, *The International Law of Property* (Oxford University Press 2014) 23. See Sections 3 and 4 below.

this chapter will briefly revisit the doctrine of autonomous interpretation in ECHR law.[12]

2.3 *The Relationship between Property Rights in the Convention and in Domestic Law*

The Court in *Marckx* saw the basic purpose of Protocol 1 Article 1 as protecting existing property rights.[13] Since then, the starting point has been that the applicant has a 'possession' if and to the extent that it exists in domestic law. In most cases, the Court has been content to accept the applicant's legal position under relevant national law, based on the view that it is a matter for national legislators to define the nature and extent of property rights.

Determining whether or not the applicant has an existing possession in domestic law is normally a relatively straightforward matter, but not always. The commercial property interests of a business, for example, may derive from complex domestic legal structures. The legal as well as the factual basis for its claim to property rights may be unclear and contested. In these situations, the Court's task is to determine whether the applicant's property rights are 'sufficiently established' under domestic law.[14]

The Court has accepted a range of legal instruments as constitutive of property rights: private-law acts such as contracts[15] and various public-law acts, including statutes,[16] administrative decisions,[17] judicial decisions[18] and arbitration awards.[19] As part of its analysis of the applicant's position under domestic law,[20] the Court also considers relevant factual circumstances, in particular whether the State has treated the applicant as the rightful owner,

12 See Chapter 3 above.

13 *Marckx v. Belgium* (n 4), para. 50.

14 *J.A. Pye (Oxford) Ltd and J.A. Pye (Oxford) Land Ltd v. the United Kingdom ('Pye v. the United Kingdom')* (44302/02) judgment [GC] 30 August 2007, para. 61, and *Matos e Silva, Lda., and Others v. Portugal* (15777/89) judgment 16 September 1996, para. 75.

15 See e.g. *Beyeler v. Italy* (33202/96) judgment [GC] 5 January 2000, paras. 104–105.

16 See e.g. *Lindheim and Others v. Norway* (13221/08; 2139/10) judgment 12 June 2012.

17 See e.g. *Pine Valley Developments Ltd and Others v. Ireland* (12742/87) judgment 29 November 1991.

18 See e.g. *Broniowski v. Poland* (31443/96) judgment [GC] 22 June 2004, paras. 130–131.

19 See e.g. *Stran Greek Refineries and Stratis Andreadis v. Greece* (13427/87) judgment 9 December 1994, para. 62.

20 The applicant's position must primarily be derived from domestic legal sources, but the Court has occasionally shown a willingness to consider the State's obligations under international law as a sufficient legal basis for proprietary interests, see e.g. *S. A. Dangeville v. France* (36677/97) judgment 16 April 2002.

for instance by claiming taxes or offering compensation in connection with expropriation.[21]

Beyeler v. Italy serves to illustrate the Court's approach. A Swiss art collector had purchased a valuable painting, which was later confiscated by Italian authorities. The conduct of the authorities demonstrated to the Court that the applicant was the rightful owner of the painting, even if that right was based on a contract which had been declared null and void. This was reinforced by the fact that the applicant had been awarded compensation, which in Italian law was characteristic of an expropriation measure. In the Grand Chamber's view, the applicant's legal position therefore amounted to a 'possession' for the purposes of Protocol 1 Article 1.[22] *Beyeler* is a special but not unique case which shows that the applicant's interest can achieve protected status under Protocol 1 Article 1 even with a weak basis in domestic law.[23]

While domestic law is the starting point for the Court's assessment, the term 'possessions' nonetheless has an autonomous meaning which is independent from any constructs in the domestic legal system. As with other autonomous terms found in the Convention, classification in national law has a relative value.[24] In practice, this means that if the applicant can demonstrate a property right which is recognised by domestic law, that interest will automatically be considered a 'possession' under the Convention.

The significance of the Court's autonomous interpretation becomes evident primarily when domestic law does *not* recognise a particular interest as a property right. That does not prevent the Court from considering the proprietary interest as a 'possession' within the meaning of Protocol 1 Article 1.[25]

---

21 See e.g. *The former King of Greece and Others v. Greece* (25701/94) judgment [GC] 23 November 2000, paras. 60–66, *Papamichalopoulos and Others v. Greece* (14556/89) judgment 24 June 1993, para. 39, *Zwierzyński v. Poland* (34049/96) judgment 19 June 2001, paras. 65–66, and *Brosset-Triboulet and Others v. France* (34078/02) judgment [GC] 29 March 2010.

22 *Beyeler v. Italy* (33202/96) judgment [GC] 5 January 2000, paras. 104–105.

23 See also *Öneryildiz v. Turkey* (48939/99) judgment [GC] 30 November 2004, where the Court recognised the applicant's proprietary interests in an illegal settlement.

24 See *Chassagnou and Others v. France* (25088/94; 28331/95; 28443/95) judgment [GC] 29 April 1999, para. 100.

25 See e.g. *Depalle v. France* (34044/02) judgment [GC] 29 March 2010, para. 68, where the Grand Chamber noted that 'the fact that the domestic laws of a State do not recognise a particular interest as a "right" or even a "property right" does not necessarily prevent the interest in question, in some circumstances, from being regarded as a "possession" within the meaning of Article 1 of Protocol No. 1'. See also *Öneryildiz v. Turkey* (n 23), paras. 124–129, and *Brosset-Triboulet and Others v. France* (n 21), para. 71.

As the Court has put it in another context, the autonomy of the term operates, as it were, one way only.[26]

The Court's doctrine of autonomous interpretation has a two-fold rationale, as explained in Chapter 3. On one hand, autonomous terms are an instrument for achieving greater unity between the legal systems of the Member States. To leave it to each individual State to define core concepts in the Convention would undermine the effectiveness of the ECHR system, in the Court's view. To the extent possible, therefore, key terms such as 'possessions' should reflect the common legal standards found in the jurisdictions of the Member States. On the other hand, adhering strictly to the domestic classification of concepts which have bearing on the rights and freedoms in the Convention may lead to results which are at odds with its object and purpose.[27]

The remainder of this chapter will demonstrate how the autonomy of the term 'possessions' has enabled developments in the material scope of Protocol 1 Article 1 along the 'rights' and 'assets' axes.

3 Rights in Property Protected by Protocol 1 Article 1

3.1 *Elements of Ownership*

The text of Protocol 1 Article 1 does not say which rights in property are protected.[28] It refers to the notion of being 'deprived of [one's] possessions' in the second sentence, and 'the use of property' in the second paragraph, but these are merely attributes of what we normally think of as property rights.

An attempt to derive conclusions from the case law should begin with the most recognisable and commonly accepted form of property right. Ownership is not a strict legal term, and no uniform legal definition of

26 See, in relation to the concept of 'criminal charge' in Article 6, *Engel and Others v. the Netherlands* (5100/71 et al.) judgment 8 June 1976, para. 81.

27 See *ibid.*, para. 81, and *Chassagnou and Others v. France* (n 24), para. 100. See also R Bernhardt, 'The Convention and Domestic Law' in R St J Macdonald et al. (eds) *The European System for the Protection of Human Rights* (Martinus Nijhoff Publishers 1993) 34.

28 See by comparison Article 9 para. 1: 'Everyone has the right to freedom of thought, conscience and religion; *this right includes* freedom to change his religion or belief and freedom, either alone or in community with others and in public or private, to manifest his religion or belief, in worship, teaching, practice and observance' (emphasis added).

ownership exists. It is commonly understood as a comprehensive set of exclusive rights to a thing.[29]

The Court's case law reflects that ownership in ECHR law encompasses at least three elements. Firstly, the notion of peaceful enjoyment of property logically presupposes physical access to it. Equally, freedom from deprivation implies an ability to access and maintain possession of one's property. *Loizidou* is a case in point: The applicant had been refused access to her home in Northern Cyprus, of which she remained the legal owner, as a result of the Turkish occupation. The Court observed that as a consequence of being denied access she had effectively lost all control over, as well as all possibilities to use and enjoy, her property.[30]

A second attribute of ownership is the owner's right to enjoy, use, exploit, or alter their 'possession' as they please.[31] The right to enjoy one's property in peace (which follows directly from the first paragraph) and to use it (which follows indirectly from the second paragraph) are the most fundamental attributes of ownership; without them, ownership is a mere formality.

Of course, all rights in property are inherently limited. For one thing, there are statutory restrictions on the use of all kinds of assets – the imposition of taxes, area planning and zoning regulations governing the use of immovable property, and so on. In the same vein, the owner is prohibited from using his or her property in ways that violate the legal rights of others. These implied limitations to the owner's rights were succinctly formulated by Judge Zekia in his separate opinion in *Handyside*: 'the owner [...] is at liberty to make use of his property in any way he likes as long as such usage does not go against the law'.[32]

The third element of ownership is the owner's right to dispose of his or her property – for example, to sell, mortgage, lease, rent out, give away or

29 The concept of ownership is understood in different ways in European legal traditions. In common law and civil law, property is traditionally defined as 'a right of a person with respect to a thing'. Property thus establishes a relationship of power between the owner and the object of ownership. In addition, property creates obligations for others to respect the owner's power over the object. See e.g. A R Çoban, *Protection of Private Property Rights within the European Convention of Human Rights* (Ashgate 2004) 12–14.

30 *Loizidou v. Turkey* (15318/89) judgment [GC] 18 December 1996, para. 63. See also *Sargsyan v. Azerbaijan* (40167/06) judgment [GC] 16 June 2015.

31 See e.g. *Kristiana Ltd. v. Lithuania* (36184/13) judgment 6 February 2018, para. 100, where the Court pointed out that '[t]he inability to develop his or her own property constitutes a limitation of the rights normally enjoyed by a property owner'.

32 *Handyside v. the United Kingdom* (n 3), separate opinion of Judge Zekia.

destroy it. In *Marckx*, the Court affirmed that 'the right to dispose of one's property constitutes a traditional and fundamental aspect of the right of property'.[33] In contrast to limited rights in property, ownership is by definition exclusive.[34] That connotation is more strongly conveyed by the French text of Protocol 1 Article 1, according to which everyone has the right to respect for his or her property ('respect de ses biens'). The Convention recognises the owner's positive rights to access, use and dispose of property, as well as the negative right to deny the same rights to others.[35]

The elements of ownership reflected in the Court's case law generally correspond to the way that the right to property is devised in many domestic jurisdictions as well as in the law of the European Union.[36] Judges on the Court rely on conceptions of property derived from their own legal experience – the 'traditional and fundamental aspects', as it referred to in *Marckx* – and it is only natural that the Court has approached the property concept in the ECHR with those conceptions in mind.

Occasionally, however, the Court has been faced with claims for protection under Protocol 1 Article 1 which test the limits of our ordinary understanding of property, particularly in the context of a human rights instrument. In *Hutten-Czapska v. Poland*, the Court was asked to decide whether Protocol 1 Article 1 entitles owners to derive profit from their property. The Court had heard applications regarding rent control legislation on several occasions prior to *Hutten-Czapska*. In *Mellacher and Others v. Austria*, for example, the contested legislation deprived the applicants of a significant part of their income from the property they owned by altering the terms of lawfully concluded contracts.[37] The question of whether such legislation can deny owners profit without violating the ECHR had not been explicitly raised, however.

---

33 *Marckx v. Belgium* (6833/74) (n 4), para. 63. See also *Zelenchuk and Tsytsyura v. Ukraine* (846/16; 1075/16) judgment 22 May 2018, para. 146, where the right to dispose of one's property is described as one of the key elements of ownership.

34 See e.g. *Chassagnou and Others v. France* (n 24), para. 74.

35 The right to deny others access to one's property is also intrinsic to the right of respect for one's home, which is protected by Article 8 of the Convention.

36 See Article 17 of the EU's Charter of Fundamental Rights, which gives everyone the right to 'own, use, dispose of and bequeath his or her lawfully acquired possessions'. See also *United States v. General Motors* 323 U.S. 373 (1945), where the US Supreme Court defined the right to property as 'the group of rights inhering in the citizen's relation to the physical thing, as the right to possess, use and dispose of it'.

37 *Mellacher and Others v. Austria* (10522/83; 11011/84; 11070/84) judgment 19 December 1989.

The facts of *Hutten-Czapska* were essentially as follows: To mitigate a housing shortage, the Polish government had introduced statutory restrictions on the right of landlords to terminate leases and impose rent increases. Under the contested laws, the levels of rent were fixed without any reasonable relationship to the costs of keeping the property in good condition. The low level of rent resulted in a significant depreciation in the value and condition of the applicant's house.

In finding Protocol 1 Article 1 to be applicable in the case, the Grand Chamber maintained that the right to profit is an important element of the right to property, and that the combination of restrictions under the impugned legislation impaired the 'very essence' of the applicant's right of property.[38] In his separate opinion, Judge Zupančič took issue with the majority's interpretation:

> The *travaux préparatoires* of Protocol No. 1 amply demonstrate the hesitations different prospective signatories had concerning its Article 1 .... These hesitations concerned the question whether the right to property is a human right at all. *A fortiori*, the right to derive profit by merely owning an apartment building cannot be seen as a human right. I think the language of Article 1 of Protocol No. 1 demonstrates this ...
>
> In other words, the question whether 'peaceful enjoyment of one's possessions' implies the 'entitlement to derive profit from one's property' must be answered in the negative. This is not the place to discuss the 'social function of property', although a clause to that effect is an integral part of many modern constitutions. Suffice it to say that a sheer profit for the landlord – in other words, income not derived from his services – is, for the tenant, of necessity a payment that is not reciprocated by a benefit.
>
> How can that be a landlord's human right?[39]

The idea that the human right to property should include a right to economic profit is a contentious one, and in a way, Judge Zupančič's dissenting opinion articulates the controversy inherent in the human right to property.

---

38 *Hutten-Czapska v. Poland* (35014/97) judgment [GC] 19 June 2006, paras. 202–203.

39 Ibid., partly concurring, partly dissenting opinion of Judge Zupančič.

As Chapter 2 demonstrated, some of the drafters advocated for limiting the right to property to the exclusion of pure economic interests such as income derived from capital and from business undertakings. Clearly, such a restrictive scope would have ruled out protection for pure economic and commercial interests.

Although the Court in *Hutten-Czapska* did not say so explicitly, it appears to have agreed with the Polish Constitutional Court when it observed that '[o]ne of the essential elements of the right of property is the possibility of deriving profit from the object of ownership, which is of particular importance in a market economy'.[40] Ostensibly, the majority took the view that in modern European societies, the right to property should include the possibility of earning a profit. They were therefore inclined to reject domestic law which is at odds with those conceptions.[41]

In subsequent practice, the Court has continued to hold that deriving a minimum level of profit from property is an element of ownership protected by Protocol 1 Article 1.[42] It should be stressed that this only implies that a right to profit is counted among the elements of ownership; the level of profit to which the owner may be entitled is a matter for consideration under the assessment of 'fair balance', which will be discussed in Part 3.

3.2 *Limited Rights in Property*

If we venture a step beyond the case of ownership, the Court has responded to claims for protection of limited rights in property. Such rights do not fit easily with our ordinary understanding of the term 'possessions' or with notions of property in domestic law more generally. By virtue of the autonomous property concept, however, the Court has gone some way in extending ECHR protection to limited rights.

---

40 This view was not among the arguments cited by the majority, but the premises reveal that it was shared by the Strasbourg Court. See also *Ibid.*, para. 239, where the Court referred to the landlords' 'entitlement to derive profit from their property' in connection with its ruling on the pilot-judgment procedure pursuant to Article 46. See generally A M Honoré, 'Ownership' in A G Guest (ed), *Oxford Essays in Jurisprudence: A Collaborative Work* (Oxford University Press 1961) 107–126, who regards the right to income from property as an element of ownership.

41 See also *Frascino v. Italy* (35227/97) judgment 11 December 2003, where the Court found that the right to construct buildings was one of the rights held by the owner of land, contrary to what Italian law allegedly permitted.

42 See e.g. *Ghigo v. Malta* (31122/05) judgment 26 September 2006, para. 66, *Lindheim and Others v. Norway* (n 16), and *Kirovogradoblenergo, PAT v. Ukraine* (35088/07) judgment 27 June 2013.

For example, the Court has viewed lease rights as a proprietary interest attracting the protection of Protocol 1 Article 1, and restrictions of rights under the lease as interference with the lessee's right to property.[43] A lease is a contractual right to property conveyed by the owner to another party for a specified time, usually in return for a periodic payment. The title to the asset remains with the lessor, whereas the lessee is granted exclusive rights pursuant to the contract.[44]

Bosphorus v. Ireland is characteristic of the Court's approach.[45] An airline charter company had leased two aircraft from the national airline of former Yugoslavia. One of the aircraft was detained at the airport in Dublin on the grounds that releasing it might violate United Nations sanctions imposed in response to human rights violations in Serbia. The *Bosphorus* judgment is significant to the interpretation of the ECHR because it clarified the circumstances in which compliance with obligations under international law can be a legitimate aim of State interference. For our present discussion, the important point is that neither the parties nor the Court had any objection to regarding the impounded aircraft as the applicant company's 'possession', even though it was clearly not its formal owner. The Grand Chamber accepted without reservations that the detention of the aircraft was an interference in the applicant company's benefit of the lease.[46]

To take another example, it is common in transactions for the seller to ensure some form of security for payment from the buyer. A security interest is normally understood as a right in a specific thing that secures the performance of an obligation, usually a debt owed to a creditor. The case of *Gasus Dosier- und Fördertechnik GmbH v. the Netherlands* was introduced above, but a few more details bear mentioning here. The applicant company had sold a concrete mixer subject to retention of title until the full price had been paid. The buyer had taken possession of the mixer in accordance with the terms of the contract. After the buyer went bankrupt, the Dutch

43 See e.g. *Posti and Rahko v. Finland* (27824/95) judgment 24 September 2002, which concerned fishing rights pursuant to a contracted lease. See also Article 1 (6) a of the Energy Charter Treaty, which defines investment as every kind of asset including property rights such as leases.

44 A lease is comparable to the civil-law concept of *usufruct*, which permits the holder to possess, use and receive the fruits from things owned by another usually for a limited time.

45 *Bosphorus Hava Yolları Turizm ve Ticaret Anonim Şirketi v. Ireland* ('*Bosphorus v. Ireland*') (45036/98) judgment [GC] 30 June 2005.

46 Ibid., para. 140. See also *Bruncrona v. Finland* (41673/98) judgment 16 November 2004, para. 79, where the Court regarded a lease as a protected proprietary interest.

tax authorities proceeded to seize and sell it. Before the Strasbourg Court, the State argued that retention of title was a security right, not a property right, and that the enjoyment of it was limited to achieving security for payment of the purchase price.

The Court responded that it was immaterial whether Gasus's right in the concrete mixer was considered a right of ownership or as a security right *in rem* under Dutch law. The seizure and sale of the concrete mixer constituted an interference with the applicant company's 'possessions' under Protocol 1 Article 1, even though it no longer had the right of use and dispose of the concrete mixer.[47] Retention of title is a special form of security, because it leaves the rights holder with formal title. It is not entirely clear whether the Court would consider other security interests, such as liens or mortgages in immovable property, in the same manner.[48]

The broader question is whether contractual rights as such attract the protection of Protocol 1 Article 1. There are indications in more recent case law that the Court answers this in the affirmative.[49] In *Kurban v. Turkey*, the applicant had undertaken to construct a flood-prevention scheme for a local river basin.[50] There was no question that as a matter of domestic law, the applicant had both the right and the obligation to perform the agreed works, and the right to obtain the agreed payment for that performance. But the Court's conclusion that the contract itself amounted to a 'possession' for the applicant is far from obvious. Extending protection to pure contractual rights would normally need to be based on the existence of legitimate expectations.[51] However, such expectations were not established in the case.[52] In the absence of a clear justification, the Court's conclusion in *Kurban* underscores the need for a more coherent adjudicatory approach to the circumstances in which contractual rights can attract the protection of Protocol 1 Article 1.

The case law is similarly inconclusive with respect to use rights.[53] The Court has occasionally dismissed tenancy rights and rights of use to

47 *Gasus Dosier- und Fördertechnik GmbH v. the Netherlands* (n 10), para. 53.

48 See, by comparison, Article 1 (6) (a) of the Energy Charter Treaty where the term 'investment' is defined as *inter alia* 'other property rights such as mortgages, liens or pledges'.

49 See e.g. *Vijatović v. Croatia* (50200/13) judgment 16 February 2016, paras. 42–43.

50 *Kurban v. Turkey* (n 6).

51 See Section 4 below.

52 *Kurban v. Turkey* (n 6), separate opinion of Judge Koskolo, para. 11.

53 The Commission considered a number of applications concerning collective use rights in property, such as grazing, hunting and fishing rights enjoyed by indigenous peoples

immoveable property owned by others,[54] and occasionally accepted such rights.[55] The crucial point appears to be the extent to which they are exclusive to the applicant. The Court's approach to use rights in other assets corroborates that the degree of exclusivity is decisive for the Court's analysis.[56]

Obviously, there are limits to which rights in property are protected under Protocol 1 Article 1. At some point, limited rights no longer have economic value for the applicant,[57] and this brings us to the question of which assets are protected under Protocol 1 Article 1 – the second axis of the property concept introduced above.

4 Assets Constituting 'Possessions' for the Purposes of Protocol 1 Article 1

4.1 *'All Kinds of Pecuniary Assets'*

The Convention organs have refrained from providing a general definition of which assets qualify as 'possessions'. As Wildhaber has remarked, the case law indicates a rather 'open judicial mind' with respect to the protected

of Northern Europe. The overall impression from that branch of case law is that collective rights may qualify as a 'possession' under Protocol 1 Article 1 if the rights are invoked by a representative organ and that individuals may invoke a right of use provided that the right is sufficiently exclusive. See e.g. *Könkämä and 38 other Saami villages v. Sweden* (27033/95) decision [EComHR] 25 November 1996. See also S Solheim, *Eiendomsbegrepet i Den europeiske menneskerettskonvensjon* [The term 'property' in the European Convention on Human Rights] (Gyldendal Oslo, 2010) 159–163.

54 See e.g. *Durini v. Italy* (19217/91) decision [EComHR] 12 January 1994.

55 See e.g. *Wittek v. Germany* (37290/97) judgment 12 December 2002, where the applicants had a right of property in their house, coupled with the right of use (usufruct) over the land belonging to the State on which the house stood, in accordance with the applicable legislation. See also *Doğan and Others v. Turkey* (8803/02 et al.) judgment 29 June 2004, para. 139, where the economic resources that the applicants derived from their rights over the common lands qualified as 'possessions' for the purpose of Protocol 1 Article 1.

56 See e.g. *Paeffgen GmbH v. Germany* (25379/04 et al.) decision 18 September 2007, where the Court recognised the exclusive rights to use internet domains registered in the name of the applicant company as a 'possession'.

57 See e.g. *Chiragov and Others v. Armenia* (13216/05) judgment [GC] 16 June 2015, para. 147, where the Court the pointed out that the right to use land under the Soviet legal system represented a 'substantive economic interest' for the applicant, and as such a 'possession' under ECHR law.

interest.[58] As a starting point, the Court has established that Protocol 1 Article 1 protects 'all kinds of pecuniary assets'.[59]

That the interest is economic in nature may be said to follow implicitly from the text – in particular the French word 'biens', which normally translates as 'assets' and conveys the notion of economic value. It is further evidenced by the State's right to 'secure the payment of taxes or other contributions or penalties' pursuant to the second paragraph. The text thus recognises the obligation to pay money as an interference in the protected right. Furthermore, the Court's response to situations where the applicant has been deprived of his or her 'possessions', which will be discussed in Chapter 8 below, strongly suggests that it views money as a substitute for property.

On its face, this interpretation implies that anything with economic value should be considered a 'possession' within the meaning of Protocol 1 Article 1, whereas anything without economic value should not. Deciding whether something has economic value is not as straightforward as it may seem, however. By one measure, a thing has economic value if it can be the object of a transaction. The Court has occasionally referred to criteria such as assignability and transferability in support of its understanding of the property concept, but it has not applied these criteria consistently.

That said, they do pertain to most tangible assets.[60] For example, it is self-evident that immovable property and physical goods constitute 'possessions' within the meaning of Protocol 1 Article 1. These assets are indisputably endowed with economic value and transferable to others. The classic

---

58 L Wildhaber, 'The Protection of Legitimate Expectations in European Human Rights Law' in M Monti et al. (eds), *Economic Law and Justice in Times of Globalisation / Wirtschaftsrecht und Justiz in Zeiten der Globalisierung, Festschrift for Carl Baudenbacher* (Nomos 2007) 255.

59 See e.g. *Kirilova and Others v. Bulgaria* (42908/98 et al.) judgment 9 June 2005, para. 104. The term 'asset' is used interchangeably with 'possession' to denote an interest with economic value. See also D J Harris et al. (n 5) 850, who refer to 'the acquired economic value of the individual interest'.

60 In the few instances where the Court has ruled out assets as incompatible *ratione materiae* with the terms of Protocol 1 Article 1, it has done so because of moral considerations or because the asset has had questionable economic value, see e.g. *Parrillo v. Italy* (46470/11) judgment [GC] 27 August 2015, para. 215, where the Grand Chamber concluded, with reference to the pecuniary and economic scope of the right to property, that human embryos cannot be reduced to 'possessions' within the meaning of Protocol 1 Article 1. See also *De la Cierva Osorio de Moscoso and Others v. Spain* (41127/98 et al.) decision 28 October 1999, where the Court held that nobiliary titles could not be regarded as 'possessions' pursuant to Protocol 1 Article 1.

illustration from the Court's jurisprudence is *Sporrong and Lönnroth v. Sweden*, which concerned planning restrictions imposed on apartment buildings in Stockholm.[61] But the Court has also considered cases involving industrial equipment or machinery,[62] shipping cargo[63] and aircraft[64] – to name but a few examples.

Property rights in tangible assets, whether moveable or immoveable, normally pose few problems in terms of the applicability of Protocol 1 Article 1. Establishing rights in these objects under domestic law is normally straightforward, since these rights often appear in official registers, deeds or other publicly available documents. It is also understood that their use is subject to legal restrictions in the public interest.[65] The question for the Court in these matters is rather whether such restrictions comply with the requirements for justified interference – lawfulness, a legitimate aim and a 'fair balance' between the general interest of the community and the requirements for the protection of the individual's fundamental rights.[66]

The extent to which rights in intangible assets are accepted as 'possessions' is less clear, at least at the margins. The Court has formulated generic tests, for example by asking whether the applicant's legal position 'gave rise to interests of a proprietary nature' or whether 'the circumstances of the case, considered as a whole, conferred on the applicant title to a substantive interest protected by Article 1 of Protocol No. 1'.[67]

In an attempt to define the nature of that interest, the property concept will now be examined through the lens of a few specific categories of intangible assets. This is a fruitful exercise not only because it shows how the Court has drawn the line between protected and unprotected interests, but also because the Court's initial analysis of the applicant's 'possession' has bearing on the discussions in later chapters. Aside from their economic

61 *Sporrong and Lönnroth v. Sweden* (7151/75; 7152/75) judgment 23 September 1982. See also *Hutten-Czapska v. Poland* (n 38).

62 See e.g. *Gasus Dosier- und Fördertechnik GmbH v. the Netherlands* (n 10).

63 *Islamic Republic of Iran Shipping Lines v. Turkey* (40998/98) judgment 13 December 2007.

64 See e.g. *Air Canada v. the United Kingdom* (18465/91) judgment 5 May 1995 and *Bosphorus v. Ireland* (n 45).

65 See e.g. *Pye v. the United Kingdom* (n 14), para. 62, where the Court stated that '[t]he applicant companies' possessions were necessarily limited by the various rules of statute and common law applicable to real estate'.

66 See Part 3 below.

67 See e.g. *Anheuser-Busch Inc. v. Portugal* (73049/01) judgment [GC] 11 January 2007, paras. 63 and 78. See also P van Dijk et al. (eds), *Theory and Practice of the European Convention on Human Rights* (5th edn, Intersentia 2018) 853.

value, assets are imbued with different legal and factual characteristics which define the applicant's initial legal position against which the impugned interference is considered. An appreciation of the Court's analysis at the admissibility stage is necessary, first, in order to understand its subsequent assessments of whether there has been interference with the applicant's right to property, how that interference manifests itself and should be categorised, and ultimately whether the interference is justified.

4.2 *The Court's Approach to Intangible Assets*

4.2.1 Intellectual Property Rights

Intellectual property rights were initially recognised as 'civil rights' pursuant to Article 6, but not as 'possessions' pursuant to Protocol 1 Article 1.[68] The Commission first argued in favour of regarding patents as 'possessions' on the grounds that they are an essential element of economic activity, and have the core characteristics of property – exclusivity and transferability.[69] Since then, the Court has found Protocol 1 Article 1 to be applicable to a range of intellectual property rights.[70]

Anheuser-Busch Inc. v. Portugal illustrates how far the Court has gone in protecting intellectual property. The applicant company had applied to register 'Budweiser' as a trademark, but the application was rejected by the Portuguese authorities because the name had already been registered by a Czechoslovak company. Ultimately, the Portuguese courts upheld the decision of the patent authorities, and set aside the registration of 'Budweiser' on behalf of the applicant company.

One would think that a trademark could constitute a 'possession' under Protocol 1 Article 1 only after it had been registered in accordance with the rules in force in the State concerned. This was essentially how the Chamber reasoned when it declared the application from Anheuser-Busch inadmissible.[71] Under Portuguese law, the company could not be sure of being the

---

68 *X v. Austria* (7830/77) decision [EComHR] 13 July 1978.

69 *Smith Kline and French Laboratories Ltd v. the Netherlands* (12633/87) decision [EComHR] 4 October 1990.

70 See e.g. *Melnychuk v. Ukraine* (28743/03) decision 5 July 2005, which confirmed that Protocol 1 Article 1 applies to copyright, and *Kamoy Radyo Televizyon Yayıncılık ve Organizasyon A.Ş. v. Turkey* (19965/06) judgment 16 April 2019, para. 37, which extended protection to trade marks, and *SIA AKKA/LAA v. LATVIA* (562/05) judgment 12 July 2016, para. 55, concerning rights to musical works. See also Article 17 of the European Union's Charter of Fundamental Rights, whose second paragraph states that intellectual property shall be protected.

71 *Anheuser-Busch Inc. v. Portugal* (73049/01) judgment 11 October 2005, para. 52.

rightful owner of the trademark until after its final registration, and then only on the condition that no objection was raised by a third party. However, the Grand Chamber concluded that the applicant company was entitled to expect that the application would be examined under the applicable legislation as long as it satisfied other relevant substantive and procedural conditions.

The Court held that the application itself 'may give rise to a variety of legal transactions, such as a sale or licence agreement for consideration' and that '[t]hese elements taken as a whole suggest that the applicant company's legal position … came within Article 1 of Protocol No. 1, as it gave rise to interests of proprietary nature'. It went on to note that 'in a market economy, value depends on a number of factors and it is impossible to assert at the outset that the assignment of an application for the registration of a trade mark will have no financial value'.[72]

The dissenting minority pointed out that it would have been more appropriate to rely on the doctrine of legitimate expectations in the case. After all, the application gave Anheuser-Busch a conditional claim to protection of the 'Budweiser' trademark, and the Court's settled case law denies the status of 'possession' to a conditional claim which has lapsed as a result of a failure to fulfil the condition.[73] Still, the majority's interpretation of Protocol 1 Article 1 in *Anheuser-Busch Inc.* has prevailed in subsequent case law, and the judgment remains a landmark case in ECHR law concerning intellectual property.

4.2.2 Goodwill

Goodwill is commonly understood as the value of a business entity not directly attributable to its assets. The Convention institutions have long recognised that the goodwill of a business may constitute a 'possession' under Protocol 1 Article 1. The Court first articulated its view in *Van Marle and Others v. the Netherlands*, where it held that the goodwill of a group of accountants should be likened to the right of property: 'by dint of their own work, the applicants had built up a clientèle; this had in many respects the nature of a private right and constituted an asset and, hence, a possession within the meaning of the first sentence of Article 1 (P1–1)'.[74] Accordingly, State acts or omissions that diminish the present value of goodwill

72 *Anheuser-Busch Inc. v. Portugal* (n 67) paras. 76–78.

73 Ibid., joint concurring opinion of Judges Steiner and Hajiyev, para. 6.

74 *Van Marle and Others v. the Netherlands* (8543/79 et al.) judgment 26 June 1986, para. 41.

may amount to interference with the right to the peaceful enjoyment of property.

The Court has resolved a number of subsequent cases based on the approach in *Van Marle*. In *Iatridis v. Greece*, for example, the Grand Chamber found that by operating a cinema for 11 years without any interference from the authorities, the applicant had a clientèle which constituted a protected asset.[75] And in *Könyv-Tár Kft and Others v. Hungary*, a case brought by schoolbook distributors, the Court concluded that clientèle was 'an essential basis for the applicant companies' established business'.[76]

The Court's willingness to define goodwill as a 'possession' may seem unproblematic in light of the economic nature of Protocol 1 Article 1 and the open-minded approach it has taken to other intangible assets, such as intellectual property. However, it is not entirely consistent with the property concept described thus far. The Convention organs have always maintained that future income cannot be regarded as a 'possession' until it has been earned or is definitely payable.[77] One could argue that goodwill has no inherent value for the business which is distinct from the present value of the future income that the business expects to generate. If we follow this line of reasoning, it is difficult to understand how the Court can distinguish protected goodwill from unprotected future income, and whether such a distinction is workable in practice at all.[78]

4.2.3 Claims

In most jurisdictions, claims are a transferable asset. A claim can come in many different forms, however – it may be undisputed or disputed, conditional or unconditional, existing or potential – which implies that its economic value cannot always be easily ascertained. Naturally, the value of a claim also depends on the identity of the debtor.

---

75 *Iatridis v. Greece* (31107/96) judgment [GC] 25 March 1999.

76 *Könyv-Tár Kft and Others v. Hungary* (21623/13) judgment 16 October 2018, para. 32.

77 See e.g. *Centro Europa 7 S.r.l. and Di Stefano v. Italy* (38433/09) judgment [GC] 7 June 2012, para. 172. In a series of admissibility decisions against the United Kingdom involving the impact of a ban on handguns, the Court took the view that complaints of reductions in goodwill were in effect claims for loss of future income, which is not protected by Protocol 1 Article 1, see e.g. *Ian Edgar (Liverpool) Limited v. the United Kingdom* (37683/97) decision 25 January 2000.

78 See *Könyv-Tár Kft and Others v. Hungary* (n 76), dissenting opinion of Judge Wojtyczek, para. 6. See also A Bhasin, 'Future Income versus Goodwill under A1P1 – A Distinction Without a Difference?' 17(3) (2012) *Judicial Review* 226–235, and Maxwell (n 7) 111–116.

Claims have posed particular problems with respect to the applicability of Protocol 1 Article 1. After all, a claim is merely a right to acquire something in the future, and the Court has repeatedly stressed that the Convention does not give anyone the right to acquire property.

As noted above, the Court determines the existence of an asset according to its legal merits under national law. A claim must be 'sufficiently established to be enforceable', according to established case law.[79] To begin with, this means that a potential or conditional claim cannot be regarded as a 'possession'. A degree of certainty is required.[80] With respect to the enforceability criterion, a claim based on a final court decision ordering payment of an obligation falls within the remit of Protocol 1 Article 1.[81] By comparison, a judgment from the lower courts will normally not be sufficiently established to generate a 'possession'.[82]

The lack of consistency on this particular point is no doubt due to the various forms of claims which the Court deals with – claims for pension rights or social benefits, claims for salary, claims for restitution of property, and so on.[83] There is also a fluid dividing line between claims which are deemed to be sufficiently established *per se*, and claims which are protected because the applicant had a legitimate expectation of obtaining effective

---

79 *Stran Greek Refineries and Stratis Andreadis v. Greece* (13427/87) judgment 9 December 1994, para. 59.

80 In one early case, *X v. Germany* (8410/78) decision [EComHR] 13 December 1979, the Commission concluded that a notary's claim for fees could be considered a 'possession' only when such a claim has come into existence on the basis of services rendered by the notary and on the basis of existing regulations for notaries' fees. The mere expectation that the regulations on fees would not be changed was not protected by Protocol 1 Article 1. In more recent practice, the Court has stated that since the article applies only to a person's existing possessions and does not create a right to acquire property, future income cannot be considered to constitute 'possessions' unless it has already been earned or is definitely payable, see *Anheuser-Busch Inc. v. Portugal* (n 67), para. 64, and *Denisov v. Ukraine* (76639/11) judgment [GC] 25 September 2018, para. 137.

81 See *Stran Greek Refineries and Stratis Andreadis v. Greece* (n 79), para. 59, where a claim against the State which was based on a final arbitration award was considered a 'possession' under Protocol 1 Article 1. See also *Sciortino v. Italy* (30127/96) judgment 18 October 2001, and *Broniowski v. Poland* (31443/96) judgment [GC] 22 June 2004.

82 See e.g. *Kopecký v. Slovakia* (44912/98) judgment [GC] 28 September 2004, para. 59. See M Sigron, *Legitimate Expectations under Article 1 of Protocol No. 1 to the European Convention on Human Rights* (Intersentia 2014) 89, who concludes that '[the] case law is not clear about whether the claim must have proceeded to final judgment'.

83 See generally T Allen (n 7) 49, and B Rainey, P McCormick and C Ovey, *Jacobs, White and Ovey: The European Convention on Human Rights* (8th edn, Oxford University Press 2020) 568–572.

enjoyment of a property right in the future.[84] The extent to which claims are protected as 'possessions' can therefore only be fully explained in the context of the Court's doctrine on legitimate expectations, which will be discussed in Section 5 below.

4.2.4 Licences

Licences under public law were initially not regarded as 'possessions' pursuant to Protocol 1 Article 1.[85] The Court took a new approach in *Tre Traktörer Aktiebolag v. Sweden*, where it concluded that the licence was one of the main prerequisites for the applicant company's ability to pursue its economic interests. Indeed, in the Court's view, retaining the licence was one of the 'principal conditions for the carrying on of the applicant company's business, and … its withdrawal had adverse effects on the goodwill and value of the restaurant'.[86]

Thus, a licence can give rise to a protected position within the meaning of Protocol 1 Article 1 if and to the extent that it establishes economic interests for the licence holder.[87] The Court's approach reflects the view that a public licence is primarily a regulatory instrument, which does not give rise to property rights in an ordinary sense. The licence holder's legal position is

84 See e.g. *Xenodochiaki S.A. v. Greece* (49213/99) decision 15 November 2001, where the Court held that the applicant's claim for rent 'constituted expectations for future income which cannot be regarded as "possessions" within the meaning of Article 1 of Protocol No. 1, since they had not been recognised and determined by a judicial decision having final effect'. See also *Smokovitis and Others v. Greece* (46356/99) judgment 11 April 2002, para. 32, where the Court concluded that the practice of domestic courts had created a legitimate expectation that they would have found in favour of the applicants, and *EEG-Slachthuis Verbist Izegem v. Belgium* (60559/00) decision 10 November 2005, where the Court considered that the applicant had, at least, a legitimate expectation that the sums paid would be reimbursed.

85 See e.g. *X v. Federal Republic of Germany* (9177/80) decision [EComHR] 6 October 1981, which concerned confiscation of a driver's license, and *Pudas v. Sweden* (10426/83) decision [EComHR] 5 December 1984.

86 *Tre Traktörer Aktiebolag v. Sweden* (10873/84) judgment 7 July 1989, para. 53. See also *Fredin v. Sweden (no. 1)* (12033/86) judgment 18 February 1991, para. 40, where the permit to exploit gravel was not in itself regarded as a 'possession', but the Court found that its revocation constituted interference with the economic interests connected with the exploitation of the gravel pit.

87 See e.g. *Megadat.com SRL v. Moldova* (21151/04) judgment 8 April 2008, *Rosenzweig and Bonded Warehouses Ltd. v. Poland* (51728/99) judgment 28 July 2005, para. 51, *Werra Naturstein GmbH & Co KG v. Germany* (32377/12) judgment 19 January 2017, para. 37, and *NIT S.r.l. v. the Republic of Moldova* (28470/12) judgment [GC] 5 April 2022, paras. 245–247.

defined by the terms of the licence, as well as by the relevant laws and regulations in force at any given time. For the holder of the licence, the licence is an accessory to other proprietary interests, since the licence gives a right to utilise property or existing facilities in a certain way.[88] That licences are not deemed to be 'possessions' in and of themselves explains why the Court has generally viewed revocation of licences affecting the running of businesses as a measure controlling the use of property under the second paragraph of Protocol 1 Article 1, and not deprivation of property under the first paragraph.[89]

5 Protection of Legitimate Expectations

5.1 *A Notable Expansion of Protocol 1 Article 1's Material Scope*

So far this chapter has shown how the right to property in the ECHR primarily provides support for rights which already exist under domestic law. By virtue of the doctrine of autonomous concepts, the Court has interpreted the term 'possessions' to include assets without a clear basis in domestic law, in respect of which the applicant can argue that he or she has a 'legitimate expectation' of obtaining effective enjoyment.[90] The protection of legitimate expectations represents a notable expansion of Protocol 1 Article 1's material scope, even though it has admittedly played a rather limited role in the case law so far.

The protection of legitimate expectations is a considerable topic in domestic as well as international law. In German constitutional law, for example, the concept of *Vertrauensschutz* denotes the principle according to which citizens' confidence is protected by the legal system.[91] Similarly, when a subject of international law makes assurances to another in a way

88 See generally I Alvik, 'Concessions in International Law' (2022) 91 *Nordic Journal of International Law* 572–576.

89 See Chapter 6 below.

90 See e.g. *Malhous v. the Czech Republic* (33071/96) decision [GC] 13 December 2000. See also P De Sena, 'Economic and Non-Economic Values in the Case Law of the European Court of Human Rights' in P-M Dupuy et al. (eds), *Human Rights in International Investment Law and Arbitration* (Oxford University Press 2009) 210, who concludes that 'the concept of possessions covers not only an actual monetary or pecuniary right, but also a legitimate and well-founded expectation of realizing an economic interest'.

91 See generally K-A Schwarz, *Vertrauensschutz als Verfassungsprinzip. Eine Analyse des Nationalen Rechts, des Gemeinschaftsrechts und der Beziehungen zwischen beiden Rechtskreisen* (Nomos 2002).

that leads the other to legitimately place trust and confidence in them, those expectations are protected as a general principle of international law.[92]

The protection of legitimate expectations is a basic concept in the law of the European Union. It occupies a lesser, but by no means negligible, place in the legal order of the ECHR. As Wildhaber has observed, legitimate expectations appear in different branches of the case law of the Convention institutions, but it is primarily in relation to Protocol 1 Article 1 that it has been invoked and adapted to the distinctive context of the Convention system.[93]

The notion of legitimate expectations has two functions in the Court's jurisprudence. One relates to the determination of whether or not the applicant has a 'possession'. In this function, the Court has identified two forms of legitimate expectations which will be discussed below. It is worth emphasising here that at the admissibility stage, the Court views a legal position based on legitimate expectations as subsidiary to one based on existing property rights. In other words, legitimate expectations become relevant when no existing 'possession' can be clearly established.[94] Legitimate expectations fulfil a second function in the 'fair balance' test, by strengthening or weakening the applicant's position in the Court's assessment of whether the impugned interference was justified.[95]

5.2 *Expectations Linked to Existing Property Rights*

The concept of 'legitimate expectations' in the context of Protocol 1 Article 1 was first developed by the Court in *Pine Valley Developments Ltd and Others v. Ireland*. The applicant companies had bought land outside Dublin in reliance on an outline planning permission which appeared in a public register. Local authorities later refused to grant them a detailed planning permission, which was required in order to develop the land as they had intended. In the ensuing legal proceedings, the Irish Supreme Court decided that the outline planning permission had been granted *ultra vires* and was therefore void. In determining whether there had been an interference with the

92 See C McLachlan, L Shore and M Weiniger, *International Investment Arbitration: Substantive Principles* (2nd edn, Oxford University Press 2017) 315.

93 L Wildhaber (n 58) 253.

94 See e.g. *Balan v. Moldova* (19247/03) judgment 29 January 2008, para. 34, where the Court found that the applicant enjoyed 'a right recognised by law and by a previous final judgment … and *not merely* a legitimate expectation of obtaining a property right' (emphasis added).

95 See Chapter 8 below.

applicant companies' right to property, the Strasbourg Court held that until the Irish Supreme Court rendered its decision, the applicants had 'at least a legitimate expectation of being able to carry out their proposed development and [that] this [had] to be regarded as a component part of the property in question'.[96]

In a similar case, *Stretch v. the United Kingdom*, the applicant was prevented from exercising an option to extend the lease of land where he carried out commercial activity. Local authorities had acted *ultra vires* in granting the option, but before the mistake came to light, the applicant had proceeded to a late stage in negotiations with his subtenants. The Court concluded that the applicant 'must be regarded as having at least a legitimate expectation of exercising the option to renew and this may be regarded, for the purposes of Article 1 of Protocol No. 1, as attached to the property rights granted to him … under the lease'.[97]

In *Kopecký v. Slovakia* the Court described the line of cases from *Pine Valley Developments* and *Stretch* as follows:

> the persons concerned were entitled to rely on the fact that the legal act on the basis of which they had incurred financial obligations would not be retrospectively invalidated to their detriment. In this class of case, the 'legitimate expectation' is thus based on *reasonably justified reliance on a legal act which has a sound legal basis and which bears on property rights*.[98]

Here, the Court formulated a general test for determining the existence of legitimate expectations under Protocol 1 Article 1. Firstly, the applicant's expectation must be founded on a legal act. In other words, the expectation must be based on a normative legal instrument that can reasonably confer a property right on the applicant. The legal act may be a contract or statute; a judicial, administrative or parliamentary decision; case law; a register; zoning plans recognising the applicant's right, and so on.[99] By contrast, a

96 *Pine Valley Developments Ltd and Others v. Ireland* (n 17), para. 51.

97 *Stretch v. the United Kingdom* (44277/98) judgment 24 June 2003, para. 35. See also e.g. *Di Marco v. Italy* (32521/05) judgment 26 April 2011.

98 *Kopecký v. Slovakia* (n 82), para. 47 (emphasis added).

99 See e.g. *CRASH 2000 OOD and Others v. Bulgaria* (49893/07) decision 17 December 2013, para. 70, and *Bata v. the Czech Republic* (43775/05) decision 24 June 2008, paras. 77–79. See generally M Sigron (n 83) 103–141.

political act or declaration is not sufficient to generate legitimate expectations protected by Protocol 1 Article 1.

Secondly, the legal act in question must have a sound legal basis. This criterion pertains to the strength of the applicant's legal position under domestic law, which must necessarily be determined on the basis of an objective interpretation.[100] Conversely, no legitimate expectation can arise where there is a dispute as to the correct interpretation and application of domestic law.[101]

Thirdly, the legal act which forms the basis for the expectations must bear on existing property rights. A legitimate expectation has no independent existence; it must be attached to a proprietary interest which is itself sufficiently established.[102] Such property rights may amount to ownership, as in *Pine Valley Developments*, but also to limited rights in property such as lease rights, as in *Stretch*.

Fourthly, the applicant must demonstrate reliance which is reasonably justified. Various factual circumstances may give rise to more or less well-founded expectations of obtaining property rights in the future.[103] By way of contrast, the hope of recognition of a property right cannot form the basis of a 'possession' within the meaning of Protocol 1 Article 1.[104] The investors in *Pine Valley Developments* and *Stretch* had made investments in reliance on rights which appeared in public registers and contracts with the appropriate public organ. It was decisive in both cases that the applicants were deemed to have acted in good faith.[105]

---

100 See e.g. *Centro Europa 7 S.r.l. and Di Stefano v. Italy* (n 77), para. 179, where the Grand Chamber noted that the company's legitimate expectation had a 'sufficient basis to constitute a substantive interest and hence a "possession"'.

101 See e.g. *Anheuser-Busch Inc. v. Portugal* (n 67), para. 65, and *Cosmos Maritime Trading and Shipping Agency v. Ukraine* (53427/09) judgment 27 June 2019, para. 99.

102 *Kopecký v. Slovakia* (n 82), paras. 45–53.

103 See e.g. *Fredin v. Sweden (no. 1)* (n 86), para. 54.

104 This criterion has been at the centre of many property restitution cases. See e.g. *Gratzinger and Gratzingerova v. the Czech Republic* (39794/98) decision [GC] 10 July 2002, para. 73, where the Court noted that 'there is a difference between a mere hope of restitution, however understandable that hope may be, and a legitimate expectation, which must be of a nature more concrete than a mere hope and be based on a legal provision or a legal act such as a judicial decision'. See also *Prince Hans-Adam II of Liechtenstein v. Germany* (42527/98) judgment [GC] 12 July 2001, para. 83.

105 L Wildhaber and I Wildhaber, 'Recent Case Law on the Protection of Property in the European Convention on Human Rights' in C Binder et al., (eds), *International Investment Law for the 21st Century: Essays in Honour of Christoph Schreuer* (Oxford University Press 2009) 661.

5.3 *A Separate Form of Expectations Linked to the Realisation of Claims?*

According to the Court in *Kopecký*, a different form of legitimate expectations emerged in the case of *Pressos Compania Naviera S.A. and Others v. Belgium*. The case concerned State liability for losses caused by negligence among operators of pilot services at sea. Under domestic rules of tort, such claims came into existence as soon as the damage had occurred. By the time the domestic courts had resolved the applicant companies' claims with final effect, however, a legal act had been passed which extinguished liability with retroactive effect for a period of thirty years without compensation. The Strasbourg Court held that the applicant companies had a legitimate expectation that their claims would be determined in accordance with the general law of tort.[106]

In *Kopecký* the Court drew a distinction between legitimate expectations relating to existing property rights on one hand, and legitimate expectations relating to the realisation of claims on the other.[107] Despite the Grand Chamber's efforts to explain this distinction, it is difficult to understand the roles that these two forms of legitimate expectations are meant to play at the admissibility stage. Indeed, this is an important reason why the doctrine on legitimate expectations in ECHR law has been described, by observers and judges alike, as vague and unsettled.[108] Both forms of expectations concern economic interests from which the applicant expected to benefit in the future: In the case of *Pine Valley Developments*, the development of land in accordance with an administrative decision; and in the case of *Pressos Compania Naviera*, a claim for damages in tort in accordance with established domestic case law. Subsequent acts by the State annulling these interests confounded the applicants' expectations.

As noted above, a claim can be regarded as a 'possession' when it is sufficiently established under domestic law. An applicant with a legally sound claim can legitimately expect that the claim will pass to judgment and enforcement, but it is difficult to see how an applicant can legitimately expect a claim to be realised if it fails the test formulated by the Court in *Kopecký*.

---

106 *Pressos Compania Naviera S.A. and Others v. Belgium* (17849/91) judgment 20 November 1995, para. 31.

107 *Kopecký v. Slovakia* (n 82), para. 48.

108 See M Sigron (n 83) 96 and further references. See also *Béláné Nagy v. Hungary* (53080/13) judgment [GC] 13 December 2016, concurring opinion of Judge Wojtyczek, para. 2, who describes the case law on legitimate expectations as 'difficult to understand, due to lack of precision and inconsistencies'.

In this respect, a claim is no different from other interests in property that the holder anticipates to realise, such as the lease option in the case of *Stretch*. Also, whether the applicant's expectations are linked to an existing proprietary interest or to the realisation of a claim may be subject to reasonable disagreement, as in the case of *Anheuser-Busch Inc.*[109]

Judging by more recent case law, the Court appears to have abandoned the distinction between claims and other assets as the basis for legitimate expectations.[110] The crux of the Court's analysis is the strength of the applicant's position in domestic law, regardless of the asset to which those expectations are attached. Thus, it is easy to agree with Wildhaber, when he argues that

> the applicability of [Protocol 1] Article 1 to claims is determined by their well-foundedness in domestic law. To say that the claimant may legitimately expect his claim to be respected or enforced adds nothing of substance; it must, after all, be generally presumed that well-founded legal claims will be protected in a State that subscribes to the rule of law. Conversely, a claim that lacks a sound basis in domestic law will lie beyond the reach of [Protocol 1] Article 1, and no expectation, however legitimate or reasonable it may be, will change that.[111]

The doctrine of legitimate expectations in ECHR law has occasionally given rise to controversy both within and beyond the Court, because it has rendered Protocol 1 Article 1 a bar to legislative changes in the Member States. As Chapter 2 showed, some of the drafters were concerned that the right to property in the ECHR would place restrictions on States' right to implement necessary economic and social policies. The case law on legitimate expectations shows that those premonitions have partly come true.

---

109 As noted above, the Grand Chamber was divided over whether the company's application for trademark registration deserved status as a 'possession' in its own right, or whether it merely provided a basis for legitimate expectations since the statutory conditions were not fulfilled, see in particular *Anheuser-Busch Inc. v. Portugal* (n 67), joint concurring opinion of Judges Steiner and Hajiyev, para. 6.

110 See *Béláné Nagy v. Hungary* (n 108), para. 79, where the Grand Chamber concluded that '[n]otwithstanding the diversity of the expressions in the case-law referring to the requirement of a domestic legal basis generating a proprietary interest, their general tenor can be summarised as follows: for the recognition of a possession consisting in a legitimate expectation, the applicant must have an assertable right which … may not fall short of a sufficiently established, substantive proprietary interest under the national law'.

111 L Wildhaber (n 58) 260.

The controversy has been most evident in cases concerning claims for social benefits. In modern European societies, many depend for their survival on welfare allowances from the State. At the same time, the State may have legitimate reasons for making changes to the welfare system from time to time, in response to societal changes and evolving views on the categories of persons who are deserving of assistance.

For a long time, the case law in Strasbourg was ambiguous with respect to the role of Protocol 1 Article 1 in these cases. The Convention organs initially drew a distinction between benefits which were paid on the basis of contributions, and those which were paid without reference to contributions. Compulsory contributions towards social insurance schemes of any kind were considered to create a right protected under Protocol 1 Article 1 only where there was a direct link between the level of contributions paid and the benefits awarded.[112] However, in a number of later cases the Court held that even a welfare benefit in a non-contributory scheme may constitute a 'possession' for the purposes of Protocol 1 Article 1.[113]

In *Stec and Others v. the United Kingdom*, the Court sought to clarify the applicability of Protocol 1 Article 1 to social benefits. The Court noted that such benefits are funded in a variety of ways: Some are paid for by contributions to a specific fund, some depend on a claimant's contribution record and many are paid for out of general taxation on the basis of a status defined by law. Given the variety of funding methods, it was no longer justified to hold that only benefits financed by contributions to a specific fund fall within the scope of Protocol 1 Article 1. However, the Court stressed that Protocol 1 Article 1 was applicable only where national law provides for an entitlement and if the applicant satisfies the relevant conditions.[114]

In *Béláné Nagy v. Hungary*, the Court took a further step in extending the application of Protocol 1 Article 1. The applicant had been granted a disability pension because her claim met the two statutory conditions relating to health and contributions. Following a reform of the method used to determine disability, her entitlement was withdrawn in 2010 because she did not meet the new health condition. Her medical condition remained the same, however. In 2012, the law was changed with respect to the contributions necessary for a disability allowance, and a requirement was introduced

112 See e.g. *Müller v. Austria* (5849/72) decision [EComHR] 16 December 1974, and *Gaygusuz v. Austria* (17371/90) judgment 16 September 1996.

113 See e.g. *Koua Poirrez v. France* (40892/98) judgment 30 September 2003, para. 37.

114 *Stec and Others v. the United Kingdom* (65731/01; 65900/01) decision [GC] 6 July 2005, paras. 48–56.

which the applicant could not meet. She complained to the Strasbourg Court that the legislative changes violated her rights under Protocol 1 Article 1, and the Court narrowly decided the case in her favour – initially with four votes against three in the Chamber,[115] and ultimately with 9 votes against 8 in the Grand Chamber.[116]

The majority of judges in the Chamber and the Grand Chamber concluded that the applicant had a legitimate expectation to receive disability pension as long as her medical condition would necessitate.[117] Yet as the dissenting minorities in both chambers pointed out, her claim for disability allowance no longer had a basis in domestic law after the changes adopted with effect from 2012. By allowing the claim to succeed, the Court had, in their view, applied the concept of legitimate expectations under Protocol 1 Article 1 in a novel way.[118] The minority in the Court's Chamber pointedly argued that 'the right to property under the European Convention on Human Rights is not an autonomous repository for economic and social rights not granted by the Member States'.[119]

When the majority found the applicant's legal position worthy of protection under Protocol 1 Article 1, they were clearly motivated by the fact that she depended on the disability allowance for survival. Also, she had acted in good faith and there were no effective transitional measures in place. The Court is understandably cautious to avoid imposing far-reaching obligations in the area of socio-economic rights.[120] After all, these parts of ECHR law are sensitive, because they require budgetary and policy choices to be made and new obligations to be reconciled with existing policies. This has led some observers to conclude that Protocol 1 Article 1 has a distinct role to play in relation to claims for social security benefits.[121] It remains to be

115 *Béláné Nagy v. Hungary* (53080/13) judgment 10 February 2015.

116 *Béláné Nagy v. Hungary* (n 108).

117 *Béláné Nagy v. Hungary* (n 115), para. 47, and ibid., para. 107.

118 *Béláné Nagy v. Hungary* (n 115), joint dissenting opinion of Judges Keller, Spano and Kjølbro, para. 9, and *Béláné Nagy v. Hungary* (n 108), joint dissenting opinion of Judges Nußberger, Hirvelä, Bianku, Yudkivska, Møse, Lemmens and O'Leary, para. 39.

119 *Béláné Nagy v. Hungary* (n 115), joint dissenting opinion of Judges Keller, Spano and Kjølbro, para. 1.

120 I Leijten 'Defining the Scope of Economic and Social Guarantees in the Case Law of the ECtHR' in E Brems and J Gerards (eds), *Shaping Rights in the ECHR: The Role of the European Court of Human Rights in Shaping the Scope of Human Rights* (Cambridge University Press 2013) 115.

121 See e.g. I Leijten, 'The Right to Minimum Subsistence and Property Protection under the ECHR: Never the Twain Shall Meet?' (2019) 21(4) *European Journal of Social Security* 308, who suggests that a legitimate expectation can more easily arise in cases where

seen, therefore, what interpretative value *Béláné Nagy* has for other areas of case law concerning the protection of legitimate expectations under Protocol 1 Article 1.

5.4 *The Rationale for Protecting Legitimate Expectations under Protocol 1 Article 1*

As argued above, the primary function of Protocol 1 Article 1 is to protect property rights which already exist in domestic law.[122] The drafters surely never anticipated that the right to property in the Convention would oblige States to safeguard interests without a basis in the national legal order. The case law regarding legitimate expectations shows how the Court has used the autonomous property concept to bring stability in situations where the national law fails to do so. It is worthwhile to consider how the Court has justified this expansion of the material scope.

Expectations can be understood as a disposition to predict that a certain event will occur, combined with an attitude of desiring and feeling entitled to rely on its occurrence. In one definition, legitimate expectations are 'beliefs about what will and ought to happen in the future that is underpinned by systems of law and by particular legal entitlements, as opposed to mere social customs, habits or conventions'.[123] The right to property makes it possible for legal subjects to entertain legitimate expectations with respect to their assets. A good legal system, it could be argued, should secure these expectations.[124]

A common feature of applications involving legitimate expectations under Protocol 1 Article 1 is that the applicants have relied on an instrument of domestic law which has been retrospectively invalidated to their detriment. Retrospective legislative interference poses a challenge to the principle of legal certainty, according to which the law must be foreseeable so as

---

the basic means of subsistence are concerned. As Leijten also observes, the Court's foray into the social and policy sphere of the political democracies – with its imposition of external solutions going against the outcome of the normal working of democratic processes at the national level – has not been universally appreciated.

122 See Section 2 above. See also T Allen (n 7) 282.

123 See A Brown, *A Theory of Legitimate Expectations for Public Administration* (Oxford University Press 2017) 54.

124 See e.g. S R Munzer, *A Theory of Property* (Cambridge University Press 1990) 23, and M Sigron (n 83) 43–70.

to allow legal subjects to rely on the law and regulate their conduct accordingly.[125] In *Béláné Nagy* the Court reasoned that:

> Respect for such reliance follows from one aspect of the rule of law, which is inherent in all the Articles of the Convention and which implies, inter alia, that there must be a measure of legal protection in domestic law against arbitrary interferences by public authorities with the rights safeguarded by the Convention …[126]

The impact of *Béláné Nagy* may be subject to debate, but if we take the Court at its word here, its rationale for protecting legitimate expectations is to uphold the rule of law.[127] As Spano has argued, from the perspective of the legal subject, the most important effect of the rule of law is precisely to create foreseeability. As long as the law is sufficiently clear and accessible ahead of time, he or she is able to find out what they can and cannot do, and the consequences of acting in one way rather than another. In a system based on the rule of law, the law empowers legal subjects to access things to which they have a rightful claim, and to avoid or mitigate any negative consequences for their existing interests. Ultimately, the rule of law thus promotes respect for personal autonomy.[128]

In the case of *ultra vires* representation, it seems arbitrary that the authorities should be allowed to treat legal subjects as owners when it is to their advantage, but refuse to do so when it is to their disadvantage.[129] In similar situations, the Court has observed that a State whose authorities have failed to observe their own internal rules and procedures should not be allowed to profit from their wrongdoing and escape their obligations. The risk of any mistake made by the authorities should be borne by the

---

125 This principle is enshrined in Article 7 of the Convention with respect to penal cases, and is regarded as inherent in the rule of law and in the law of the Convention. See Chapter 9 below.

126 *Béláné Nagy v. Hungary* (n 108), para. 78.

127 See also *Béláné Nagy v. Hungary* (n 108), para. 99, where the Grand Chamber majority noted that '[t]he change in the law effectively imposed on a certain category of insured persons, including the applicant, a condition whose advent had not been foreseeable during the relevant potential contributory period and which they could not possibly satisfy once the new legislation entered into force – a combination of elements which is ultimately difficult to reconcile with the rule of law'.

128 R Spano, 'The Rule of Law as the Lodestar of the European Convention on Human Rights: The Strasbourg Court and the Independence of the Judiciary' (2021) *European Law Journal* 2.

129 M Sigron (n 83) 159.

State and the errors must not be remedied at the expense of the individual concerned.[130] While such considerations do not figure in the rationale for protecting legitimate expectations, they are intrinsic to the concepts of legitimate expectations in prominent European legal cultures from which the Convention emanates.

At this point, the distinction between formal and substantive conceptions of the rule of law should be recalled. In a formal sense, the rule of law implies that Protocol 1 Article 1 should recognise a 'possession' only if and to the extent that it exists in domestic law, and go no further in protecting the applicant's interests. Conceived in this way, the rule of law leaves no room for protecting the applicant's interests in preserving the *status quo* on the basis of 'a careful consideration of the individual circumstances of the case', as the Court did in *Béláné Nagy*.[131]

On the other hand, if 'possessions' were protected under the Convention only to the extent to which they exist and enjoy protection under domestic law, the Court's role would be limited to making sure that domestic law has been applied correctly. The autonomy of the term 'possessions' would be illusory, and protection for expectations based on legal acts deemed invalid *ultra vires*, as in the case of *Pine Valley Developments* and *Stretch*, would be impossible. Such a conclusion clearly contradicts the Court's conception of the rule of law. But applied in this manner, the rule of law is not just a formal concept; it is also concerned with the substance of the law. Accordingly, at least in some cases, the ECHR requires that domestic laws respect citizens' legitimate expectations.

6 Conclusion

The term 'possessions' is crucial in the context of Protocol 1 Article 1, since it defines and delineates the provision's material scope of application. With respect to existing property rights, the discussions in this chapter have given substance to and offered evidence for the 'formula' in *Gasus* that the right to property in the Convention is not limited to ownership of physical

130 See e.g. *Lelas v. Croatia* (55555/08) judgment 20 May 2010, para. 74.

131 *Béláné Nagy v. Hungary* (n 108), para. 89. See also *Stec and Others v. the United Kingdom* (n 114), para. 51, where the Court similarly held that '[w]here an individual has an assertible right under domestic law to a welfare benefit, the importance of that interest should also be reflected by holding Article 1 of Protocol No. 1 to be applicable'.

goods. The autonomous property concept has enabled the Court to extend protection to a range of other rights and assets as well.

Along the 'rights' axis, property in ECHR law is understood as legal rights in property which are exclusive to the applicant. Owners of property are free to access, use or dispose of their possessions, and they are protected against interference from others that would conflict with these rights. By incorporating these elements, the Court has developed a property concept reflecting the traditional notions of property in the laws of the Member States. Furthermore, the Court has come to view the right to profit as an element of ownership, which is of particular importance in a modern, market-based economy.

The Court has also brought limited rights in property, such as lease rights and security interests, into the ambit of Protocol 1 Article 1. The ostensible motivation lies in the need to ensure that the right to property is effective in practice: taking a formalistic approach to the applicant's legal position would be atypical of a court which prides itself on looking beyond appearances and investigating the realities in the situation complained about.[132] Moreover, the development of the property concept at this point may be said to reflect the harmonising role of the Court's jurisprudence.[133] Limiting the scope of Protocol 1 Article 1 to formal ownership would preclude individuals in jurisdictions where such ownership, for whatever reason, is less prevalent.

Along the 'assets' axis, property is generally understood as objects with economic value. Here, developments appear to have been motivated by the need to ensure equal treatment to various types of assets and by a pragmatic recognition of the difficulty in drawing clear lines between protected and non-protected interests. With economic value as a common denominator, there are few rational reasons to treat some assets less favourably than others at the admissibility stage. Rather, it is preferable to treat all forms of property in the same manner, and balance the interests involved in the subsequent justification assessment.

---

132 See e.g. *Sporrong and Lönnroth v. Sweden* (n 61), para. 63.

133 See *A, B and C v. Ireland* (25579/05) judgment [GC] 16 December 2010, joint partly dissenting opinion of Judges Rozakis, Tulkens, Fura, Hirvelä, Malinverni and Poalelungi, para. 5, where the minority noted that 'one of the paramount functions of the case-law is to gradually create a harmonious application of human rights protection, cutting across the national boundaries of the Contracting States and allowing the individuals within their jurisdiction to enjoy … equal protection regardless of their place of residence'.

The Court continues to recite the *dictum* from *Marckx* that Protocol 1 Article 1 does not give anyone a right to acquire property, but as this chapter has shown, it is difficult to draw the line between existing 'possessions' and assets in respect of which the applicant may be said to entertain legitimate expectations. The Court's case-by-case approach makes it necessary to explain why the lines are drawn where they are drawn. The problem is exacerbated by the fact that the Court in hard cases rarely takes pains to identify the protected 'possession', but instead refers more generally to the economic interests at stake for the applicant.[134] In the interest of clarity and consistency, it would serve the Court well to treat the applicant's initial legal position with more methodological transparency and openness.[135]

The role of legitimate expectations is particularly unclear in case law dealing with intangible assets. Future income is not protected by Protocol 1 Article 1, but expectations founded on existing rights in goodwill, intellectual property, claims, and licences can be protected and thus indirectly safeguard future income. Clarifying the principles which define the scope of Protocol 1 Article 1 with respect to intangible assets in particular is paramount, as a growing proportion of society's economic values consists of intangible assets, due to developments in technology and in financial markets and due to the growth in intellectual property.[136]

While a gradual, *ad hoc* approach may have prevailed in the case law with respect to existing assets, the Court has sought to offer a more principled justification for extending protection to legitimate expectations. The protection of legitimate expectations in ECHR law cannot be explained by reference to common property standards among the Member States. Rather, the Court's concern is that adhering to the domestic classification of 'possessions' in some situations leads to results which are at odds with the Convention's object and purpose, specifically the rule of law.

---

134 See e.g. *Werra Naturstein GmbH & Co KG v. Germany* (n 87), para. 37, and *Kristiana Ltd. v. Lithuania* (36184/13) judgment 6 February 2018, para. 91.

135 As Judge Koskelo argued in her separate opinion in *Kurban*, such a state of affairs creates difficulties not least at the domestic level, where the primary responsibility of ensuring compliance and respect for the protected Convention rights lies, see *Kurban v. Turkey* (n 6), concurring opinion of Judge Koskelo, para. 2.

136 See E Nordtveit, 'The Changing Role of Property Rights: An Introduction' in E Nordtveit (ed), *The Changing Role of Property Law: Rights, Values and Concepts* (Edward Elgar Publishing 2023), 8, who refers to the trends of digitisation, de-materialisation, and commodification of property.

CHAPTER 5

Protection of Whose Property Rights?

1 Introduction

Chapter 4 dealt with the material scope of the right to property in the Convention. The present chapter deals with the question of whose property rights are protected – the personal scope of Protocol 1 Article 1. Given that the objective is to account for the developments in the case law, the focus will be on how the Court has determined whose property rights deserve Convention protection and whose property rights do not.

Whose property rights are protected by the Convention is a substantive question in the sense that the person or entity alleging a violation must fall within the ambit of the terms of Protocol 1 Article 1. As will be briefly shown in Section 2, the article contains no limitations in this respect. Whose property rights are protected is also a procedural question in the sense that the Court must have jurisdiction and the applicant must have legal standing under the Convention in order for his or her complaint to be considered on the merits.[1] Thus, the articles governing the Court's jurisdiction and the Convention's enforcement machinery effectively delimit the personal scope of the right to property. These articles, which will be examined in Sections 3 and 4, respectively, apply to all of the rights in the ECHR, but the subject matter of the right to property has allowed the Court to develop the principles used to determine whose rights are ultimately protected by the Convention.

2 The Starting Point: 'Every Natural or Legal Person'

There is a distinction in ECHR law between rights and freedoms which can be enjoyed only by human beings and those which apply to physical and

1 If the applicant lacks standing before the Court, the application is to be dismissed as incompatible with the Convention *ratione personae* without examination on the merits, pursuant to Article 35 paras. 3 and 4. The Court's *competence ratione personae* has two components: the application must be brought against a State party to the Convention, and by a natural or legal person with standing before the Court in accordance with the terms of Article 34. The following discussion concerns the latter component.

 | DOI:10.1163/9789004735088_006

legal persons alike. Most of the Convention's rights generally apply to everyone ('Everyone has the right …'), as do its freedoms ('No one shall be subjected to …'). Although the term 'everyone' may be said to encompass both legal and natural persons, it is normally used only in reference to natural persons. The French version speaks of 'toute personne', which perhaps offers more freedom of interpretation with respect to whether or not non-natural persons are to be included.

These open-ended terms notwithstanding, it is well established that some rights and freedoms are by their nature susceptible of being exercised only by natural persons. These rights include the right to life pursuant to Article 2[2]; the prohibition against torture, inhuman and degrading treatment pursuant to Article 3[3]; freedom from slavery under Article 4; freedom from arbitrary detention under Article 5[4]; and the right to marry under Article 12.

Convention rights which are deemed applicable to legal persons include the right to a fair hearing under Article 6 para. 1[5]; freedom from punishment without law under Article 7[6]; the right to an effective remedy under Article 13[7]; freedom from non-discrimination under Article 14[8]; and the right to protection from the abuse of restrictions under Article 18.[9]

Between these two categories is a third group of rights whose applicability to legal persons must be determined on a case-by-case basis: the right to respect for private and family life, home and correspondence under Article 8[10]; freedom of conscience, thought and religion under

---

2 See e.g. *Comingersoll S.A. v. Portugal* (35382/97) judgment [GC] 6 April 2000, concurring opinion of Judge Rozakis, joined by Judges Sir Nicolas Bratza, Caflisch and Vajić.

3 See e.g. *Identoba and Others v. Georgia* (73235/12) judgment 12 May 2015, para. 45, where the Court held that 'it is inconceivable that physical integrity, susceptible to be enjoyed by human beings, could be attributed to the first applicant, a legal person'.

4 See e.g. *Wouterse, Marpa Zeeland BV and Metal Welding Service B.V. v. the Netherlands* (46300/99) decision 1 October 2002.

5 See e.g. *Västberga Taxi Aktiebolag and Vulic v. Sweden* (36985/97) judgment 23 July 2002, and *Terra Woningen B.V. v. the Netherlands* (20641/92) judgment 17 December 1996.

6 See e.g. *G.I.E.M. S.r.l. and Others v. Italy* (1828/06; 34163/07; 19029/11) judgment [GC] 28 June 2018.

7 See e.g. *The Communist Party of Russia and Others v. Russia* (29400/05) judgment 19 June 2012.

8 See e.g. *Pine Valley Developments Ltd and Others v. Ireland* (12742/87) judgment 29 November 1991.

9 See e.g. *OAO Neftyanaya Kompaniya Yukos v. Russia* (14902/04) judgment 20 September 2011.

10 Legal persons have a right to respect for their 'correspondence' and 'home', but not for 'family life', see e.g. *Société Colas Est S.A. and Others v. France* (37971/97) judgment

Article 9[11]; freedom of expression under Article 10[12]; freedom of peaceful assembly and freedom of association under Article 11[13]; and the right to compensation for non-pecuniary damage under Article 41.[14]

In contrast to every other article in the ECHR, the text of Protocol 1 Article 1 makes clear that the right to peaceful enjoyment of possessions extends to '[e]very natural or legal person'. The second sentence states that '[n]o one' shall be subjected to deprivation of their possessions except as provided for by national and international law, and necessarily encompasses the same sphere of persons as the first sentence does.

An early draft of Protocol 1 Article 1 made the right to property applicable to 'individuals and corporate bodies'.[15] Although the *travaux préparatoires* do not say so explicitly, these terms were probably inspired by the wording of Article 17 of the Universal Declaration of Human Rights, which extends to collective ownership ('alone as well as in association with others') and which the drafters sought to espouse. From the outset, it appears to have been uncontroversial that the Convention should protect the property rights of legal persons on par with those of individuals.

The lack of controversy is somewhat surprising, given the popular belief that human rights can only be enjoyed by human beings. For example, Donnelly has argued that 'the very term human rights points to a source: humanity, human nature, being a person or human being. Legal rights have law as their source; contractual rights arise from contracts, and thus, human rights have humanity or human nature as their source.'[16]

The drafters of the ECHR, however, clearly envisaged Convention protection for legal persons. The text of Protocol 1 Article 1 provides specific recognition of the general notion that corporate bodies have rights under the

---

16 April 2002. See also *Verein Klimaseniorinnen Schweiz and Others v. Switzerland* (53600/20) judgment [GC] 9 April 2024, paras. 521–526.

11 See e.g. *Kontakt-Information-Therapie and Hagen v. Austria* (11921/86) decision [EComHR] 12 October 1988 and *X and Church of Scientology v. Sweden* (7805/77) decision [EComHR] 5 May 1979.

12 See e.g. *Autronic AG v. Switzerland* (12726/87) judgment 22 May 1990, para. 47.

13 See e.g. *A. Association and H. v. Austria* (9905/82) decision [EComHR] 15 March 1984, and *Slavic University in Bulgaria and Others v. Bulgaria* (60781/00) decision 18 November 2004.

14 See e.g. *Comingersoll S.A. v. Portugal* (35382/97) judgment [GC] 6 April 2000, para. 35.

15 'Supplementary Report of the Committee to the Consultative Assembly' 8 August 1950, *Travaux Préparatoires*, vol IV, 822.

16 J Donnelly, *Human Rights, Individual Rights and Collective Rights* in J Berting et al. (eds), *Human Rights in a Pluralist World. Individuals and Collectivities* (Praeger 1990), quoted in T R G van Banning, *The Human Right to Property* (Intersentia 2002) 170.

Convention.[17] Evidence of the same is found in the first paragraph of Article 10, which provides that the right of freedom of expression 'shall not prevent States from requiring the licensing of broadcasting, television or cinema enterprises'.

The introductory words in Protocol 1 Article 1 were later changed to '[e]very natural or legal person', which was the form in which the article was adopted in 1952. In a substantive sense, these terms do not exclude anyone as holders of property rights. Lack of compatibility with the personal scope of Protocol 1 Article 1 is therefore no grounds for the Court to dismiss a complaint. The Court has never quarrelled with the notion that companies and organisations have the right to the peaceful enjoyment of their 'possessions'. At this particular point, it is fair to say that the jurisprudence under Protocol 1 Article 1 has been relatively static – in contrast to the more dynamic case law pertaining to for example Articles 8 and 10.[18]

3 Limitations Derived from the Court's Jurisdiction

The analysis of the personal scope of Protocol 1 Article 1 could end here, but as alluded to in the introduction, the terms '[e]very natural or legal person' provide no more than a starting point for determining whose property rights are protected. Obviously, the protection derived from Protocol 1 Article 1 cannot extend further than the States' obligation under Article 1 to 'secure to everyone within their jurisdiction the rights and freedoms defined in ... this Convention'.[19] That obligation includes the right to property if and to the extent that the State has ratified the First Additional Protocol.

---

17 D J Harris et al., *Law of the European Convention on Human Rights* (4th edn, Oxford University Press 2018) 849–850.

18 See, in particular, M Emberland, *The Human Rights of Companies - Exploring the Structure of ECHR Protection* (Oxford University Press 2006) 110–154.

19 The principles of the territorial application of the ECHR are well covered in the literature, and will not be reiterated in detail here. According to the case law, the State is responsible for everyone within its territorial jurisdiction, including nationals, non-nationals and stateless persons. The Court has formulated two exceptions to this principle: the State may be held responsible for acts performed by its authorities (or producing effects) outside its own territory, (i) where the State through diplomatic and consular agents has exercised authority and control over persons, and (ii) where the State has exercised effective control over an area, see e.g. *Al-Skeini and Others v. the United Kingdom* (55721/07) judgment [GC] 7 July 2011. As noted by Harris et al., the jurisdiction of the Court in practice overlaps with that of the Contracting States; consequently, the concept of the Court's jurisdiction *ratione loci* has been all but

As long as a Member State has jurisdiction over the person and property in question, the protection deriving from the Convention's substantive rights applies in full.[20] As a consequence, the protection offered by Protocol 1 Article 1 extends to persons domiciled outside the Council of Europe area with economic interests in a Member State – for example, American and Iranian companies, which have appeared as applicants before the Court in the past.[21]

In the context of Protocol 1 Article 1, it has been maintained that non-nationals enjoy stronger protection against deprivation of property than nationals of the respondent State. This argument has been framed not as a matter of the Court's jurisdiction, but as a substantive aspect said to follow from 'the general principles of international law' referred to in the second sentence.[22] This reference was mentioned briefly in Chapter 2 above and will be revisited in Chapter 8 below. Suffice it for now to say that Protocol 1 Article 1 does not differentiate *prima facie* between legal subjects within the State's jurisdiction.[23]

4 Limitations Derived from the Convention's Enforcement Machinery

It follows from the discussions so far that the personal scope of the right to property is defined by the limits of the Court's jurisdiction. The sphere of

---

replaced by an examination of whether the applicant is within the respondent State's jurisdiction, see D J Harris et al., *Law of the European Convention on Human Rights* (4th edn, Oxford University Press 2018) 102. See also P van Dijk et al. (eds), *Theory and Practice of the European Convention on Human Rights* (5th edn, Intersentia 2018) 11–20.

20 As noted above, while the term 'everyone' in Article 1 is normally used to describe natural persons, it does not *per se* exclude legal persons. In this respect, the ECHR differs from the International Covenant on Civil and Political Rights, whereby States undertake to respect the rights of individuals only, see Article 2 para. 1. See also Article 1 para. 2 of the American Convention on Human Rights, which makes clear that '[f]or the purposes of this Convention, "person" means every human being'.

21 See e.g. *Anheuser-Busch Inc. v. Portugal* (73049/01) judgment [GC] 11 January 2007, and *Islamic Republic of Iran Shipping Lines v. Turkey* (40998/98) judgment 13 December 2007.

22 See *James and Others v. the United Kingdom* (8793/79) judgment 21 February 1986, para. 63. See also U Kriebaum, 'Is the European Court of Human Rights an Alternative to Investor-State Arbitration?' in P-M Dupuy et al. (eds), *Human Rights in International Investment Law and Arbitration* (Oxford University Press 2009) 242.

23 See by comparison Article 16, which restricts the political activity of 'aliens', and Protocol 4 Article 3, which makes the right to access and reside in the country applicable to nationals only.

persons protected by the Convention's substantive rights is further limited by the articles governing the ECHR's enforcement machinery – in particular, the right of individual application under Article 34, which states:

> The Court may receive applications from any person, non-governmental organisation or group of individuals claiming to be the victim of a violation by one of the High Contracting Parties of the rights set forth in the Convention or the Protocols thereto. The High Contracting Parties undertake not to hinder in any way the effective exercise of this right.

The requirements in Article 34 are well-covered in the literature about ECHR law, and there is no need to review them in detail here.[24] What is important to note is that complaints relating to the right to property have occasionally presented the Court with practical and interpretative difficulties, in particular related to the standing of legal persons. Although these issues do not have bearing on the interpretation of Protocol 1 Article 1 directly, the Court has, in response to complaints concerning the right to property, developed principles clarifying the personal scope of the Convention as a whole. The case law in this area is therefore worth a closer look.

4.1 *The 'Victim' Requirement*

The first issue relates to the requirement in Article 34 that the applicant claims to be a 'victim of a violation' of the Convention or its Protocols. The word 'victim' suggests that the alleged violation must have affected the applicant directly, and this is also how it has been understood in practice.[25] In cases involving natural persons, the 'victim' requirement poses few problems, since the person pursuing the application to the Court is normally identical to the person claiming to have suffered a Convention violation.

In cases involving legal persons, on the other hand, the limits of the Convention's personal scope are more unclear. At least, with respect to complaints relating to the right to property, the notion of being directly affected by a violation has occasionally given rise to difficult questions in practice. Since Protocol 1 Article 1 primarily protects economic interests, and virtually

24 See e.g. D J Harris et al., *Law of the European Convention on Human Rights* (4th edn, Oxford University Press 2018) 83–98.

25 See e.g. *Skubenko v. Ukraine* (41152/98) decision 6 April 2004, where the Court noted that 'the word "victim" in the context of Article 34 denotes the person directly affected by the act or omission in issue'.

any economic loss attributable to State activity or inactivity is treated as interference, as will be shown in the next chapter, the subject matter opens the door for persons other than the directly affected entity to claim 'victim' status.

Shareholders in a company are a case in point. Shares are 'possessions' for the purposes of Protocol 1 Article 1. Thus, shareholders are entitled to 'victim' status under Article 34 with respect to interference directly affecting the value of their shares.[26] But even if the shareholder is not directly affected by a State measure, any adverse effect on the company's activities indirectly affects the shareholder's financial interests as well. In this situation, the shareholder is liable to seek Protocol 1 Article 1 protection.

The prevailing rule in ECHR law is that it is up to the company, and not its shareholders, to take action when the company's rights are infringed upon. When shareholders appeal for 'victim' status on account of interference which has affected the company's business, they are effectively requesting to be identified with the company – an exercise often referred to as 'lifting the corporate veil'.[27] In response to such requests – and primarily within the context of Protocol 1 Article 1 complaints – the Court has developed an 'indirect victim' doctrine under which acts prejudicial to the company in exceptional circumstances can give the shareholders the status as applicants under Article 34.[28]

---

26 See *Albert and Others v. Hungary* (5294/14) judgment [GC] 7 July 2020, para. 134, where the Court summed up the relevant jurisprudence by stating that acts affecting the rights of the shareholders are distinct from measures affecting the company in that 'both the nature of such acts and their alleged effect impact the shareholders' legal rights both directly and personally and go beyond merely disturbing their interests in the company by upsetting their position in the company's governance structure'.

27 The term is most often used in international law as a reference to the act of disregarding the legal entity in the interests of third parties who have dealings with the company. As noted by the International Court of Justice in the *Case Concerning the Barcelona Traction, Light & Power Co Ltd (Belgium v. Spain) (Merits)* [1970] ICJ Rep 3, 36, para. 56: 'The wealth of practice already accumulated on the subject in municipal law indicates that the veil is lifted, for instance, to prevent the misuse of the privileges of legal personality, as in certain cases of fraud or malfeasance, to protect third persons such as a creditor or purchaser, or to prevent the evasion of legal requirements or of obligations'. ECHR law is primarily concerned with the opposite situation, in which the 'corporate veil' is lifted from within, to the benefit of the shareholders.

28 See e.g. *Vallianatos and Others v. Greece* (29381/09; 32684/09) judgment [GC] 7 November 2013, para. 47, where the Court noted that '[t]he word "victim", in the context of Article 34 of the Convention, denotes the person or persons directly or indirectly affected by the alleged violation ... Hence, Article 34 concerns not just the direct victim or victims of the alleged violation, but also any indirect victims to whom the violation

The case law shows that the 'indirect victim' approach may be justified in two situations. In one group of cases, the Court has allowed shareholders to proceed with complaints where it is impossible for the company to pursue the application in its own name.[29] Overwhelmingly, it has refused to examine cases brought by individual shareholders due to lack of standing, but in a few instances, the Court has acknowledged that exceptional circumstances precluded the company from bringing the case. This group has included cases where an appointed official tasked with looking after the company's interests was unable or unwilling to apply to the Strasbourg Court in respect of the alleged violation,[30] or where the alleged violation concerned a matter of disagreement between the trustee and the shareholders, such as the removal of a manager and the appointment of a trustee.[31]

In the second group of cases, the Court has conferred 'indirect victim' status on shareholders in situations where the applicant is the sole shareholder of the company, and where the company merely serves as a 'vehicle' for the owner's business ventures.[32] This group has included cases brought by shareholders of small or family-owned companies or cooperatives[33] or where one shareholder in a family-owned firm has lodged an application to the Court without any objection from the remaining shareholders.[34] In these situations, the company and its shareholders are so closely identified

---

would cause harm or who would have a valid and personal interest in seeing it brought to an end'.

29 See e.g. *Agrotexim and Others v. Greece* (14807/89) judgment 24 October 1995, para. 66, *Olczak v. Poland* (30417/96) decision 7 November 2002, para. 59, and *Albert and Others v. Hungary* (5294/14) judgment [GC] 7 July 2020, para. 126.

30 See e.g. *Credit and Industrial Bank v. the Czech Republic* (29010/95) judgment 21 October 2003, para. 51, *Capital Bank AD v. Bulgaria* (49429/99) decision 9 September 2004, and *International Bank for Commerce and Development AD and Others v. Bulgaria* (7031/05) judgment 2 June 2016, paras. 90–92.

31 See e.g. *G.J. v. Luxembourg* (21156/93) judgment 26 October 2000, paras. 23–24, and *Veselá and Loyka v. Slovakia* (54811/00) decision 13 December 2005.

32 See e.g. *Pine Valley Developments Ltd and Others v. Ireland* (12742/87) judgment 29 November 1991, para. 42, where the Court found that '[the applicant companies] were no more than vehicles through which Mr Healy proposed to implement the development ... On this ground alone it would be artificial to draw distinctions between the three applicants as regards their entitlement to claim to be "victims" of a violation'.

33 See e.g. *Yarrow and Others v. the United Kingdom* (9266/81 et al.) decision [EComHR] 28 January 1983, *S.C. Fiercolect Impex S.R.L. v. Romania* (26429/07) 13 December 2016, paras. 38–41, and *Vujović and Lipa D.O.O. v. Montenegro* (18912/15) judgment 20 February 2018, paras. 29–30.

34 See e.g. *KIPS DOO and Drekalović v. Montenegro* (28766/06) judgment 26 June 2018, paras. 86–87.

with each other that it would be artificial, in the Court's view, to distinguish between the two.

4.2 'Non-Governmental Organisations'

The second issue related to the standing of legal persons under Article 34 concerns the scope of the term 'non-governmental organisation'. Distinguishing between public and private legal subjects may have been straightforward when the Convention was written, but as European societies have developed, the lines separating public and private ownership have become more blurred. Public authorities today are owners of various assets in addition to exercising the regulatory power vested in the State.[35] Also, public authorities act in various ways in a private capacity as parties to contracts involving property rights – as seller or buyer, as landowner or lessee, as service provider or procurer, and so on.

This convergence of roles and interests held by public and private actors has occasionally posed difficulties with respect to establishing legal standing under Article 34 for entities closely linked to the State. Complaints relating to Protocol 1 Article 1 have enabled the Court to confront this issue. In *Danderyds kommun v. Sweden*, a case brought by a Swedish municipality, it responded that:

> ... it is not only the central organs of the State that are clearly governmental organisation [sic] ... but also decentralised authorities that exercise public functions, notwithstanding the extent of their autonomy vis-à-vis the central organs. This is the case even if the municipality is claiming that in this particular situation it is acting as a private organ.[36]

---

35 See e.g. E Nordtveit, 'The Changing Role of Property Rights: An Introduction' in E Nordtveit (ed), *The Changing Role of Property Law: Rights, Values and Concepts* (Edward Elgar Publishing 2023) 2–3.

36 *Danderyds kommun v. Sweden* (52559/99) decision 7 June 2001. The test in *Danderyds kommun*, which emphasised the exercise of public functions, codified previous decisions from the Convention organs in response to applications from territorial authorities, see e.g. *16 Austrian Communes and Some of Their Councillors v. Austria* (5767/72 et al.) decision [EComHR] 31 May 1974, and *Ayuntamiento de Mula v. Spain* (55346/00) decision 1 February 2001. The essential holding in *Danderyds kommun* has been maintained and further clarified in the Court's subsequent practice, see e.g. *Breisacher v. France* (76976/01) decision 26 August 2003.

The Court went on to hold that 'to consider a Swedish municipality a non-governmental organisation is clearly contradicted by the fact that its acts can engage the responsibility of the Swedish State under the Convention'.[37] The principle here is that the Convention cannot bestow human rights and the obligation to observe those rights on the same legal subject. The symmetry in the ECHR system mandates that the sphere of legal subjects entitled to rights and freedoms must be distinct from the sphere of legal subjects which are obligated to 'secure' those same rights and freedoms under Article 1. Thus, the term 'non-governmental organisations' must be interpreted in a way which prevents a State from acting as both an applicant and a respondent party before the Court.

The same reasoning applies to legal entities which participate in the exercise of governmental powers or run a public service under government control. As a means of distinguishing between 'governmental' and 'non-governmental' entities, the Court has developed a functional test pertaining to the entity's institutional and operational independence from the State:

> In order to determine whether any given legal person other than a territorial authority falls within [the 'non-governmental' organisation] category, account must be taken of its legal status and, where appropriate, the rights that status gives it, the nature of the activity it carries out and the context in which it is carried out, and the degree of its independence from the political authorities.[38]

In this test, the Court takes into account a variety of factors, none of which appears to be decisive on its own. The entity's legal status is no more than a starting point: The Court has considered private-law companies as 'governmental organisations' and public-law entities as 'non-governmental organisations'.[39]

One important factor is the legal context in which the entity operates. Companies with monopoly status or other special privileges in law have been deemed to be 'governmental organisations'.[40] Conversely, companies

37 Ibid.

38 *Islamic Republic of Iran Shipping Lines v. Turkey* (40998/98) judgment 13 December 2007, para. 79. See also *Radio France and Others v. France* (53984/00) decision 23 September 2003, para. 26.

39 See, respectively, e.g. *State Holding Company Luganksvugillya v. Ukraine* (23938/05) decision 27 January 2009 and *The Holy Monasteries v. Greece* (13092/87; 13984/88) judgment 9 December 1994, para. 49.

40 See e.g. *Renfe v. Spain* (35216/97) decision [EComHR] 8 September 1997.

that do not enjoy any powers beyond those conferred by ordinary law in the exercise of their activities have been considered 'non-governmental'. In this assessment, it is relevant whether the same services are operated by private actors and whether the applicant company is subject to the jurisdiction of the ordinary courts rather than the administrative courts.[41]

Another important factor is the nature of the entity's activities. Companies performing traditional public functions such as utilities[42] and railways,[43] as well as the more modern functions such as managing State property,[44] have been deemed to belong to the 'governmental' sphere. Companies engaged in ordinary commercial business, on the other hand, have been presumed to be non-governmental organisations.[45]

The Court's overriding concern is whether the applicant company enjoys sufficient institutional and operational independence from the State.[46] The criteria applied by the Court to define the sphere of 'non-governmental organisations' under Article 34 mirror those it applies to determine whether the State can be held responsible under Article 1 for the acts of a body which is not formally a public authority.[47] In particular, complaints relating to Protocol 1 Article 1 have allowed the Court articulate criteria for deciding whether or not the State is liable for the debts of a State-owned company.[48]

---

41 See e.g. *Islamic Republic of Iran Shipping Lines v. Turkey* (n 38), para. 81.

42 *JKP Vodovod Kraljevo v. Serbia* (57691/09; 19719/10) decision 16 October 2018.

43 *Renfe v. Spain* (n 40).

44 See e.g. *State Holding Company Luganksvugillya v. Ukraine* (n 39).

45 *Islamic Republic of Iran Shipping Lines v. Turkey* (n 38), para. 79.

46 Ibid., para. 81. The Court found that the applicant company was a 'non-governmental organisation', despite the fact that it was wholly owned by the Iranian State and that a majority of the members of the board of directors were appointed by the State. The Court emphasised that the applicant company was legally and financially independent from the State and was run as a commercial business.

47 See *Kotov v. Russia* (54522/00) judgment [GC] 3 April 2012, para. 95, where the Grand Chamber noted that '[d]espite the difference between the concept of "governmental organisation" and that of "public authority", the pattern of analysis used by the Court in these two situations is similar'. See also *Ljubljanska banka d.d. v. Croatia* (29003/07) decision 12 May 2015, para. 53, where the Court held that the criteria used in the context of State responsibility under Article 1 'apply with equal force in the context of determining whether a (State-owned) company may be considered a "non-governmental organisation" within the meaning of Article 34'.

48 See e.g. *Ališić and Others v. Bosnia and Herzegovina, Croatia, Serbia, Slovenia and the former Yugoslav Republic of Macedonia* (60642/08) judgment [GC] 16 July 2014, paras. 114–115.

5 Conclusion

Protocol 1 Article 1 is unique among the rights and freedoms in the Convention in that it formally equates natural and legal persons as holders of the right to property. Whose property rights are protected by the ECHR is therefore easily established in a substantive sense. It is obvious that the right to property cannot extend further than the States' obligation to secure the same right under Article 1 of the Convention, and that the personal scope of the right to property is delimited by the principles governing the Court's jurisdiction. More importantly, the sphere of persons protected by Protocol 1 Article 1 is defined by the Convention's enforcement machinery, in particular right of individual application under Article 34. Difficult issues relating to the standing of legal persons have required an adjudicatory response, and as this chapter has shown, the subject matter of Protocol 1 Article 1 has provided the Court with an opportunity to clarify the principles that determine whose rights are ultimately protected by the Convention.

The 'indirect victim' doctrine demonstrates that the Court's occasional sympathy for shareholders' interests rests squarely on practical considerations. The Court has emphasised the need to avoid the risk of competing claims in Strasbourg made on behalf of the same company, and the risk of differences of opinion among shareholders or between shareholders and a board of directors as to the most appropriate way of reacting to an infringement of the company's rights.[49] Only when it is impossible for the company to pursue the application in its own name, or when the shareholder owns all or most of the company, will the Court have no objection to allowing the shareholder to appear on behalf of the company.

The Court's interpretation of the term 'non-governmental organisation' reflects the need to interpret the Convention in a manner which ensures internal consistency and harmony between its provisions.[50] The term 'non-governmental organisation' rules out protection for the property interests of public organs, even when they are acting in a private capacity. With respect to entities which participate in the exercise of governmental powers or run a public service under government control, the Court has developed a functional test mirroring the assessment it carries out to determine whether the State can be held responsible for acts or omissions of those entities under Article 1. The Court's primary concern has been to prevent a State from

49 See *Agrotexim and Others v. Greece* (n 29), para. 66, and *Albert and Others v. Hungary* (n 29), paras. 136–137.

50 See e.g. *Johnston and Others v. Ireland* (9697/82) judgment 18 December 1986, para. 57.

acting as both an applicant and a respondent party in Strasbourg and thus maintain a form of symmetry in the ECHR system.

These jurisprudential developments testify to a rather pragmatic reading of the provisions governing the Convention's enforcement machinery. But at the heart of the Court's reasoning lies the fundamental objective of the ECHR as an instrument for protecting human rights. This was aptly illustrated by the Grand Chamber's decision in the inter-State case of *Slovenia v. Croatia*. The case was originally brought by a bank owned by the Slovenian State complaining that the non-enforcement of judgments in its favour violated its rights under Article 6 and Protocol 1 Article 1. The Court declared the application inadmissible because the bank was deemed to be controlled by the government and thus lacked standing to lodge an application.[51]

Slovenia proceeded to file an inter-State application under Article 33, alleging that Croatia was responsible for the violations. The Court responded that if an organisation is not entitled to submit an individual application pursuant to Article 34, then it cannot be recognised as a victim of a violation of any Convention rights. According to the very nature of the Convention, the Court said, it is always the individual, and not the State, who is directly or indirectly harmed by a violation. To hold otherwise would be to contradict the very object and purpose of the ECHR. Furthermore, should the Court find a violation in a case brought on behalf of an entity lacking sufficient institutional and operational independence from the State, and award a sum of money as just satisfaction, then the eventual final beneficiary of the Court's judgment would be the State.[52]

In the case of *Slovenia v. Croatia* Article 33 was invoked for the first time for the protection of the interests of legal, rather than natural, persons. The Court took the opportunity to address the fundamental question of whether the Convention's rights and freedoms extend to entities controlled by the State at all. It answered in the negative. The purpose of Convention's enforcement machinery, then, is to provide private entities with a venue for appealing to the Court. By implication, Protocol 1 Article 1 exists to protect private property, and not public property.

---

51 *Ljubljanska banka d.d. v. Croatia* (n 47).

52 *Slovenia v. Croatia* (54155/16) decision [GC] 18 November 2020, para. 66–67.

CHAPTER 6

The Merits of the Court's 'Three Rules' Approach

1 Introduction: The Notion of Interference in Convention Rights in General and the Right to Property in Particular

So far Part 2 has discussed developments in the case law with respect to Protocol 1 Article 1's material and personal scope of protection. In order for the State's responsibility under the ECHR to be engaged, the applicant must also be able to show that his or her property rights have been interfered with, either by the State or by a private party. The present chapter seeks to define the characteristics of State interference in the right to property, and to analyse the different forms of interference that Protocol 1 Article 1 has been understood to reflect.[1]

The notion of interference is significant because it has presented the Court with a dilemma which goes to the heart of the right to property as a human right: Should protection under Protocol 1 Article 1 be limited to freedom from arbitrary deprivation of property, as the drafters intended? The Court settled this question early on by making all forms of interference in the right to property justiciable under broadly similar requirements. Yet the dilemma persists because deprivation measures must, as a rule, be accompanied by compensation if they are to be consistent with Protocol 1 Article 1. Other forms of interference will often comply even if no compensation is paid. The Court has failed to clearly articulate the principles it applies to distinguish deprivation from other forms of interference in the right to property, and the criteria emerging from the case law remain elusive.

By way of introduction, a few words should be said about what generally characterises interference in Convention rights. Interference functions both as a requirement for admissibility and as a defining element in the Court's examination of the merits of the complaint. In its function as an

1 In this section, the word 'interference' is used for convenience to denote both acts by public authorities affecting the individual's property rights, and the State's failure to ensure the effective exercise of the right guaranteed by Protocol 1 Article 1. These two aspects of the State's undertaking to 'secure' the Convention rights and freedoms pursuant to Article 1 are referred to as the States' negative and positive obligations, respectively. The book will touch on the extent of States' positive obligation to secure the right to property later in the chapter, and in more detail in later chapters.

 | DOI:10.1163/9789004735088_007

admissibility requirement, an interference renders the applicant a *prima facie* victim of a violation.[2] As an element in the Court's substantive analysis, the nature and severity of the intrusion into the applicant's sphere of interests have a bearing on the outcome of the 'fair balance' assessment.[3]

In practice, however, the distinction between the Court's assessment of admissibility and its examination of the merits of the complaint is not watertight. The respondent State may have raised preliminary objections which invite the Court to examine the character of the interference at the admissibility stage. In such cases, where the objections are closely linked to the merits of the application, the Court often considers them jointly.[4]

Most of the qualified rights in the Convention define interference in rather broad terms. Article 8 para. 2 prohibits 'interference by a public authority' in the right to private and family life except in certain situations. Article 9 para. 2 conceives of 'limitations' to freedom of thought, conscience and religion. Article 10 para. 2 envisages 'formalities, conditions, restrictions or penalties' curtailing the freedom of expression. Article 11 para. 2 refers to 'restrictions' on the freedom of assembly and association. In the same vein, Protocol 4 Article 2 para. 3 governs 'restrictions' on freedom of movement, whereas Protocol 7 Article 2 para. 2 talks of 'exceptions' to the right of appeal in criminal matters.

These general terms are ostensibly chosen to encompass all forms of interference, legal as well as physical.[5] On a close reading, the words 'limitations' and 'formalities' in Articles 9 and 10, respectively, evoke interference in the individual's legal sphere. These connotations are logical in light of the fact that attempts by a State to restrain the freedom of conscience and expression often take a legal form, censorship being a case in point. On the other hand, the word 'restrictions' in Article 11 imparts the notion of physical restraints, which is equally reasonable since the act of peaceful assembly presupposes a degree of physical freedom. Nonetheless,

2 Absent a *prima facie* violation the Court shall reject the application as inadmissible, in accordance with Article 35 para. 3. See Chapter 5 above.

3 See Part 3 below.

4 See e.g. *Kurban v. Turkey* (75414/10) judgment 24 November 2020, para. 61 where the Court recalled that 'questions relating to the applicability of qualified rights under the Convention and the existence of an interference, the latter forming part of the merits of the relevant complaints, are often inextricably linked'.

5 See by comparison the former Article 50 (present Article 41), according to which 'a *decision* or a *measure* taken by a legal authority or any other authority of a High Contracting Party' could give rise to a claim for just satisfaction (emphasis added).

the above-mentioned articles describe State interference in a manner which does not exclude any forms or manifestations in practice.

By contrast, the text of Protocol 1 Article 1 does not refer to 'interference' or any similar general term. It identifies two specific forms of interference: being 'deprived' of one's possessions and subjected to 'control' with the use of one's property. Whereas deprivation is generally prohibited unless carried out in accordance with applicable rules of domestic and international law, control of the use of property in the general interest is permitted as long as it is lawful and the State deems it to be necessary. On its face, the second paragraph formulates a broad reservation which leaves no doubt as to the State's right to regulate private property; indeed, the *travaux préparatoires* intimate that the drafters' intention was to circumscribe the political and economic prerogatives of the States.[6] On a strict interpretation, therefore, the text of Protocol 1 Article 1 – read both in isolation and alongside the other qualified articles in the Convention – conceives of deprivation of property as the only relevant form of interference.[7]

It follows from the discussions above that interference in Convention rights must be established in the specific context of the protected interest. Determining the existence of a 'possession' and the existence of interference are separate exercises in the admissibility assessment, but it would be wrong to view these questions entirely in isolation. At least, doing so would be taking a more formalistic approach to the applicability of Protocol 1 Article 1 than what the Court's case law reflects. Whether the applicant has a legal position protected by Protocol 1 Article 1 must be determined in the light of the alleged interference, and *vice versa*: the existence and nature of the interference must be determined in the light of the proprietary interest initially held by the applicant.

Chapter 4 showed that the concept of property in ECHR law can be mapped along two axes. Along the first axis, 'possessions' are powers or privileges in law deriving from ownership as well as from exclusive, limited rights in property. In this sense, interference implies a detrimental change to the applicant's legal position under domestic law. Since ownership under the ECHR is understood to encompass the right to access, use and dispose of one's property, any limitation of those privileges will, in principle, constitute interference. Limitations may take the form of legal impediments, such

6 T Allen, *Property and the Human Rights Act 1998* (Oxford University Press 2005) 25.

7 The second sentence of Protocol 1 Article 1 is structurally similar to Article 2 para. 2, which sets the parameters for the lawful deprivation of life, and Article 5 para. 1, which provides the conditions according to which someone can be deprived of his or her liberty.

as prohibitions of certain acts or the imposition of new obligations, or physical restrictions or hindrance. And since the Court has held that owners are entitled to derive profit from their property, restrictions in that entitlement also by definition constitute interference.

Along the second axis, 'possessions' are understood as any asset with objective economic value to which the applicant's rights are attached. Interference must therefore, as a general rule, entail some adverse economic effect for the applicant.[8] On its face, this interpretation suggests that even the slightest reduction in the value of the applicant's 'possession' amounts to interference. However, the Convention organs have long applied a *de minimis* threshold to complaints concerning the right to property.[9] With the entry into force of Protocol 14, the Court shall now dismiss an individual application if it considers that the applicant has not suffered a 'significant disadvantage'.[10]

The premises of *Pine Valley Developments Ltd. and Others v. Ireland* show how the Court maintains a conceptual distinction between the applicant's rights in property and the economic value of the asset, and how it gauges the effects of the interference along both axes. On one hand, the Court noted that the applicant company retained substantive privileges or powers in its property after the Supreme Court's decision – specifically, the right to lease out the land or use it for other purposes. On the other hand, the Court observed that the land retained economic value, as demonstrated by the

8 However, it would be incorrect to say that it is always necessary to demonstrate economic loss. See e.g. *Chassagnou and Others v. France* (25088/94; 28331/95; 28443/95) judgment [GC] 29 April 1999, where the Court concluded that a statutory obligation to allow hunting on the applicants' land amounted to a violation of Protocol 1 Article 1. The applicants did not frame their case in terms of economic loss, but were opposed to hunting on ethical grounds. However, the majority of complaints reflect an economic impact.

9 See e.g. *Langborger v. Sweden* (11179/84) judgment 22 June 1989, para. 41, where the Court held that the impugned legislative measure, which impacted the applicant's financial position to a negligible extent, failed to reach the threshold of interference under Protocol 1 Article 1.

10 See Protocol 14 Article 12. What constitutes a 'significant disadvantage' depends on the circumstances of the case, including the nature of the right violated, the seriousness of the alleged violation and the potential consequences of the violation for the applicant's personal situation. The purpose of the admissibility criterion is to enable a more rapid treatment of cases without merit and to allow the Court to concentrate on its central mission of providing legal protection of human rights at the European level, see *Explanatory Report to Protocol No. 14 to the Convention for the Protection of Human Rights and Fundamental Freedoms, Amending the Control System of the Convention* (Council of Europe Treaty Series No. 194), para. 39.

fact that it had subsequently been sold, albeit at a price of one-tenth of what the applicant companies had originally paid.[11]

This chapter will now look closer at the different forms of interference that Protocol 1 Article 1 has been understood to reflect. As intimated by the text and the drafting history, the right to property in the ECHR was conceived as a safeguard against arbitrary deprivation of property. In keeping with that intention, the Convention organs initially left it to the States to determine the justification of measures which did not amount to deprivation.[12] In the landmark judgment in *Sporrong and Lönnroth v. Sweden*, the Court established that

> [Protocol 1 Article 1] comprises three distinct rules. The first rule, which is of a general nature, enounces the principle of peaceful enjoyment of property; it is set out in the first sentence of the first paragraph. The second rule covers deprivation of possessions and subjects it to certain conditions; it appears in the second sentence of the same paragraph. The third rule recognises that the States are entitled, amongst other things, to control the use of property in accordance with the general interest, by enforcing such laws as they deem necessary for the purpose; it is contained in the second paragraph.[13]

A few years later, in *James and Others v. the United Kingdom*, the Court added that '[t]he three rules are not, however, "distinct" in the sense of being unconnected. The second and third rules are concerned with particular instances of interference with the right to peaceful enjoyment of property and should therefore be construed in the light of the general principle enunciated in the first rule'.[14]

---

11 *Pine Valley Developments Ltd and Others v. Ireland* (12742/87) judgment 29 November 1991, para. 56.

12 See e.g. *Handyside v. the United Kingdom* (5493/72) judgment 7 December 1976, para. 62, where the Court maintained that '[the second] paragraph sets the Contracting States up as sole judges of the "necessity" for an interference. Consequently, the Court must restrict itself to supervising the lawfulness and the purpose of the restriction in question'.

13 *Sporrong and Lönnroth v. Sweden* (7151/75; 7152/75) judgment 23 September 1982, para. 61. *Sporrong and Lönnroth* has long been viewed as one of the most important judgments the Court's case law in relation to Protocol 1 Article 1, see e.g. L Sermet, 'The Right to Property under the European Convention on Human Rights' (2007) Council of Europe *Human Rights Handbook Series* 10.

14 *James and Others v. the United Kingdom* (8793/79) judgment 21 February 1986, para. 37.

The 'three rules' formula from *Sporrong and Lönnroth* has since become part of the Strasbourg liturgy in cases involving Protocol 1 Article 1. It is repeated so often that it is easy to forget that the 'three rules' are a product of the Court's interpretation, which has expanded the scope of Protocol 1 Article 1 in a radical manner. Indeed, some observers have called the 'three rules' a 'judicial reconstruction' and an effective 'restatement' of the right to property in the Convention.[15]

Whatever the most apt description might be: Once these 'rules' have been introduced, they should serve clearly defined purposes and be foreseeable for applicants as well as for States. The principle of legal certainty – which the Court sees as an inherent element of the rule of law – requires some preconception of how the Court is likely to treat a given interference.[16] At a minimum, it should be possible to answer two basic questions: What are the conditions for placing interference into one category rather than another? And, linked to this, what are the legal consequences of the categorisation?

The remainder of this chapter is devoted to analysing the three 'rules' in Protocol 1 Article 1 with the aim of answering these questions. Section 2 examines the characteristics of deprivation of property under the second sentence of the first paragraph. Section 3 deals with measures deemed to 'control the use of property' within the meaning of the second paragraph. Section 4 surveys other forms of interference – sometimes referred to as interference with the 'substance of ownership' – which the Court considers under the general principle in the first sentence of the first paragraph. Section 5 concludes by reviewing the merits of the Court's 'three rules' approach.

2 Characteristics of Deprivation of Property

Depriving someone of their property is undoubtedly the most significant restriction which can be imposed by State authorities on the right to the

---

15 See T Allen (n 6) 37, and C Rozakis and P Voyatzis, '"Le Droit au Respect de ses Biens": Une Clause Déclaratoire ou une "Omnibus" Norme' in H Vandenberghe et al. (eds), *Propriété et Droits de l'Homme / Property and Human Rights* (Bruylant 2006) 5, who argue that *Sporrong and Lönnroth* constituted 'une veritable réformulation' of the right to property in the Convention.

16 See Chapter 10 below.

peaceful enjoyment of one's possessions.[17] The drafters were preoccupied with the arbitrary taking of property. The earliest drafts referred to the right to property in Article 17 the Universal Declaration of Human Rights, the scope of which is limited to arbitrary deprivation, and delegates in the Consultative Assembly pointed to the fact that totalitarian regimes were known to confiscate private property in order to suppress their political opponents.[18] They sought to design Protocol 1 Article 1 as a bulwark against such abuse of power in Europe in the future, and to provide a guarantee that deprivation of property would take place only where it was lawful and necessary in the interests of the community.

This was how the second sentence of Protocol 1 Article 1 was understood by the Convention organs in the early years.[19] For example, the Commission observed that

> [a]lthough there is no reference to 'expropriation' as such in the Article, its wording, especially the phrase 'deprived of his possessions except in the public interest' and the reference to the 'general principles of international law' shows clearly that it is intended to refer to formal (or even de facto) expropriation, that is to say *the action whereby the State lays hands – or authorises a third party to lay hands – on a particular piece of property* for a purpose which is to serve the public

17 See *James and Others v. the United Kingdom* (n 14), para. 71, where the Court called deprivation 'the most radical kind' of interference with the right to peaceful enjoyment of property. See also P van Dijk et al. (eds), *Theory and Practice of the European Convention on Human Rights* (5th edn, Intersentia 2018) 867. The Court's approach to interference in the right to property is to first determine whether there has been a deprivation of the applicant's 'possessions', since deprivation is the most severe intrusion into the right to property. If the interference in question falls short of deprivation, the Court considers whether it can be classified as 'control [of] the use of property'. In other words, it considers the application of the general principle only after having ruled out the particular instances of interference contained in the second and third sentences.

18 See e.g. remarks by Arthur Sundt (Norway) in the Consultative Assembly's session on 8 September 1949, *Travaux Préparatoires* vol II, 70.

19 See e.g. *de Buck v. Belgium* (1420/62) decision [EComHR] 18 December 1963, and *Powell and Rayner v. the United Kingdom* (9310/81) decision [EComHR] 19 January 1989, where the Commission noted that Protocol 1 Article 1 is 'mainly concerned with the arbitrary confiscation of property'. See also *Marckx v. Belgium* (6833/74) judgment 13 June 1979, dissenting opinion of Judge Fitzmaurice, para. 20, where the purpose of Protocol 1 Article 1 was understood to be 'to prevent the arbitrary seizures, confiscations, expropriations, extortions, or other capricious interferences with peaceful possession'.

> interest. This interpretation is confirmed by the 'Travaux préparatoires' for Article 1 of the First Protocol.[20]

As this interpretation suggests, the hallmark of deprivation is the transfer of property rights, by operation of law or by the exercise of legal power to the same effect.[21] Accordingly, the effects of the interference on the applicant appear to be key to the distinction between deprivation and non-deprivation measures.

Formal deprivation can be readily ascertained if a transfer of title has taken place. The Court's case law offers myriad examples, but most of the complaints relate to the amount of compensation. The loss caused by the State's action is normally an acknowledged part of the scheme, and the amount of compensation offered for that loss will form an essential element in the Court's justification assessment.[22]

Loss of title is not required for finding that deprivation of property has taken place. As the Court has frequently put it, '[i]n the absence of a formal expropriation, [it] must look behind the appearances and investigate the realities of the situation complained of'.[23] The notion of deprivation includes measures where the applicant retains title to the property, but where all substantive rights have been effectively removed – what is often referred to as *de facto* expropriation.[24] In practice, the Court has developed a strict test, and asked whether the property has lost meaningful alternative use, and whether the applicant's right has been deprived of its substance or

20 *Bramelid and Malmström v. Sweden* (8588/79; 8589/79) decision [EComHR] 12 October 1982, 82 (emphasis added).

21 See also *Sporrong and Lönnroth v. Sweden* (n 13) para. 63, where the Court equated formal expropriation with 'a transfer of ownership', and *The Holy Monasteries v. Greece* (13092/87; 13984/88) judgment 9 December 1994, where a statutory provision giving the possession of the applicant's property to the State was substantially a transfer of ownership constituting 'deprivation'.

22 See Chapter 8 below.

23 See e.g. *Sporrong and Lönnroth v. Sweden* (n 13) para. 63.

24 In international investment law, *de jure* and *de facto* expropriation are referred to as direct and indirect expropriation, respectively, see R Dolzer and C Schreuer, *Principles of International Investment Law* (Oxford University Press 2012) 101. See also generally V Lowe, 'Regulation or Expropriation?' (2002) 55 *Current Legal Problems* 447–466, R Dolzer, 'Indirect Expropriations: New Developments?' (2003) 11 *NYU Environmental Law Journal* 64–93, L Y Fortier and S L Drymer, 'Indirect Expropriation in the Law of International Investment: I Know It When I See It, or Caveat Investor' (2004) 19 *ICSID Review Foreign Investment Law Journal* 293–327, and U Kriebaum, 'Regulatory Takings: Balancing the Interests of the Investor and the State' (2007) 8 *Journal of World Investment and Trade* 717–744.

otherwise been rendered worthless.[25] The loss of property rights must also be instantaneous[26] and irreversible.[27]

The case of *Sporrong and Lönnroth* illustrates the Court's approach to *de facto* expropriation. The applicants' properties had been subjected to expropriation permits and prohibitions on construction, which had been left in force over a long time. Title had remained in the applicants' names and they were entitled to use, sell, devise, donate or mortgage their properties if they wished. Reiterating that the Convention is intended to guarantee rights that are practical and effective, the Court found that 'although [the applicants' right to property] lost some of its substance, it did not disappear. The effects of the measures involved are not such that they can be assimilated to a deprivation of possessions'.[28]

Such statements support the observation that the effects on the applicant's legal position are the defining characteristic of deprivation of property. The case law shows that only a complete inability to exercise the rights of ownership will suffice for *de facto* expropriation.[29] The value of the land may be reduced and the owner may be unable to utilise the property in the most profitable way, but *de facto* expropriation will normally not be found as long as the applicant can continue to access and use the property.[30]

25 *Pine Valley Developments Ltd and Others v. Ireland* (12742/87) judgment 29 November 1991, para. 56.

26 Deprivation of property is an instantaneous act which does not produce a continuing situation of interference. See e.g. *Malhous v. the Czech Republic* (33071/96) decision [GC] 13 December 2000. Other forms of interference, for example those designed to control the use of property, may create a continuing violation.

27 Deprivation measures are by definition permanent. See e.g. *Prötsch v. Austria* (15508/89) judgment 15 November 1996, para. 42, where the Court held that the provisional transfer of land could not, by its very nature, amount to deprivation.

28 *Sporrong and Lönnroth v. Sweden* (n 13) para. 63 (emphasis added). The same test was applied in *Matos e Silva, Lda., and Others v. Portugal* (15777/89) judgment 16 September 1996, where a part of the applicants' land had been earmarked for the creation of a nature reserve. No formal expropriation measures were put in place and the applicants remained registered owners, but their ability to use the land or enter into dealings with it had been severely restricted. The Court noted that '[a]lthough the right in question had lost some of its substance, it had not disappeared … all reasonable manner of exploiting the property had not disappeared seeing that the applicants continued to work the land' (para. 85).

29 D J Harris et al., *Law of the European Convention on Human Rights* (4th edn, Oxford University Press 2018) 864.

30 M Pellonpää, 'Reflections on the Notion of "Deprivation of Possessions" in Article 1 of the First Protocol of the European Convention on Human Rights', in P Mahoney et al.

Given this rigorous standard, it is not surprising that few examples of *de facto* expropriation can be found in the case law.[31]

It seems natural that the effects have a central role to play where the interference involves a transfer of property to the State. In this situation, the State's obligation to offer compensation for the property taken serves as a restraint on self-interested acts of public authorities. The significance of the effects is less clear when property is compulsorily transferred between private parties.

Two judgments against the United Kingdom serve to illustrate this point. In both cases, the applicants had permanently lost beneficial ownership over the land. The effects on their property rights were the same. In *James*, the plenary Court concluded that the owners had been deprived of their possessions by the operation of domestic legislation which allowed tenants to buy their long-leasehold properties in central London.[32] In *Pye*, land registered in the name of the applicant companies was transferred to a couple who had occupied it for twelve years, pursuant to English land law rules on adverse possession. The Grand Chamber viewed the interference as control of the use of property, not as deprivation.[33]

In *Pye*, the Court reasoned that the rules on adverse possession were 'not *intended* to deprive paper owners of their ownership', but constituted a small piece of a larger system of property law, with which it was reluctant to interfere.[34] According to the minority, however, any legislative measure which brings about a transfer of property from one individual to another must amount to deprivation of possessions within the meaning of the second sentence.[35] The minority focused exclusively on the consequences of the interference, and in so doing, it essentially applied the same reasoning that the Court had relied on in *James* when it found the rule on deprivation

(eds), *Protecting Human Rights: The European Perspective. Studies in Memory of Rolv Ryssdal* (Heymann 2000) 1099.

31 See e.g. *Papamichalopoulos and Others v. Greece* (14556/89) judgment 24 June 1993. The applicants' land had never been formally transferred from the applicants, but they had no access and could not utilise it. In particular, the Court emphasised that the applicants had, to no avail, brought proceedings in order to obtain restitution or compensation. The situation was therefore not temporary; indeed, it had persisted for 25 years.

32 *James and Others v. the United Kingdom* (n 14) para. 38.

33 *Pye v. the United Kingdom* (44302/02) judgment [GC] 30 August 2007, para. 66.

34 Ibid. (emphasis added).

35 Ibid., joint dissenting opinion of Judges Rozakis, Bratza, Tsatsa-Nikolovska, Gyulumyan and Šikuta, para. 6.

applicable. To be sure, the result in *Pye* would have been more persuasive if the majority had explained why the situation in *James* was not analogous. In any event, by emphasising that the purpose of the measure was to redistribute property, the Court introduced another criterion for distinguishing deprivation from other forms of interference.

Deprivation aims at the situation where the substance of the right to property has been transferred or extinguished, but how such transfer or extinguishment manifests itself must be determined specifically in light of the asset in question.[36] The case law shows that most assets are susceptible to deprivation within the meaning of Protocol 1 Article 1, but not all. For example, goodwill is considered a 'possession', but when the State causes a business to cease its operations by removing its licence or making it illegal, such acts are deemed to be controlling the use of property rather than depriving the business of its goodwill.[37]

To take another example, the extinction of a pending claim against public bodies can affect the applicant and benefit the State in a manner similar to ordinary expropriation. In this line of case law, the choice of the applicable rule appears to be determined by the strength of the applicant's position in domestic law, in addition to the effects and the purpose of the interference.

In the case of *Pressos Compania Naviera S.A.*, the applicants were deprived of their claims in tort against the State by new legislation which denied them the opportunity to sue in respect of negligence by sea pilots.[38] In *Stran Greek Refineries v. Greece*, the Court concluded that a similar legislative annulment of an arbitration award made in the applicants' favour did not constitute deprivation, but fell to be considered under the general

36 See e.g. *Olczak v. Poland* (30417/96) decision 7 November 2002, where the applicant's shareholding had been reduced from 45 per cent to 0.4 per cent following a decision to increase the share capital by the board of receivers of a limited liability bank. Since the decision entailed a severe reduction in the value of the applicant's shares, it amounted to deprivation of property, in the Court's view.

37 See e.g. *Tre Traktörer Aktiebolag v. Sweden* (10873/84) judgment 7 July 1989, para. 53, and *Könyv-Tár Kft and Others v. Hungary* (21623/13) judgment 16 October 2018, para. 43. The Commission also established that the elements of ownership – the owner's right to access, use and dispose of the property – are not separate property rights susceptible of deprivation within the meaning of the first paragraph; rather they must be viewed as a whole, see *Mellacher and Others v. Austria* (10522/83; 11011/84; 11070/84) report [EComHR] 11 July 1988, paras. 185–186.

38 *Pressos Compania Naviera S.A. and Others v. Belgium* (17849/91) judgment 20 November 1995, para. 34.

principle in the first paragraph.[39] And in *Béláné Nagy v. Hungary*, the majority viewed the legislative reform as a measure depriving the applicant of the entirety of her disability benefits, whereas the dissenting minority required the reform to be justified under the first sentence of the first paragraph.[40]

On the whole, the effects of the interference is a natural starting point for the Court when it decides whether the interference amounts to deprivation of property, but the case law is neither transparent nor consistent with respect to where the analysis goes from there. Other factors such as the purpose of the interference, the type of asset involved, and the applicant's position in domestic law also have a role to play, but it is unclear how these factors are to be weighed.

As a result, analogous situations have been subsumed under different rules, and judges have taken diverging views on the same set of facts. This divergence would be unproblematic if the requirements for justification were identical, but as a rule, only deprivation of property obligates the State to offer compensation. To define more accurately deprivation of property within the meaning of the Convention, it is necessary take a closer look at the scope and function of the other two rules that Protocol 1 Article 1 has been understood to reflect.

3 Control of the Use of Property

As already noted, the text of the second paragraph of Protocol 1 Article 1 is not concerned with the rights of individuals. Rather, it is formulated as a reservation designed to safeguard the rights of the Member States. The gist of the second paragraph is that the right to the peaceful enjoyment of property and the right to protection against deprivation enshrined in the first paragraph 'shall not … in any way impair' the State's right to regulate private property. Furthermore, the phrase 'as it deems necessary' appears to cast the State as the sole judge of whether or not regulation is justified.

The second paragraph denotes the act of interference as 'to enforce … laws' in English and 'mettre en vigueur les lois' (literally: enact such laws

39 *Stran Greek Refineries and Stratis Andreadis v. Greece* (13427/87) judgment 9 December 1994, para. 68.

40 See, respectively, *Béláné Nagy v. Hungary* (53080/13) judgment [GC] 13 December 2016, para. 124, and *Béláné Nagy v. Hungary* (53080/13) judgment [GC] 13 December 2016, joint dissenting opinion of Judges Nußberger, Hirvelä, Bianku, Yudkivska, Møse, Lemmens and O'Leary, para. 20.

or put such laws into effect) in French. On a close reading, the words 'to' in English (essentially: in order to) and 'pour' in French suggest that controlling the use of property or securing the payment of certain claims must be the purpose of the State's measure. 'Control' and 'réglementer', respectively, are the operative terms, but the purpose of enforcing or enacting laws is important because these words convey the method by which the State's control of the use of property is to be achieved. The wording thus lends some support to the conclusion that the purpose of the interference is relevant to the categorisation.

The drafters considered several versions of the second paragraph. In August 1950, the Consultative Assembly adopted a proposal according to which the right to property and the protection against arbitrary confiscation 'shall not however be considered as infringing, in any way, the right of a State to pass necessary legislation to ensure that the said possessions are utilised in accordance with the general interest'.[41] Later, the second paragraph was amended to make clear that the right to property 'does not prevent the state from collecting taxes, or applying other regulatory measures to the whole of property of individuals in question'.[42] By conceiving of the relevant act of the State as 'pass[ing] necessary legislation' and 'applying regulatory measures', the drafters clearly had regulation of property in mind.

The Convention organs have opted to define 'control' measures negatively in light of deprivation measures proscribed by the first paragraph.[43] Whereas deprivation has been understood as the complete loss or transfer of property rights from the owner to the State or to a third party, 'control [of] the use of property' involves no transfer of ownership. The owner retains ownership of the possession, but is restricted in the use of it.[44] In

---

41 'Recommendation no. 24' 25 August 1950, *Collected Edition of the Travaux Préparatoires*, Council of Europe, Doc H(61)4, vol IV, 946.

42 'Commentary by the Secretariat General on the draft Protocol' 18 September 1951, *Travaux Préparatoires*, vol VIII, 10.

43 See A R Çoban, *Protection of Property Rights Within the European Convention on Human Rights* (Ashgate 2004) 125, who concludes that the second paragraph 'encompasses all measures taken by public authorities to regulate the use of property which do not amount to deprivation'. However, the Court has applied the first sentence of the first paragraph, to which the discussions return in Section 4 below, to deal with measures which defy classification as either deprivation or control of the use of property.

44 See e.g. *Gillow v. the United Kingdom* (9063/80) report [EComHR] 3 October 1984, para. 148, where the Commission observed that 'deprivation of property is inherently more serious than the control of its use, where full ownership is retained'.

Banér v. Sweden, the Commission explained the difference between deprivation and control in the following way:

> Legislation of a general character affecting and redefining the rights of property owners cannot normally be assimilated to expropriation even if some aspect of the property right is thereby interfered with or even taken away. There are many examples in the Contracting States that the right to property is redefined as a result of legislative acts. Indeed, the wording of Article 1 para. 2 (Art. 1–2) shows that general rules regulating the use of property are not to be considered as expropriation. The Commission finds support for this view in the national laws of many countries which make a clear distinction between, on the one hand, general *legislation redefining the content of the property right* and expropriation, on the other.[45]

Accordingly, the term 'control' is aimed at general rules restricting or redefining the content of property rights, whereas 'deprivation' involves the transfer or loss of property rights. In practice, however, the difference is one of degree rather than kind: If regulation goes too far, it will eventually amount to deprivation.[46]

Needless to say, all forms of property regulation have the effect of restricting or redefining private property rights. The scope of the second paragraph is therefore almost infinite in practice. When distinguishing deprivation of property from other forms of interference, the Court begins by looking at the effects on the applicant's legal position – that is, whether the applicant has been subjected to the loss or transfer of property rights or merely restrictions through general rules. This is consistent with the analysis above.

As noted there, however, the interference must be assessed in light of the asset in question and the circumstances as a whole. The effects of the

---

45 *Banér v. Sweden* (11763/85) decision [EComHR] 9 March 1989 (emphasis added).

46 See e.g. *Pennsylvania Coal Co. v. Mahon* 260 U.S. 393, 415 (1922), where Justice Holmes observed that 'while property may be regulated to a certain extent, if regulation goes too far, it will be recognized as a taking'. See also *Starrett Housing Corporation v. Government of the Islamic Republic of Iran*, Interlocutory Award 19 December 1983, 4 Iran-US Claims Tribunal, para. 66, where the tribunal held that 'it is recognized in international law that measures taken by a State can interfere with property rights to such an extent that these rights are rendered so useless that they must be deemed to have been expropriated, even though the State does not purport to have expropriated them and the legal title to the property formally remains with the original owner'.

interference on the applicant's property interests are sometimes overruled by other factors. To take one obvious example, taxation in principle involves the permanent transfer of property rights, since it deprives the legal subject of the amount of money to be paid. Yet the power to secure the payment of taxes falls squarely within the scope of the second paragraph as a means of controlling the use of property, which is explicitly recognised as the prerogative of the State.

In the same vein, the Convention organs have subsumed seizure and confiscation of property used for or derived from criminal activities under the second paragraph, even though such measures entail a transfer of property rights to the authorities.[47] Clearly, it would not be acceptable if the right to the peaceful enjoyment of property should give the applicant a claim for compensation against the State following the permanent seizure of property as part of criminal proceedings. Such a right would defeat the very purpose of the penalty.

That Protocol 1 Article 1 does not offer full protection to possessions which have been unlawfully acquired is to be expected – indeed, this principle is recognised in other legal systems as well.[48] What this shows is that the purpose of the interference is not only relevant to the categorisation; in some situations, it effectively determines the choice of the applicable rule.[49] The examples of confiscation and taxation measures may be plain enough, but the observation underscores the need for a more principled approach to the categorisation of interference.

---

47 The case law shows that when confiscation is ordered at the same time as the conviction, interference is viewed as 'secur[ing] the payment of penalties', see e.g. *Phillips v. the United Kingdom* (41087/98) judgment 5 July 2001, para. 51. When confiscation is ordered independently of any criminal proceedings, because property is presumed to be of unlawful origin or used for unlawful activities, the Court has generally viewed the interference as control of the use of property, see *AGOSI v. the United Kingdom* (9118/80) judgment 24 October 1986, para. 51, *Air Canada v. the United Kingdom* (18465/91) judgment 5 May 1995, paras. 33–34, *Forminster Enterprises Limited v. the Czech Republic* (38238/04) judgment 9 October 2008, para. 63, *Bowler International Unit v. France* (1946/06) judgment 23 July 2009, paras. 36–41, *S.C. Fiercolect Impex S.R.L. v. Romania* (26429/07) judgment 13 December 2016, para. 57, and *Credit Europe Leasing Ifn S.A. v. Romania* (38072/11) judgment 21 July 2020, para. 70. See also *Bosphorus v. Ireland* (45036/98) judgment [GC] 30 June 2005, paras. 141–142, where the Court applied the latter criterion to measures aimed at enforcing international sanctions.

48 See e.g. Article 17 of the Charter of Fundamental Rights of the European Union, which limits the right to property to lawfully acquired possessions.

49 See e.g. *Bruncrona v. Finland* (41673/98) judgment 16 November 2004, para. 79, where the Court arrived at the general principle *inter alia* because the 'interference was not *intended* as a means of controlling the applicants' property' (emphasis added).

4 The General Principle

Before concluding on the merits of the Court's 'three rules' approach, a few words on the function of the first sentence are in order. The principle that everyone is entitled to the peaceful enjoyment of their possessions was long considered a meta norm, but over time, the Court has come to treat it as a third category of interference in property rights which it sometimes refers to as interference with the 'substance of ownership'.[50] As Rozakis and Voyatzis have observed, the general principle has developed into a complementary and distinct norm in the context of Protocol 1 Article 1.[51]

The wording itself provides little support for such an interpretation. The introductory sentence has a purely declaratory content. As with many of the qualified rights in the Convention, one would expect the introductory sentence to proclaim the right or freedom to be protected, and leave it to the ensuing text to spell out permissible limitations of that right. The *travaux préparatoires*, for their part, do not divulge any intention on the part of the drafters to imbue the first sentence with autonomous normative content distinct from the rest of the article.[52]

The Court first identified interference with the 'substance of ownership' in the case of *Sporrong and Lönnroth*. In that case, it concluded that the expropriation permits issued in respect of the applicants' properties amounted to neither deprivation nor control of the use of property; consequently, the general principle applied.[53] The impression left by the case law is that of a residual category of interference, whose scope of applicability is defined negatively in relation to the other two categories.[54] The function of the general principle as a catch-all category has also been noted in the legal

---

50 See e.g. *Young, James and Webster v. the United Kingdom* (7601/76; 7806/77) judgment 13 August 1981, dissenting opinion of Judge Sørensen, joined by Judges Vilhjálmsson and Lagergren, para. 5.

51 C Rozakis and P Voyatzis (n 15) 5.

52 See e.g. L Sermet (n 13) 22, who calls interference with the substance of ownership 'a purely judicial construct'.

53 *Sporrong and Lönnroth v. Sweden* (n 13), para. 60.

54 The subsidiary character of the general principle implies that once the Court has considered the merits of the complaint in light of the rules on 'deprivation' and 'control', there is no room for an independent assessment under the general principle. See *James and Others v. the United Kingdom* (n 14), para. 71, where the Court – after having concluded that the contested legislation amounted to *de jure* deprivation of their property rights – dismissed the applicability of the first sentence.

literature.[55] For the purposes of our present discussion, it is worth considering whether the scope of the general principle can be defined in positive terms.

To this end, at least a few tendencies are discernible. One tendency is that the Court has recourse to the general principle when the State's interference has left the applicant in a legally uncertain or precarious state for a long period of time. Even if the applicant has formally retained his or her right to property, the State's acts or omissions may have rendered the enjoyment of that right uncertain, for example through preparatory measures with a view to land consolidation or expropriation. The situation in *Sporrong and Lönnroth*, where the expropriation permits left the applicants' rights 'precarious and defeasible', is illustrative.[56]

A second tendency is that the Court has examined interference under the general principle because of the legal and factual complexity of the impugned measure.[57] In *Jokela v. Finland*, for example, the Court observed that a decision to expropriate would normally fall to be considered under the 'deprivation' rule, while a decision regarding inheritance tax would fall under the 'control' rule. However, given the close factual and legal relationship between these decisions – involving a comparison between the valuation methods for the expropriation of land and the levying of tax with respect to it – it was not possible to subsume the totality of the interference under either of the two rules. The Court therefore considered the merits of the case in the light of the general principle.[58]

---

55 See e.g. L Sermet (n 13) 29, who asks: 'It surely serves as a kind of catch-all category for any kind of interference which is hard to pin down?' See also F Sudre '"Le Droit au Respect de ses Biens" au Sens de la Convention Européenne des Droits de l'Homme' (2005) 3 *Cahiers du GRIDAUH* 74–75, and P van den Broek, 'The Protection of Property Rights under the European Convention on Human Rights' (1986) 13(1) *Legal Issues of Economic Integration* 66.

56 *Sporrong and Lönnroth v. Sweden* (n 13), para. 60. See also *Cooperativa La Laurentina v. Italy* (23529/94) judgment 2 August 2001, para. 64, where prohibition of construction was left in force for 35 years due to the failure of the municipal authorities in Rome to adopt a plan. See Chapters 8 and 10 below.

57 See e.g. *Broniowski v. Poland* (31443/96) judgment [GC] 22 June 2004, and *Kurban v. Turkey* (n 4). See also C Rozakis and P Voyatzis (n 15) 18, who refer to 'la fluidité de la situation incriminée', noting that 'plus les éléments de fluidité co-existent dans une affaire, plus la probabilité de faire appel à la norme générale s'accroît'.

58 *Jokela v. Finland* (28856/95) judgment 21 May 2002, para. 50. See also *Beyeler v. Italy* (33202/96) judgment [GC] 5 January 2000, para. 106, *Sovtransavto Holding v. Ukraine* (48553/99) judgment 25 July 2002, para. 93, and *O.B. Heller, a.s., and Československá obchodní banka, a.s. v. the Czech Republic* (55631/00; 55728/00) decision 9 November 2004. See also *Lekić v. Slovenia* (36480/07) judgment [GC] 11 December 2018, para. 93, where

A third tendency is that the Court has applied the general principle if the case raises the issue of positive obligations under Protocol 1 Article 1.[59] As noted in Chapter 3 above, in order for the Convention to be effective, States must be obligated to do more than merely refrain from interfering with the rights and freedoms. They also have to implement positive measures to ensure that individuals can take advantage of their rights under the Convention.[60] Accordingly, the Court has developed the doctrine of positive obligations as a means of ensuring effective protection of the rights and freedoms in the ECHR.[61]

The Court first established the existence of positive obligations in relation to the right to property in *Öneryıldız v. Turkey*. An explosion in a household refuse dump had caused a landslide, which killed a large number of persons burying eleven slum houses situated below it, including the applicant's home. The Grand Chamber emphasised that '[g]enuine, effective exercise of the right protected by Article 1 of Protocol No. 1 (P1–1) does not depend merely on the State's duty not to interfere, but may require positive measures of protection, particularly where there is a direct link between the measures an applicant may legitimately expect from the authorities and his effective enjoyment of his possessions'.[62]

Since then, claims arising from the failure on the part of the State to take positive action to protect property have been examined in many cases, primarily in the light of the general rule in the first sentence. The extent of States' positive obligations under Protocol 1 Article 1 will be discussed in later chapters, but it is important to note here that the boundaries of the State's positive and negative obligations under Protocol 1 Article 1 do not

---

the authorities' decision to hold the applicant personally liable for a company's debt amounted to an interference with the peaceful enjoyment of his possessions under Protocol 1 Article 1. The wider context of the case – including the decision to remove the applicant's company from the public register – led the Court to examine it in the light of the general principle.

59 See e.g. *Öneryildiz v. Turkey* (48939/99) judgment [GC] 30 November 2004, para. 133.

60 *Marckx v. Belgium* (6833/74) judgment 13 June 1979, para. 31. See generally A Mowbray, *The Development of Positive Obligations under the European Convention on Human Rights by the European Court of Human Rights* (Hart Publishing 2004), and A Mowbray, 'The Creativity of the European Court of Human Rights' (2005) 5 *Human Rights Law Review* 72.

61 See Article 1, which obligates States to 'secure' the rights and freedoms set out in the Convention. See also *Bistrović v. Croatia*, para. 33, where the Court noted that positive obligations are 'inherent in ensuring the effective exercise of the rights guaranteed by the Convention'.

62 *Öneryildiz v. Turkey* (n 59), para. 134.

lend themselves to precise definition. Whether a case is analysed in terms of a positive duty of the State or in terms of interference by a public authority, the criteria applied by the Court for assessing the justification do not differ in substance.[63]

5 Conclusion

The Court's 'three rules' approach to interference in the right to property is an important development in the history of the right to property in the Convention. It represents a radical departure from the original intention behind Protocol 1 Article 1, which was to provide protection against arbitrary deprivation of property. By introducing the 'three rules', the Court expanded the scope of the right to property to include all forms of interference and imbued the article with a new purpose.

In so doing, the Court has not expressly relied on its teleological interpretative method, but the impression left by the case law – and the premises of *Sporrong and Lönnroth* in particular – is that the 'three rules' have been introduced to ensure that the right to the peaceful enjoyment of property is practical and effective.[64] Demonstrating that such jurisprudential development have taken place is one thing, however. They should also be held up against the ideals of judge-made law. In order for the ECHR system itself to be effective, the rules emerging from the Court's judgments must be as consistent and foreseeable as possible. After all, these are ideals that the Court applies in its evaluation of domestic legal systems.

The Court's case law does not fully live up to these expectations, as this chapter has shown. The essential problem is that the Court has failed to articulate the principles distinguishing deprivation from other forms of interference in the right to property. Instead, it has taken a pragmatic, case-by-case approach to this important distinction, and left it to observers to deduce the general criteria.

The Court's starting point is the effect of the interference on the applicant's legal position: deprivation involves the permanent loss of property rights, whereas 'control' means that the applicant retains ownership of his or her possessions, but is restricted in his or her use of them. But other

63 See e.g. *Sargsyan v. Azerbaijan* (40167/06) judgment [GC] 16 June 2015, para. 220.

64 As will be shown in Chapter 8 below, the Court in *Sporrong and Lönnroth* also established the 'fair balance' test in Protocol 1 Article 1 as a means of ensuring that the right to property is effective.

factors such as the type of the asset and the applicant's position in domestic law also have a role to play, and in a few specific situations, the purpose of the interference takes precedence over the effects.

Protocol 1 Article 1 does provide for arguments relating to the aim and purpose of the interference to be taken into account, but the appropriate place for such arguments is the justification stage. As Gerards and Senden have argued, the structure of rights should direct the Court to first define the *prima facie* right at stake, before reviewing the justification advanced by the State. In line with the idea that fundamental rights can be limited, the second step allows public and other interests to be balanced against the interests of the individual. In order for the protection of human rights to be real and not illusory, however, defining the right should be done autonomously and without reference to State concerns and other general interests.[65]

The conclusions in the present chapter confirm that the distinction between deprivation and non-deprivation measures remains 'an untidy and unsatisfactory one'.[66] It is problematic that the Court has failed to develop precise criteria for making the distinction, because it opens the door to subjective views and differential treatment of analogous cases.[67] As long as that is the case, the choice of the applicable rule makes the Court's assessment vulnerable to arbitrary outcomes, and it is difficult for those bound by the Convention to determine how the principles apply to the facts before them. This is something of a paradox in view of the importance that the Court attaches to the principle of legal certainty and the rule of law when evaluating judge-made law in domestic jurisdictions.[68]

65 J Gerards and H Senden, 'The Structure of Fundamental Rights and the European Court of Human Rights' (2009) 7 *International Journal of Constitutional Law* 638.

66 D Anderson, 'Compensation for Interference with Property' (1999) *European Human Rights Law Review* 553. See also M Frigo, 'Peaceful Enjoyment of Possessions, Expropriation and Control of the Use of Property in the System of the European Convention on Human Rights' (2001) 10 *Italian Yearbook of International Law* 45, who refers to the 'vague interpretative tools' and 'elusive criteria' used by the Court when distinguishing between the two concepts, and A R Çoban, *Protection of Private Property Rights within the European Convention of Human Rights* (Ashgate 2004) 118, who claims that 'the distinction between deprivation and control [of] use does not seem acceptable'.

67 This appears to conform to the observation made in US law that 'whether a particular restriction will be rendered invalid by the government's failure to pay for any losses proximately caused by it depends largely "upon the particular circumstances [in that] case"', see *Penn Central Transportation Co. v. City of New York* 438 U.S. 104, 124 (1978).

68 See e.g. *OAO Neftyanaya Kompaniya Yukos v. Russia* (14902/04) judgment 20 September 2011, paras. 565–575, where the Court held that the Convention does not prevent

A second problem is that the Court has developed the general principle as a stand-alone category of interference, without defining its scope and function. The case law does not yield any clear criteria for the types of cases falling into this category, beyond a few broad tendencies outlined above. And even with the possibility of resorting to the catch-all category, the Court has occasionally refrained from categorising the interference altogether.[69]

It is understandable that the Court finds it difficult in practice to determine under which 'rule' a particular interference is to be subsumed. The 'three rules' approach is designed to promote consistency, but the alleged violation may not be easily assimilated to measures found in the existing case law, or there may be a series of measures consisting of disparate decisions belonging to different areas of domestic law. The Court's reluctance to identify the relevant rule suggests that it views the categorisation of the interference as less important to the outcome of a case than the justification assessment. That impression is reinforced whenever the Court makes reference to its earlier decisions related to Protocol 1 Article 1 irrespective of which particular rule it may have applied in those cases.

An ostensible explanation for why the Court sometimes appears unconcerned with the choice of the applicable rule is that the conditions for justified State interference have gradually converged and are nominally the same. The interference must comply with the principle of lawfulness and pursue a legitimate aim by reasonably proportionate means.[70] Several observers have noted how the Court over time has brought together the tests it applies in relation to different forms of interference with the right to property, with the result that the questions the Court asks in each of these

---

the gradual development of domestic case law as long as it is compatible with the requirement of foreseeability. The Court concluded that the change in domestic courts' interpretation of the rules on the statutory time bar and the effect of this change on the company's tax assessment proceedings – effectively a *Lex Yukos*, in the applicant company's view – violated the lawfulness principle in Protocol 1 Article 1. See Chapter 10 below.

69 See e.g. *Stretch v. the United Kingdom* (44277/98) judgment 24 June 2003, para. 36, and *Klaus and Yuri Kiladze v. Georgia* (7975/06) judgment 2 February 2010, para. 75.

70 See *N.K.M. v. Hungary* (66529/11) judgment 14 May 2013, para. 44, where the Court noted that 'the classification of a general measure taken in furtherance of a social policy of redistribution as a "control of use" of property rather than a "deprivation" of possessions is not decisive in so far as the principles governing the question of justification are substantially the same, requiring both a legitimate aim and the preservation of a fair balance between the aim served and the individual property rights in question'.

circumstances give rise essentially to the same set of issues.[71] Wildhaber has observed that the interconnectedness of the different parts of Protocol 1 Article 1 is such that whatever part the Court considers applicable to a given set of facts, the substantive analysis varies little.[72] Schutte has referred to 'the construction of one general test'.[73] Myklebust and Allen have both concluded that the distinction between the 'three rules' has lost its original meaning and no longer performs an important function.[74]

The issue of compensation remains the principal reason why it matters whether a given interference falls into one category or the other. As long as that is the case, it is necessary to maintain a distinction between deprivation and non-deprivation measures.[75] In some cases the choice of the applicable rule effectively decides the outcome of the Court's 'fair balance' assessment, because the applicant has been denied compensation where he or she was entitled to it. In these situations, there is a risk that the 'three rules' approach is reduced to an *ad hoc* assessment of whether the interference is so severe that it would be unreasonable to require the applicant to accept it without compensation.[76] This entraps the Court in a circular argument: Because the interference does not reasonably warrant compensation, it should not be categorised as deprivation, and because it is not deemed to be deprivation, no compensation is required.

The judgment in *Pye* epitomises this problem. The majority in the Grand Chamber acknowledged that the economic loss to the applicant companies

---

71 See e.g. B Rainey, P McCormick and C Ovey, *Jacobs, White and Ovey: The European Convention on Human Rights* (8th edn, Oxford University Press 2020) 561 and 580–581, and D J Harris et al. (n 29) 894.

72 L Wildhaber, 'The Protection of Legitimate Expectations in European Human Rights Law' in M Monti et al. (eds), *Economic Law and Justice in Times of Globalisation / Wirtschaftsrecht und Justiz in Zeiten der Globalisierung, Festschrift for Carl Baudenbacher* (Nomos 2007) 255.

73 C B Schutte, *The European Fundamental Right of Property: Article 1 of Protocol No. 1 to the European Convention of Human Rights: Its Origins, Its Workings and Its Impact on National Legal Orders* (Kluwer 2004) 29.

74 See, respectively, I E Myklebust, 'The Protection of Private Ownership Rights in the ECHR and Norwegian Planning and Building Law' (2014) 32 *Nordic Journal of Human Rights* 225 and T Allen (n 6) 121–122.

75 See W Peukert, 'Protection of Ownership under Article 1 of the First Protocol to the ECHR' (1981) 2 *Human Rights Law Journal* 54, who notes that '[a] distinction between the two types of interference can in fact only be justified if one assumes that in principle there is a duty to pay compensation on expropriation'.

76 See e.g. D Anderson (n 66) 554, who suggests that the Court has been reluctant to classify interference as deprivation because of the presumption that compensation must be paid when a person is deprived of property.

would be substantial – estimated by the British Government in 2002 to be GBP 2.5 million – but took the principled view that limitation rules must be applied regardless of the size of the claim if they are to fulfil their purpose. The minority considered the effects on the applicant companies to be 'exceptionally serious', since the limitation clauses effectively deprived the applicant companies of their property with no form of compensation.[77] The minority found a violation of the 'fair balance' principle in Protocol 1 Article 1, whereas for the majority, striking down legislation in a longstanding and complex area of private law appears to have been a bridge too far.

Allen has pointed out that the Court's 'three rules' approach has a practical function in that it helps structure the Court's examination of cases where it is satisfied that Protocol 1 Article 1 is applicable. The large number of applications filed underscores the need for a structuring principle. The categorisation of measures makes it possible for the Court to confront the unique problem of whether or not a given interference involves the taking of property, and the existence of the general principle allows the Court to create a fluid space where the scope of the first sentence can be adapted at its discretion without having to follow strict predetermined criteria.[78] If anything, the case law conveys this sense of judicial pragmatism.

Still, defining the nature of the interference remains paramount for the justification assessment. The 'fair balance' test is decided in large part by how the interference affects the applicant's interests. Limitations on the actions of the authorities are primarily established by assessments of proportionality: the greater the legitimacy of an encroachment, the more a citizen will be expected to tolerate.[79]

By extension, the scope of the State's margin of appreciation depends on the severity of the intrusion into the applicant's sphere of interests.[80] The margin of appreciation afforded in instances of deprivation of property is narrower than in instances of control of the use of property. This flexibility is also reflected in the text: States have a right to control the use of property, but no 'right' to deprive anyone of their possessions; such highly intrusive State action will be subjected to heightened scrutiny by the Court.

Finally, the categorisation is relevant to the determination of the proper remedy applicable in case of violation. In cases of deprivation, the principle

---

77 *Pye v. the United Kingdom* (n 33).

78 T Allen (n 6) 103.

79 I E Myklebust (n 74) 225.

80 *Hatton and Others v. the United Kingdom* (36022/97) judgment [GC] 8 July 2003, paras. 103 and 123.

of *restitutio in integrum* is most appropriate under Article 41.[81] Compensation for deprivation should, as a rule, correspond to the full value of the property, whereas there is more room for discretion in cases of less severe forms of interference.[82]

Given these implications, it remains for the Court to develop a framework of clear criteria defining the scope of deprivation of property. Devising such a framework lies beyond the scope of this book and the capacities of its author, but the categorisation of the interference has too great an impact on the outcome of the individual case to justify the sparse doctrinal treatment the Court has given it thus far. Without a clearer analysis, the Court's approach makes the protection offered by Protocol 1 Article 1 unpredictable for applicants as well as for Member States, in a manner which can potentially undermine the effectiveness of the right to property in the ECHR.[83] Worse, there is a risk that a provision which to an increasing extent is viewed as key to safeguarding the rule of law can, paradoxically undermine it.

81 See e.g. *Hentrich v. France* (13616/88) judgment 22 September 1994, para. 71.

82 M Pellonpää (n 30) 1089–1090.

83 See e.g. L Sermet (n 13) 22, who observes that the lack of clear criteria for distinguishing between different types of interference represented a threat to the effectiveness and security of the European human rights system.

PART 3

CHAPTER 7

The Three Dimensions of the Court's Justification Assessment

As Part 2 demonstrated, the Court has taken an expansive approach to the scope of the right to property in the ECHR. Protocol 1 Article 1 extends to virtually all rights in assets belonging to physical as well as legal persons. Furthermore, the article offers protection against all forms of interference.

The wide scope of application makes it important to understand the limits of permissible State intervention in the right to property. The Court has held that '[t]he essential object of Article 1 of Protocol No. 1 is to protect a person against *unjustified* interference by the State with the peaceful enjoyment of his or her possessions'.[1] The objective in Part 3 is to explain the dynamics of the Court's justification assessment.

Clearly, the right to peaceful enjoyment of property in the ECHR was not conceived as an absolute right in the same mould as, for example, the protection against torture or slavery.[2] The very existence of the second paragraph of Protocol 1 Article 1 testifies to the fact that the drafters sought to encapsulate the inherently limited nature of the right to property. At the same time, the text is vague with respect to the circumstances under which the right to property may be justifiably restricted by the State.

Broadly speaking, the Court has come to approach the legitimacy of interference in the right to property under Protocol 1 Article 1 using much the same methodology as it has adopted in relation to other qualified rights protected by the Convention, in particular Articles 8–11 and Protocol 4 Article 2.[3] When it has established an interference with the right to property, the Court embarks on a further examination to determine whether the interference is justified on the basis of three questions: Firstly, whether the interference is lawful; secondly, whether the interference pursues a

1 See e.g. *Sargsyan v. Azerbaijan* (40167/06) judgment [GC] 16 June 2015, para. 219 (emphasis added).

2 See by comparison Article 3 ('No one shall be subjected to torture or to inhuman or degrading treatment or punishment') and Article 4 para. 1 ('No one shall be held in slavery or servitude').

3 See e.g. B Rainey, P McCormick and C Ovey, *Jacobs, White and Ovey: The European Convention on Human Rights* (8th edn, Oxford University Press 2020) 560.

 | DOI:10.1163/9789004735088_008

legitimate aim in the public or general interest; and thirdly, whether the State has struck a 'fair balance' between the general interest of the community and the requirements for the protection of the individual's fundamental rights.

These three questions appear as distinct in the case law, but in practice, they converge and overlap in various ways. They reflect three basic considerations which the Court must take at the justification stage: firstly, that the right to property must be practical and effective, not theoretical and illusory; secondly, that the sovereignty of the Member States must be respected; and thirdly, that the rule of law must prevail whenever the State interferes with private property rights.

Thus, at a conceptual level, three dimensions of the Court's assessment can be identified. The substantive dimension is concerned with the material relationship between the interference and the aim pursued. The institutional dimension is concerned with the nature and intensity of the Court's review, and flows from the basic notion that the Court's responsibility for securing the Convention's rights and freedoms is subsidiary to that of the Contracting States. The procedural dimension is concerned with the function of Protocol 1 Article 1 as a safeguard against arbitrary interference in property rights.[4]

Chapter 8 below explores jurisprudential developments in the substantive dimension. The 'fair balance' requirement is the Court's primary means of ensuring that Convention rights are real and effective. The requirement does not appear in the text of Protocol 1 Article 1, but has been read into the article and formulated as a test whereby the interference is unjustified when the applicant has been forced to bear an 'individual and excessive burden'. The case law reflects that the Court's scrutiny under this heading has become more intensive over time.

---

4 This conceptual analysis builds on the distinction between the formal and substantive aspects of the 'fair balance' test made in P van Dijk et al. (eds), *Theory and Practice of the European Convention on Human Rights* (5th edn, Intersentia 2018) 864. See also J Christoffersen, *Fair Balance: Proportionality, Subsidiarity and Primarity in the European Convention on Human Rights* (Martinus Nijhoff Publishers 2009) and G Letsas, 'Two Concepts of the Margin of Appreciation' (2006) 26 (4) *Oxford Journal of Legal Studies* 705–732 who contemplate similar models. Because of the overlap between the requirements of lawfulness, legitimate aim and 'fair balance', these aspects have been developed further and extrapolated to the justification assessment as a whole. The conceptualisation introduced here is applicable, with appropriate modifications, to the other qualified rights in the Convention as well.

Chapter 9 analyses the evolution of the Court's review in the institutional dimension. There is a tension running through the history of the ECHR between effective protection of human rights and fundamental freedoms on the one hand, and respect for the sovereignty of the Member States on the other. Throughout the Court's history, the margin of appreciation has been the Court's tool for finding the appropriate balance between these interests.[5] The chapter examines the rationale for what has traditionally been a deferential stance on the part of the Court in matters concerning Protocol 1 Article 1, and accounts for the development towards 'deeper subsidiarity' which has become increasingly evident in recent years.

Chapter 10 studies the emergence of a procedural dimension in the Court's justification assessment. The requirement that interference in the right to property must be lawful follows directly from the text, and the Court has developed additional requirements based on the principle of legal certainty. The law cannot secure the rule of law by itself, however. Even though Protocol 1 Article 1 does not contain any explicit procedural rights, the Court has understood the rule of law to imply that domestic law must provide a measure of protection in the form of procedural safeguards against arbitrary interference by public authorities. Anyone subjected to interference in the right to property must be granted access to effective proceedings, and such proceedings must afford the applicant a minimum of fairness.

The three dimensions of the Court's justification assessment have separate functions which are clearly important in their own right, but they should not be viewed in isolation. By regarding the interaction between them as dynamic and not static, it is possible to come to a better understanding of the developments in the Court's case law under Protocol 1 Article 1 at the justification stage.

5 As Christoffersen has observed, the principles of proportionality and subsidiarity (margin of appreciation) entail 'concurrent application of different kinds of principles weighing in the overall balance. On the one hand, we have the substantive principles protecting individual rights and whatever countervailing interest may weigh in the balance, and on the other hand we have the formal principles that are not directly concerned with the substantive issues, but with the vertical power balance between international review and national autonomy', see Christoffersen (n 4) 235. See also L R Glas, *The Theory, Potential and Practice of Procedural Dialogue in the European Convention on Human Rights System* (Intersentia 2015) 24–28.

CHAPTER 8

Substantive Dimension: A Heightened Level of Scrutiny

1 Introduction: The 'Fair Balance' Requirement, Its Legal Basis and Construction

The most contentious requirement for justified interference under Protocol 1 Article 1 is that the impugned measure must strike a 'fair balance' between the demands of the general interest of the community and the requirements for the protection of the individual's fundamental rights.[1] In a substantive sense, the Court's 'fair balance' assessment may be said to entail consideration of various competing interests with the aim of achieving a measure of fairness.[2] Interference in the right to property is generally deemed to be unjustified if the applicant has been forced to bear an 'individual and excessive burden'.[3] This chapter will show how the Court's 'fair balance' assessment has evolved to reflect a heightened level of scrutiny with regard to the substantive elements under that heading.

The requirement that interference with property rights must observe a 'fair balance' between the rights of the individual and the interests of the community does not appear directly in the text of Protocol 1 Article 1. Indeed, the drafting history shows that many of the drafters did not want the right to property in the Convention to become an instrument for reviewing regulatory controls on substantive grounds. The fact that the Court today sees it as its mandate to rule on the necessity of all forms of property interference makes it important to identify the legal basis for the 'fair balance' test in Protocol 1 Article 1. An effort to do so will be made in the present

1 See e.g. D Rook, *Property Law and Human Rights* (Blackstone 2001) 69, who describes the 'fair balance' test as the main battleground for litigation.

2 See e.g. *Beyeler v. Italy* (33202/96) judgment [GC] 5 January 2000, para. 114, where the Court noted that 'ascertaining whether such a balance existed requires an overall examination of the various interests in issue'.

3 See e.g. *Sporrong and Lönnroth v. Sweden* (7151/75; 7152/75) judgment 23 September 1982, para. 73, and *Gasus Dosier- und Fördertechnik GmbH v. the Netherlands* (15375/89) judgment 23 February 1995, para. 67. In other judgments, the Court has referred to a 'disproportionate and excessive burden', see e.g. *Beyeler v. Italy* (n 2), para. 122.

 | DOI:10.1163/9789004735088_009

introduction, before attention is directed at the jurisprudential developments in the substantive dimension.

In *Sporrong and Lönnroth v. Sweden*, the Court established that it

> must determine whether a fair balance was struck between the demands of the general interest of the community and the requirements of the protection of the individual's fundamental rights ... The search for this balance is *inherent in the whole of the Convention* and is also *reflected in the structure of* [*Protocol 1*] *Article 1*.[4]

The final sentence of the cited passage is the primary object of interest here. Two assertions warrant closer scrutiny. First, let us consider the proposition that the search for a 'fair balance' is 'inherent in the whole of the Convention'. The principle of 'fair balance' has several functions in the interpretation and application of the ECHR. It is an interpretative tool used for delimiting the material scope of the Convention's rights and obligations – explicitly, such as in Article 2 para. 2, as well as implicitly, such as in Article 5 para. 1 and Article 6.[5] The exercise of balancing competing rights and interests is also intrinsic to the Court's doctrine of positive obligations.[6]

More importantly, striking a 'fair balance' is a method used by the Court to reconcile individual rights with other Convention rights and legitimate public interests. In this context, the principle acts as a requirement for justified interference.[7] This function of the 'fair balance' requirement in ECHR law is most evident in the express limitation clauses found in the second paragraphs of Articles 8–11 and Protocol 4 Article 2, which make the exercise of the freedoms subject to what is deemed to be 'necessary in a democratic society'.

'Fair balance' has also been used by the Court as a test to determine whether the State has justifiably restricted rights which *prima facie* do not

---

4 *Sporrong and Lönnroth v. Sweden* (n 3), para. 69 (emphasis added).

5 See e.g. *Vasileva v. Denmark* (52792/99) judgment 25 September 2003, paras. 36–37, where the Court derived from Article 5 para. 1 the implicit requirement that 'a balance must be drawn between the importance in a democratic society of securing the immediate fulfilment of the obligation in question, and the importance of the right to liberty'.

6 A Mowbray, 'A Study of the Principle of Fair Balance in the Jurisprudence of the European Court of Human Rights' (2010) *Human Rights Law Review* 308.

7 J J Cremona, 'The Proportionality Principle in the Jurisprudence of the European Court of Human Rights' in U Beyerlin et al. (eds), *Recht zwischen Umbruch und Bewahrung – Festschrift für Rudolf Bernhardt* (Springer Verlag 1995), 328. 'Fair balance' is referred to here interchangeably as a requirement and a test.

permit such restrictions, such as the right of access to court under Article 6 para. 1 and the right to education under Protocol 1 Article 2, or whether the State has imposed a reasonable justification for differential treatment pursuant to Article 14.[8] Indeed, the Court has applied the test in the vast majority of Convention rights, albeit in different forms. It is therefore correct to say that the search for a 'fair balance' as a means of defining permissible restrictions of rights pervades the Court's case law.[9]

An early draft of the Convention included a general limitation clause, which allowed for rights to be restricted 'with the sole object of ensuring the recognition and respect for the rights and freedoms of others, or with the purpose of satisfying the just requirements of public morality, order and security in a democratic society'.[10] The text which was ultimately adopted did not comprise a general limitation clause, however. Instead, in line with a proposal by the United Kingdom delegation, the words 'necessary in a democratic society' were inserted into the limitation clauses in Articles 8–11.

In one of its very first judgments, the so-called *Belgian Linguistic case*, the Court held that:

> ... the general aim set for themselves by the Contracting Parties through the medium of the European Convention on Human Rights, was to provide effective protection of fundamental human rights ... The Convention therefore implies a just balance between the protection of the general interest of the Community and the respect due to fundamental human rights while attaching particular importance to the latter.[11]

It transpires that the 'fair balance' test was introduced by the Court as a method of ensuring that the Convention is effective as an instrument for

---

8 See, in relation to Article 6, *Golder v. the United Kingdom* (4451/70) judgment 21 February 1975, para. 38, and *Al-Dulimi and Montana Management Inc. v. Switzerland* (5809/08) judgment [GC] 21 June 2016, para. 129, where the Court observed that 'the right of access [to court] by its very nature calls for regulation by the State'.

9 In contrast to the rights qualified by express or implied limitations, Articles 3, 4, and 7, as well as the internal aspect of Article 9, are widely recognised as absolute rights, where the 'fair balance' test has no role to play in practice.

10 'Report of the Legal Committee to the Consultative Assembly' 5 September 1949 *Travaux Préparatoires* vol I, 105. The general limitation clause in the draft Convention was inspired by Article 29 para. 2 of the Universal Declaration of Human Rights, which has a similar wording.

11 *Belgian Linguistic case* (1474/62 et al.) judgment 23 July 1968, para. 5.

safeguarding human rights. Put differently, weighing the rights of the individual against the interests of the community in search of a 'just' or 'fair' balance is and has always been a way for the Court to operationalise the effectiveness principle. The notion of effective rights thus commits the Court to carry out a material review of the respondent State's acts and omissions, and not simply defer to the assessments made by the national authorities.

As might be expected, the whole notion of balancing has been controversial from the very beginning. In his dissenting opinion in the *Belgian Linguistic case*, Judge Wold objected that the majority's interpretation was 'a very dangerous road to embark upon', because it 'carries the Court into the very middle of the internal political questions of each Member State, which it has never been the intention that the Court should deal with'.[12] In its very first judgments, the Court acknowledged the inherent tension between effective human rights protection on one hand, and the sovereignty of the Member States on the other. The Court has sought to manage this conflict through the margin of appreciation doctrine, which will be discussed in Chapter 9 below.

Returning to the Court's *dictum* in *Sporrong and Lönnroth*, let us consider the 'structure' of Protocol 1 Article 1 as the source of the 'fair balance' test.[13] The provision governs deprivation of possessions 'in the public interest' and control of the use of property 'in accordance with the general interest'. On a strict reading, the text requires only that the interference be rationally connected with a legitimate aim in society's interest. As long as these criteria are satisfied, the required balance will apparently be struck without leaving any role or mandate for the Court to assess the fairness of the interference. The words 'as it deems necessary' in the second paragraph might be read as prescribing proportionality, but that part of the text expressly leaves it to the State to assess whether or not the interference is, in fact, necessary.[14]

In its first judgments concerning Protocol 1 Article 1, the Court restricted itself to supervising the lawfulness and the purpose of the impugned

12 Ibid., dissenting opinion of Judge Wold.

13 See also *Hutten-Czapska v. Poland* (35014/97) judgment [GC] 19 June 2006, para. 167, where the Grand Chamber reiterated that '[t]he concern to achieve this balance is reflected in the structure of Article 1 of Protocol No. 1 as a whole'.

14 See by comparison Articles 8–11 para. 2, according to which interference is disproportionate if it is not deemed 'necessary in a democratic society'. Since this phrase, which does not appear in Protocol 1 Article 1, is viewed as the textual source of the 'fair balance' requirement under those rights, it is not obvious that the test applies to the right to property.

interference.[15] The Court clearly took a different approach in *Sporrong and Lönnroth*, but it is difficult to see how the structure of Protocol 1 Article 1 can provide a legal basis for the 'fair balance' test. It is more accurate to say that the search for a 'fair balance' derives from the Convention as a whole, as a general means of ensuring the effective enjoyment of rights.

It is therefore easy to agree with Allen when he observes that the Court's approach in *Sporrong and Lönnroth* was far from given. The Court could have drawn on principles of protection of property rights in national or international legal systems: In national law, it might have looked to constitutional rights protecting property owners, and in international law, it might have found inspiration in other human rights treaties or in economic or investment treaties for determining the State's obligations *vis-à-vis* property owners.[16]

Instead, the Court relied on a general notion inherent in the whole of the Convention, and held that the right to property could not be effectively protected as long as its review was limited to strict tests of lawfulness and legitimacy. The Court's interpretation reflects the idea that the Convention and its Protocols represent an integrated, coherent instrument not only with respect to the procedure for protecting rights, but also with respect to their content. Further, it suggests that the right to property in the ECHR has more in common with other qualified Convention rights than with constitutional norms protecting private property rights. This has some important implications which will be explored later in this chapter. But first a terminological clarification is in order.

The 'fair balance' principle was first introduced in the context of Protocol 1 Article 1 in the case of *Sporrong and Lönnroth* (although its origins can be traced back to the earliest days of the Court). A few years later, in *James and Others v. the United Kingdom*, the Court expounded on the principle as follows:

> [n]ot only must a measure depriving a person of his property pursue, on the facts as well as in principle, a legitimate aim 'in the public interest', but there must also be a reasonable relationship of proportionality between the means employed and the aim sought to be realised ... This latter requirement was expressed in other terms in the Sporrong

15 See *Handyside v. the United Kingdom* (5493/72) judgment 7 December 1976, para. 62, and *Marckx v. Belgium* (6833/74) judgment 13 June 1979, para. 64.

16 T Allen, 'Compensation for Property under the European Convention on Human Rights' (2007) *Michigan Journal of International Law* 297.

> and Lönnroth judgment by the notion of the 'fair balance' that must be struck between the demands of the general interest of the community and the requirements of the protection of the individual's fundamental rights ...[17]

As this passage intimates, the Court basically understands proportionality and 'fair balance' as expressions of the same legal norm. Statements to the same effect are found in various places in the case law and in the literature.[18] However, in logical terms, proportionality and 'fair balance' are two distinct concepts. The principle of proportionality, on one hand, is concerned with the interests or aims of one party and the method chosen to further them. The fundamental question is whether there is a proportional or reasonable relationship between means and ends – hence the Confucian imperative: 'Do not use a cannon to kill a mosquito'. The 'fair balance' test, on the other hand, is ostensibly concerned with the disparate interests of the parties and whether or not the balance between them is fair.

In the general literature on ECHR law, Arai-Takahashi has described proportionality as 'a modified and more specific version' of 'fair balance'.[19] In line with this, Matscher has viewed 'fair balance' as an expression of the proportionality principle.[20] Mowbray has identified the assessment of proportionality as one of the two central elements of the fundamental principle of 'fair balance', the other being the State's positive obligation to secure Convention rights.[21]

---

17 *James and Others v. the United Kingdom* (8793/79) judgment 21 February 1986, para. 50.

18 See e.g. *Hutten-Czapska v. Poland* (n 13), para. 167, where the Court pointed out that '[the proportionality requirement] is expressed by the notion of a "fair balance" that must be struck between the demands of the general interest of the community and the requirements of the protection of the individual's fundamental rights'. See also L Lavrysen, 'System of Restrictions' in P van Dijk et al. (eds), *Theory and Practice of the European Convention on Human Rights* (5th edn, Intersentia 2018) 316, who notes that 'the Court is more likely to use the proportionality language in the context of negative obligations and the "fair balance" language in the context of positive obligations. However, the fair balance and proportionality language are often used interchangeably by the Court, indicating that they can be considered to be synonymous'.

19 Y Arai-Takahashi, *The Margin of Appreciation Doctrine and the Principle of Proportionality in the Jurisprudence of the ECHR* (Intersentia 2002) 193.

20 F Matscher, 'Methods of Interpretation of the Convention' in R St J Macdonald et al. (eds), *The European System for the Protection of Human Rights* (Martinus Nijhoff Publishers 1993) 79.

21 A Mowbray (n 6) 308.

In the literature related to Protocol 1 Article 1 specifically, Rook has observed that '[t]he European Court assesses proportionality by means of a fair balance test in which it weighs various competing factors', and that 'the principle of proportionality is expressed as the "fair balance" test'.[22] Lang has concluded that the test of proportionality and 'fair balance' are one and the same thing in the Court's practice.[23]

It is difficult to draw any firm conclusions from these observations, except that there is an intricate relationship between proportionality and 'fair balance' warranting further investigation. To better understand how the Court's case law has developed in the substantive dimension, it can be fruitful to explore these two ideas further on a conceptual level.

2 A Conceptual Approach to Proportionality

The notion of 'fair balance' in ECHR law has been subjected to thorough theoretical analysis in recent decades.[24] The objective here is not to take issue with the various conceptions, but rather to establish a framework within which developments in the Court's substantive justification assessment can be better understood. Still, it is hoped that the conclusions drawn from the analysis of the case law regarding property rights can shed light on the different constructions of 'fair balance' in legal doctrine.

Proportionality is a fundamental concept of justice. The word derives from the Latin term *pro portio*, which means 'in equal shares', and conveys the notion of equal distribution of weight to different interests. The principle is found in the Old Testament in the form of the principle of reciprocity – 'an eye for an eye, and a tooth for a tooth' – and in Roman law in the form of *lex talionis* – the law of retaliation. Today, it applies in various areas of international law as well as in the constitutional and administrative law of many domestic jurisdictions.

On a conceptual level, different ways of structuring the proportionality test are possible. One common approach, which is inspired by German

22 D Rook (n 1) 5 and 68.

23 R Lang, 'Unlocking the First Protocol: Protection of Property and the European Court of Human Rights' (2008) 29 *Human Rights Law Journal* 208.

24 See, in particular, Y Arai-Takahashi (n 19) *of Appreciation Doctrine in the Jurisprudence of the European Convention on Human Rights* (Intersentia 2002) and J Christoffersen, *Fair Balance: Proportionality, Subsidiarity and Primarity in the European Convention on Human Rights* (Martinus Nijhoff Publishers 2009).

constitutional law, is to distinguish between three questions when determining whether or not a restriction of a fundamental right is proportional.[25] Firstly, was the interference suitable for achieving the aim sought to be achieved? Secondly, was the interference strictly necessary in the sense that no other, less restrictive measure existed which would have been equally effective in achieving the aim pursued? And thirdly, was the measure proportional in the strict sense?[26] The remainder of this section will look briefly at these questions and their relevance for the interpretation of Protocol 1 Article 1.

2.1 *Suitability*

The first question is whether the interference was suitable for facilitating or achieving the aim pursued. The notion of suitability suggests that a causal link must exist between means and ends, which invites the decision-maker to compare potential scenarios based on the information available. Furthermore, suitability appears to require a degree of effectiveness in the sense that the choice of the contested measure must be supported by empirical evidence demonstrating its ability to advance or achieve the pursued aim.[27] Put differently, the reasons for introducing a measure will not be sufficient if that measure does not substantially contribute to the achievement of a certain goal.[28]

The notion of effective means has some resonance in the context of the ECHR, but the Court's review is primarily focused not on the efficacy but on the legitimacy of the pursued aim: Provided the legislature stayed within its margin of appreciation, it is not for the Court to say whether the means chosen represented the best solution for dealing with the problem, or whether the State should have exercised its discretion in another way. The margin of appreciation, accordingly, applies both to the means to be em-

25 See, generally, R Alexy, *A Theory of Constitutional Rights* (Oxford University Press 2010), and, in relation to the law of the European Union, J Schwarze, *European Administrative Law* (Sweet & Maxwell 2006).

26 This sequence is logical in a methodological sense: the suitability test eliminates unsuitable means, the test of strict necessity allows for a comparison of suitable means, and the question of whether the means chosen are acceptable is a matter of balancing.

27 J Christoffersen (n 24) 166.

28 J Gerards, 'How to Improve the Necessity Test of the European Court of Human Rights?' (2013) 11 *International Journal of Constitutional Law* 467.

ployed and to the question of whether the consequences are justified in the general interest.[29]

The Court has made clear that the notion of 'necessity' in the second paragraph of Article 10 implies that the interference must respond to a 'pressing social need' and be supported by 'relevant and sufficient reasons'.[30] It has relied on neither of these standards in the context of Protocol 1 Article 1.[31] In *James*, the Court observed that 'a measure must be both *appropriate* for achieving its aim and not disproportionate thereto'.[32] This interpretation suggests that the 'appropriateness' of the measure – which is another word for suitability – is a requirement in its own right. In practice, it is an indistinguishable part of the Court's substantive proportionality assessment, which is integrated in such a way that the more significant the interference, the more credible the information must be to justify its application.[33] Still, the Court's review of suitability is generally not very rigorous, owing in part to the margin of appreciation doctrine.[34]

2.2 *Strict Necessity*

The second question in the proportionality test is whether the chosen measure was strictly necessary, in the sense that no other, less restrictive measures existed which would have been equally suitable in view of the aim pursued. At a conceptual level, a test of strict necessity can be separated into several subquestions: Were other suitable means available to promote the same aim? Were these means less restrictive of the right? Were they as effective as the impugned measure in promoting the same end?

This approach can prove difficult to follow in practice, however, and the Court has also rejected it as a method of Convention interpretation. If the 'fair balance' assessment in the ECHR were premised on a test of strict necessity, States would always be obligated to choose the least onerous means.

29 See e.g. *G.I.E.M., S.r.l. and Others v. Italy* (1828/06; 34163/07; 19029/11) judgment [GC] 28 June 2018, para. 293.

30 *Handyside v. the United Kingdom* (n 15), paras. 48–50, and *The Sunday Times v. the United Kingdom (No. 1)* (6538/74) judgment 26 April 1979, para. 62.

31 As Gerards has pointed out, it is unlikely that the Court will apply these standards, which at any rate have a rather vague content, beyond the case law involving privacy or freedom of expression, see J Gerards 'How to Improve the Necessity Test of the European Court of Human Rights?' (2013) 11 *International Journal of Constitutional Law* 467.

32 *James and Others v. the United Kingdom* (n 17), para. 50 (emphasis added).

33 See J Christoffersen (n 24) 191.

34 See Chapter 9 below.

This is clearly not the case. The possibility of providing a higher level of protection does not suffice to establish a violation. Therefore, the availability of better solutions or less onerous means does not *per se* warrant the conclusion that the Convention has been violated. As Christoffersen has argued, the minimum nature of the States' obligations under the ECHR justifies a categorical rejection of the 'strict necessity' test.[35]

In its interpretation of Protocol 1 Article 1, the Court dismissed the 'strict necessity' test early on in *James and Others v. the United Kingdom*. The question was whether the statutory right of tenants to enfranchise their home violated the landlords' right to property under the Convention. The landlords maintained that the 'fair balance' requirement in Protocol 1 Article 1 would be satisfied only if no other less drastic remedy existed for the perceived social injustice. The Court responded as follows:

> This amounts to reading a test of strict necessity into the Article, an interpretation which the Court does not find warranted. The availability of alternative solutions does not in itself render the leasehold reform legislation unjustified; it constitutes one factor, along with others, relevant for determining whether the means chosen could be regarded as reasonable and suited to achieving the legitimate aim being pursued, having regard to the need to strike a 'fair balance'. Provided the legislature remained within these bounds, it is not for the Court to say whether the legislation represented the best solution for dealing with the problem or whether the legislative discretion should have been exercised in another way ...[36]

This passage makes clear that States are not obligated under Protocol 1 Article 1 to choose the least restrictive measure when interfering with property rights. Whether alternative, less restrictive means of achieving the same objective existed may be a relevant factor in the Court's 'fair balance' assessment, but it is not decisive.[37] In this connection it suffices that the State has

35 J Christoffersen (n 24) 111–135.

36 *James and Others v. the United Kingdom* (n 17), para. 51.

37 See also *Mellacher and Others v. Austria* (10522/83; 11011/84; 11070/84) judgment 19 December 1989, para. 53, where the Court maintained that '[t]he possible existence of alternative solutions does not in itself render the contested legislation unjustified', and *Tre Traktörer Aktiebolag v. Sweden* (10873/84) judgment 7 July 1989, para. 39, where the Court accepted the balance struck by the authorities, even though less severe measures under the legislation in force could have been taken.

considered less restrictive measures, and based its choice of the more restrictive ones on sufficient reasons.

Some observers have noted that the Court appears increasingly willing to integrate a form of the strict necessity test in its proportionality assessment.[38] In *Nada v. Switzerland*, for example, the Court held with respect to Article 8 that 'for a measure to be regarded as proportionate and as necessary in a democratic society, the possibility of recourse to an alternative measure that would cause less damage to the fundamental right in issue whilst fulfilling the same aim must be ruled out'.[39] Similarly, in *Mouvement Raëlien Suisse v. Switzerland*, the Court held in relation to Article 10 that 'the authorities are required, when they decide to restrict fundamental rights, to choose the means that cause the least possible prejudice to the rights in question'.[40]

A similar development is taking place in the case law concerning Protocol 1 Article 1 as well. In *Zelenchuk and Tsytsyura v. Ukraine*, for example, the Court concluded that the availability of alternative solutions and the lack of consistent reasons given for not adopting those solutions and keeping in place the most restrictive one must have 'substantial weight' in the assessment of proportionality.[41] And in *Kurban v. Turkey*, the Court maintained that 'the fair balance principle would *at least require* that a less severe measure alleviating the financial burden placed on the applicant be applied'.[42] Statements to this effect suggest that the Court's categorical rejection of the 'strict necessity' test in *James* may have lost some of its validity. At least, the Court appears to be placing increasing emphasis on the existence and availability of less intrusive means as an argument in the 'fair balance' assessment.[43]

---

38 E Brems and L Lavrysen, 'Don't Use a Sledgehammer to Crack a Nut: Less Restrictive Means in the Case Law of the European Court of Human Rights' (2015) 15 *Human Rights Law Review* 139–168.

39 *Nada v. Switzerland* (10593/08) judgment [GC] 12 September 2012, para. 183.

40 *Mouvement Raëlien Suisse v. Switzerland* (16354/06) judgment [GC] 13 July 2012, para. 75.

41 *Zelenchuk and Tsytsyura v. Ukraine* (846/16; 1075/16) judgment 22 May 2018, paras. 122–130. See also *Arsovski v. The former Yugoslav Republic of Macedonia* (30206/06) judgment 7 February 2019, where the Court emphasised that the aim might have been achieved through a partial relinquishment rather than a full expropriation of the applicant's property.

42 *Kurban v. Turkey* (75414/10) judgment 24 November 2020, para. 86 (emphasis added).

43 See Section 3 below.

2.3 *Proportionality in the Strict Sense*

The third question is whether the impugned measure was proportional in a strict sense to the aim pursued. A measure may be suitable and strictly necessary, but still be disproportionate if the State's aim in the particular instance did not justify the means – that is, if the advantages of the interference did not outweigh the disadvantages. In this assessment, the importance of the aim and the severity and impact of the interference are the primary factors: The greater the public gain to be achieved by the legitimate aim, the greater the burden the property owner can be expected to bear.

Proportionality in the strict sense is an integral part of the Court's assessment of 'fair balance', but, as will become clear in the remainder of this chapter, 'fair balance' has a wider scope, which allows the Court to take into account all relevant factual and legal circumstances in the case at hand. Mowbray is therefore correct to conclude that in cases of State interference, the 'fair balance' principle enables the Court to conduct an assessment of, among other things, the proportionality of the interference.[44]

That being said, it is important to bear in mind that when the Court uses the term 'proportionality' or similar, derived words ('proportional', 'disproportionate', etc.), it normally refers to 'proportionality' in the wide sense, which it uses synonymously and interchangeably with 'fair balance'. Here, the discussions will mainly refer to 'fair balance' when referring to the justification requirement generally, and to proportionality when referring to the relationship between means and ends specifically (proportionality in the strict sense).

2.4 *The Structure of the Court's Substantive Assessment under Protocol 1 Article 1*

Identifying the relevant elements of the proportionality test is one thing. Determining how those elements interact in practice is another. Conceptually, the proportionality test can be structured either as a strict vertical test, whereby proportionality is dependent on the fulfilment of the requirements in turn, or as a flexible horizontal test which takes account of the requirements in an overall assessment.

There appears to be consensus that the proportionality test in ECHR law is horizontally structured.[45] As Greer has pointed out, 'in most cases which

44 A Mowbray (n 6) 308.

45 J Christoffersen (n 24) 68–76.

reach the European Court of Human Rights the principles of suitability and strict necessity will already have been answered in the affirmative, and [the three-part] test will have collapsed into a single "balancing" exercise'.[46] A horizontal test of proportionality is consistent with the Court's general argumentative mode, which tends to be discursive rather than dogmatic. The Court is not prone to a style which requires it to first look at some arguments and build its conclusion on those arguments alone. Rather, it tends to rely on a number of different arguments, none of which appear to be more important or decisive than the others.

Building on this initial analysis of the legal basis and conceptual elements of the 'fair balance' test, the developments in the Court's jurisprudence concerning Protocol 1 Article 1 will now be examined further. Under the 'fair balance' assessment, the Court embarks on an overall examination of the various interests involved.[47] There is no fixed list of relevant factors under Protocol 1 Article 1; they vary from case to case, depending on the facts and the nature of the interference concerned. However, it is possible to identify and systematise the most prominent elements in the assessment, and consider how the Court's treatment of these elements has developed over time.

To that end, Section 3 begins by looking briefly at the importance of the aim of the interference. Sections 4 and 5 juxtapose the public interest against the effects on the applicant and the issue of compensation. These three sections are concerned with proportionality in the strict sense. The remaining two sections consider elements in the broader 'fair balance' assessment – in Section 6, the applicant's legitimate expectations and acceptance of risk, and in Section 7, the conduct of the parties.

3 The Weight of the Public Interest

In a substantive sense, 'fair balance' implies that the interference must be justified in the public interest. As the Court has put it, '[t]he burden borne by the applicant … must be weighed against the general interest of the community'.[48] The Court's review of the means and ends chosen by the State is

46 S Greer, *The European Convention on Human Rights – Achievements, Problems and Prospects* (Cambridge University Press 2006) 212.

47 *Broniowski v. Poland* (31443/96) judgment [GC] 22 June 2004, para. 151.

48 *O'Sullivan McCarthy Mussel Development Ltd v. Ireland* (44460/16) judgment 7 June 2018, para. 123.

qualified by the margin of appreciation, but the Court has always applied a minimum of scrutiny to the realities behind the aim pursued.[49]

A classic illustration from the case law is *Stran Greek Refineries and Stratis Andreadis v. Greece*. The applicant had entered into a contract with the Greek State, which at the time was governed by a military junta, to build a crude oil refinery. He then transferred all his rights and obligations to the applicant company. After democracy had returned, the State terminated the contract, and a subsequent arbitration award made in favour of the company was later declared invalid pursuant to a law passed by the Greek Parliament. The Court held that, in the absence of due compensation, the applicants were effectively being penalised for entering into a legal relationship with the former dictatorial regime. This view was material for the Court's conclusion that the legislature had upset the 'fair balance' that must be struck between the protection of the right of property and the requirements of the public interest.[50]

As indicated above, there are signs in more recent case law that the Court subjects the aim pursued to a heightened level of scrutiny. One example is found in the case of *Könyv-Tár KFT and Others v. Hungary*, where the Court was unconvinced that the monopolisation of schoolbook distribution would serve the interests of the parents and pupils, as the State claimed.[51] More specifically, as discussed in Section 2.2 above, the Court sees it as increasingly relevant whether the State had alternative, less restrictive means of achieving the objective.[52] As part of this assessment, it

---

49 See also Chapter 9 below.

50 *Stran Greek Refineries and Stratis Andreadis v. Greece* (13427/87) judgment 9 December 1994, paras. 72–75.

51 *Könyv-Tár Kft and Others v. Hungary* (21623/13) judgment 16 October 2018, para. 46. See also *Megadat.com SRL v. Moldova* (21151/04) judgment 8 April 2008, para. 68, where the government was able to cite only theoretical and abstract negative consequences of the applicant company's failure to comply with a procedural requirement, *Tkachevy v. Russia* (35430/05) judgment 14 February 2012, para. 50, where the Court concluded that the public interest underlying the expropriation of the applicants' flat had not been 'clearly and convincingly shown', and *G.I.E.M., S.r.l. and Others v. Italy* (n 29), para. 299, where it questioned whether confiscation of the applicants' properties had actually contributed to the aim in question.

52 See e.g. *Vistiņš and Perepjolkins v. Latvia* (71243/01) judgment [GC] 25 October 2012, para. 129, where the Court considered it relevant that the State had failed to show that the aim of optimising management of the port in Riga could not be fulfilled by less drastic measures than expropriation compensated for by purely symbolic sums. See also D J Harris et al., *Law of the European Convention on Human Rights* (4th edn, Oxford University Press 2018) 887.

also requires that the public interest be able to sustain the effects of the interference over time.[53]

4 Effects on the Applicant

4.1 *Economic Effects*

The second part of the substantive 'fair balance' assessment concerns how the interference affects the applicant's property rights. In this analysis, the Court must take account of the interests that Protocol 1 Article 1 protects, and ascertain how these interests have been affected by the interference. Chapter 4 showed that the primary purpose of the right to property in the ECHR is to protect economic interests. The economic effects of the interference are therefore the natural starting point.

It is self-evident that the economic effects of an interference with the right to property depend on the character and severity of the measure. Deprivation of property has markedly different effects than regulation, and this, in turn, has implications for the Court's 'fair balance' assessment. The Convention organs have long acknowledged that 'the measure of proportionality clearly differs in the application of the two rules since … deprivation of property is inherently more serious than the control of its use, where full ownership is retained'.[54]

In instances of deprivation, the economic effects and the issue of compensation are at the heart of the Court's 'fair balance' assessment: the essential test is whether the compensation awarded reasonably reflects the value of the property taken; compensation equal to the full market value of the property typically represents a proportional solution, in the Court's view. However, contrary to what is provided for in many constitutions, compensation less than the market value is not in itself sufficient to establish a breach of Protocol 1 Article 1. Indeed, this is an important consequence of the fact

---

53 See e.g. *Islamic Republic of Iran Shipping Lines v. Turkey* (40998/98) judgment 13 December 2007, para. 98. See also *Bittó and Others v. Slovakia* (30255/09) judgment 28 January 2014, para. 109, where the Court considered the mismatch between the government policy plans which envisaged the introduction of market-level rents and the lack of actual progress in that direction as a factor in assessing the proportionality of the rent-control measures.

54 *Gillow v. the United Kingdom* (9063/80) report [EComHR] 3 October 1984, para. 148. See also *Gasus Dosier- und Fördertechnik GmbH v. the Netherlands* (n 3), para. 59, where the Court affirmed that the strictness with which it supervises proportionality depends on the type of interference concerned.

that the Court has addressed the compensation issue under the heading of 'fair balance'.

With respect to interference not amounting to deprivation, States have no general obligation to offer compensation, but payment of some form of compensation is a relevant factor when the Court evaluates the 'fair balance' of the measure.[55] In fact, it appears increasingly often to expect the State to offer compensation as a means of 'softening the blow' to the applicant's interest, especially where the measure has substantial economic consequences.

A line of cases concerning land and housing shows how the Court has come to evaluate the economic effects of property regulation.[56] In the first place, the Court focuses on the owner's economic outcome compared to the market value of the property or another similar objective benchmark.[57] In the case of *Hutten-Czapska v. Poland*, for example, it appears to have been decisive that the statutory rent was not sufficient to cover even necessary maintenance expenses.[58] Furthermore, the Court takes into account the entirety of costs and liabilities arising from the owner's position under domestic law – for example the applicant's tax burden.[59] It considers the extent to which the regulation interferes with the owner's freedom of contract and contractual relations more generally. Finally, as will be explained further in Chapter 10 below, the Court ascertains that procedural safeguards are in place ensuring that the operation of the rent-control system and its impact on the landlords' property rights are neither arbitrary nor unforeseeable.[60]

---

55 See e.g. *Brosset-Triboulet and Others v. France* (34078/02) judgment [GC] 29 March 2010, para. 94.

56 See, in particular, *Mellacher and Others v. Austria* (n 37), *Hutten-Czapska v. Poland* (n 13), paras. 223–225, *Urbárska obec Trenčianske Biskupice v. Slovakia* (74258/01) judgment 27 November 2007, and *Lindheim and Others v. Norway* (13221/08; 2139/10) judgment 12 June 2012, para. 129.

57 See also a series of cases against Malta, where the statutory rent for houses was extremely low and demonstrably below market rates: *Ghigo v. Malta* (31122/05) judgment 26 September 2006, para. 66, *Edwards v. Malta* (17647/04) judgment 24 October 2006, para. 75, *Cassar v. Malta* (50570/13) judgment 30 January 2018, and *Edward Zammit Maempel and Cynthia Zammit Maempel v. Malta* (3356/15) judgment 15 January 2019.

58 See *Hutten-Czapska v. Poland* (n 13), para. 198. See also *R & L, s.r.o. and Others v. the Czech Republic* (37926/05 et al.) judgment 3 July 2014, para. 104, where the statutory rent was demonstrably below maintenance costs.

59 See e.g. *Zelenchuk and Tsytsyura v. Ukraine* (n 41), para. 139.

60 See e.g. *Amato Gauci v. Malta* (47045/06) judgment 15 September 2009, para. 58, and ibid., para. 103.

4.2 *Non-Economic Effects*

Interference with the right to property occasionally affects non-economic interests. An ample illustration is found in *Chassagnou and Others v. France*, where the applicants had been forced to accept hunting on their land, even though they were opposed to hunting on conscientious grounds.[61] The Court concluded that this obligation violated the applicants' right to property under Protocol 1 Article 1.

Similarly, in *N.K.M. v. Hungary*, the applicant had been subjected to a new tax on severance pay at a time when she was unemployed. The unexpected and swift nature of the change of the tax regime, which made any preparation virtually impossible for those concerned, exposed the applicant to personal hardship. The Court further noted that the tax was directly deducted by the employer from the severance, and did not allow for any individualised assessment of the applicant's situation. This was sufficient for the Court to conclude that the 'fair balance' was upset.[62]

Even though applicants overwhelmingly frame the impact of the impugned interference in terms of economic loss, the judgments in *Chassagnou* and *N.K.M.* demonstrate that the Court occasionally attaches weight to the subjective, non-economic effects as well. Not every interference with the right to property can be compensated in monetary terms. At least, this holds true for individuals invoking Protocol 1 Article 1 in defence of their personal interests in property. Thus, the Convention is concerned with the social function of property not only when considering the public interest involved, but also in the assessment of the applicant's interests.[63]

The Court's scrutiny is further heightened when the interference creates a danger of abuse of power, for example if the impugned measure targeted only a certain group of individuals who were singled out.[64] In this situation, the State must provide the applicant with safeguards against arbitrariness

61 *Chassagnou and Others v. France* (25088/94; 28331/95, 28443/95) judgment [GC] 29 April 1999. See also *Lallement v. France* (46044/99) judgment 11 April 2002, where parts of the applicant's agricultural property had been expropriated and the parties agreed that he had received reasonable compensation for the expropriated parts. The applicant had had the opportunity to demand that the authorities buy the whole farm at market price, but because he did not want to give up the family home, the Court would not fault him for having refrained from making such a claim.

62 *N.K.M. v. Hungary* (66529/11) judgment 14 May 2013, para. 70. See also *R.Sz. v. Hungary* (41838/11) judgment 2 July 2013, para. 59.

63 T Allen (n 16) 319.

64 See e.g. *Hentrich v. France* (13616/88) judgment 22 September 1994, para. 47, and *R.Sz. v. Hungary* (n 62), para. 60.

and a reasonable opportunity of putting the case before the responsible authorities and effectively challenging the measures interfering with their possessions.[65] Conversely, if the interference at issue was generally applicable, there is less reason for the Court to conclude that it imposed an 'individual and excessive burden' on the applicant.

5 The Issue of Compensation

5.1 *A Material Factor in the Court's 'Fair Balance' Assessment*

Any loss caused by the interference will, of course, be offset by any monetary compensation received by the applicant. The amount and terms of compensation are therefore a material factor in the Court's 'fair balance' assessment under Protocol 1 Article 1. However, the importance of compensation varies in the Court's assessment depending on which of the 'three rules' is at stake. Deprivation of property without payment of an amount reasonably related to its market value normally upsets the 'fair balance'. Still, as the balancing metaphor suggests, there may be circumstances where the public interest outweighs the need to protect the individual's right to property.

That the issue of compensation is at the heart of the Court's 'fair balance' assessment is perhaps to be expected, considering that Protocol 1 Article 1 has been understood to primarily protect economic interests. Indeed, as Frowein has put it: without a right to compensation, the right of property would be meaningless.[66]

The text of Protocol 1 Article 1 is silent on the issue of compensation, however. As shown in Chapter 2, several States objected to the inclusion of a compensation clause. Some delegates were concerned that the words 'arbitrary confiscation' would be understood as guaranteeing a right to compensation. In the end, the phrase 'subject to the conditions provided for by law' was deemed adequate, as some right to compensation would normally be provided for in domestic legislation concerning expropriation of property.[67] The drafters probably never intended Protocol 1 Article 1 to do more

65 See e.g. *Microintelect OOD v. Bulgaria* (34129/03) judgment 4 March 2014, paras. 38–50. See also Chapter 10 below.

66 J Frowein, 'The Protection of Property' in R St J Macdonald et al. (eds), *The European System for the Protection of Human Rights* (Martinus Nijhoff Publishers 1993) 515.

67 'Commentary by the Secretariat General on the draft Protocol' 18 September 1951, *Travaux Préparatoires*, vol VIII, 8–10.

than provide an international guarantee that States would adhere to national law when exercising their powers over property.[68]

This was also how the article was understood in the early years. The Commission decided that the State had no duty to pay compensation unless this was provided for in domestic law.[69] In *Sporrong and Lönnroth*, the Court rejected the notion that the substantive protection under Protocol 1 Article 1 would be limited to the protection offered by domestic law. In that case, the applicants' properties had been subject to expropriation permits and prohibitions on construction for an extensive period. The Court concluded that a 'fair balance' could have been obtained only if the applicants had been given 'the possibility of seeking a reduction of the time-limits *or of claiming compensation*'.[70] This falls short of stating that a right to compensation follows from Protocol 1 Article 1, but instead links the issue to the 'fair balance' assessment. Still, by recognising that the Convention contains some form of obligation for the State to award compensation, the Court clearly departed from the purpose of Protocol 1 Article 1 as it was conceived by the drafters.

The Court further developed its understanding of the compensation issue in *James*:

> under the legal systems of the Contracting States, the taking of property in the public interest without payment of compensation is treated as justifiable only in exceptional circumstances not relevant for present purposes. As far as Article 1 (P1–1) is concerned, the protection of the right of property it affords would be largely illusory and ineffective in the absence of any equivalent principle. Clearly, compensation terms are material to the assessment [of] whether the contested legislation respects a fair balance between the various interests at stake and, notably, whether it does not impose a disproportionate burden on the applicants …[71]

Here, the Court first referred to the 'legal systems of the Contracting States' to justify its interpretation of Protocol 1 Article 1 with respect to the issue. But the argument is not entirely convincing, as many European constitutions require payment of just compensation in all cases where property is

68 T Allen (n 16) 289.

69 See e.g. *Gudmundsson v. Iceland* (511/59) decision [EComHR] Yearbook III (1960), 394.

70 *Sporrong and Lönnroth v. Sweden* (n 3), para. 73 (emphasis added).

71 *James and Others v. the United Kingdom* (n 17), para. 54.

taken for public use.[72] As the remainder of the cited passage reflects, the real rationale appears to have been that the right to property in the Convention would be 'largely illusory and ineffective' without an obligation for States to pay compensation in the event of expropriation.[73] Rather than say so explicitly, the Court chose to express that obligation through the 'fair balance' principle.

In the literature, Allen has concluded that Protocol 1 Article 1 contains an 'implied right to compensation'.[74] Ress has noted that the principle of compensation is 'clearly established' through the proportionality requirement.[75] Pellonpää has observed that the search for a fair balance 'requires compensation corresponding to the full value of the property, payment without unreasonable delay and in a manner guaranteeing its economic value'.[76] Lang has concluded that the presence or absence of compensation forms part of the proportionality enquiry.[77]

Observers may articulate this point in different ways, but the legal reality is the same. Owing to the Court's flexible application of the 'fair balance' requirement, Protocol 1 Article 1 does not guarantee a right to compensation in all circumstances. In this respect, the Convention differs from rules of property protection in the written constitutions of the United States and many European countries, which guarantee full compensation whenever private property is expropriated.[78]

---

72 See generally T Allen, *Property and the Human Rights Act 1998* (Oxford University Press 2005) 167–170.

73 See also *Lithgow and Others v. the United Kingdom* (9006/80 et al.) judgment 8 July 1986, para. 109, where the Court held that the States' obligation to pay compensation 'derives from an implicit condition in Article 1 of Protocol No. 1 (P1-1) read as a whole ... rather than from the "public interest" requirement itself. The latter requirement relates to the justification and the motives for the actual taking'.

74 T Allen (n 16) 288.

75 G Ress, 'Reflections on the Protection of Property under the European Convention on Human Rights' in S Breitenmoser et al., *Human Rights, Democracy and the Rule of Law. Liber Amicorum Luzius Wildhaber* (Nomos 2007) 632.

76 M Pellonpää, 'Reflections on the Notion of "Deprivation of Possessions" in Article 1 of the First Protocol of the European Convention on Human Rights', in P Mahoney et al. (eds), *Protecting Human Rights: The European Perspective. Studies in Memory of Rolv Ryssdal* (Heymann 2000) 1087.

77 R Lang (n 23) 211.

78 See by comparison Article 17 of the EU's Charter of Fundamental Rights: 'No one may be deprived of his or her possessions, except in the public interest and in the cases and under the conditions provided for by law, *subject to fair compensation being paid in good time for their loss*' (emphasis added). Under the Takings Clause of the Fifth Amendment to the United States Constitution, the taking of property for public use

As a condition for justified interference, the 'fair balance' requirement in Protocol 1 Article 1 has more in common with the proportionality test applied in the context of other qualified rights in the ECHR, notably Articles 8–11 and Protocol 4 Article 2. These principles have common origins, and there are trends in the case law affecting their application in similar ways. Arguments about the strict necessity of the impugned measure have become increasingly prominent in the Court's reasoning, as already discussed. And as the next two chapters will show, the Court has subjected the State's justification under these articles to process-based review and procedural control.[79]

In substantive terms, these norms are not identical, however. The threshold for violation of Protocol 1 Article 1 – that the applicant has been forced to bear an 'individual and excessive burden' – is high relative to those other rights. In relation to Article 8, the Court finds an interference to be unjustified if it is 'disproportionate to the legitimate aim pursued'.[80]

Furthermore, the Court generally conceives of a core of Convention rights in the sense that limitations can never go so far as to affect the 'very substance' of the right concerned.[81] In Protocol 1 Article 1 cases, that language has been reserved for forms of interference which the Court is unable to categorise as either deprivation or control of the use of property.[82] But if we were to define the 'very substance' of the right to property in the ECHR as it is reflected in the case law, it must be to protect property holders from expropriation without compensation. In this sense, payment of compensation has a role in justifying interference under Protocol 1 Article 1 which it does not have in relation to other Convention rights.[83] This difference is

can be justified only if compensation is paid. In effect, finding that the Takings Clause is applicable necessarily leads to the conclusion that compensation must be paid; the State cannot argue that no compensation is required because the specific circumstances are exceptional. See generally T Allen, 'The Human Rights Act (UK) and Property Law' in J McLean (ed), *Property and the Constitution* (Hart Publishing 1999) 150, and A J van der Walt, *Constitutional Property Clauses* (Kluwer 1999).

79 See Chapters 9 and 10 below.

80 See e.g. *Dudgeon v. the United Kingdom* (7525/76) judgment 22 October 1981, paras. 51–53.

81 See e.g. *Young, James and Webster v. the United Kingdom* (7601/76; 7806/77) judgment 13 August 1981, dissenting opinion of Judge Sørensen, joined by Judge Vilhjálmsson and Judge Lagergren, para. 5.

82 See Chapter 6 above.

83 See T Allen (n 16) 316, who refers to the example of freedom of religion under Article 9: 'showing that a compelling public interest outweighs the individual's interests may

reflective of the primary role of Protocol 1 Article 1, which is to protect economic interests.

5.2 *The Market-Value Standard*

This sub-section looks at the level of compensation required in cases concerning deprivation of property. The intention here is not to recapitulate all the details in the protection offered by Protocol 1 Article 1, but the issue of compensation is important enough to warrant some further study. The Court laid down the ground rules in *James*:

> the taking of property without payment of an amount reasonably related to its value would normally constitute a disproportionate interference which could not be considered justifiable under Article 1 (P1–1). Article 1 (P1–1) does not, however, guarantee a right to full compensation in all circumstances. Legitimate objectives of 'public interest', such as pursued in measures of economic reform or measures designed to achieve greater social justice, may call for less than reimbursement of the full market value. Furthermore, the Court's power of review is limited to ascertaining whether the choice of compensation terms falls outside the State's wide margin of appreciation in this domain ...[84]

Here, the Court established that the 'fair balance' principle implies that the owner should be given compensation 'reasonably related to [the property's] value' in the event of deprivation. Of course, what is reasonable will depend on the circumstances of a given case, and the State has a wide margin of appreciation in determining the amount and terms of compensation.[85] As a standard of compensation, the Convention requires an amount equal to the market value for the typical taking of property for public use – what may be referred to as a market-value standard.[86]

justify an interference with freedom of religion, but showing that the state paid her money as a substitute for the opportunity to exercise her belief does not'.

84 *James and Others v. the United Kingdom* (n 17), para. 54. See also *Lithgow and Others v. the United Kingdom* (n 73), para. 121.

85 See Chapter 9 below.

86 The Court uses the terms 'full value', 'market value' and 'full market value' synonymously, see e.g. *The Holy Monasteries v. Greece* (13092/87; 13984/88) judgment 9 December 1994, para. 71, where the Court assumed that the formulas in *James* and *Lithgow* implied market value. See also *Pincová and Pinc v. the Czech Republic* (36548/97) judgment 5 November 2002, para. 53, and *Pyrantienė v. Lithuania* (45092/07) judgment 12 November 2013, para. 66.

The Court's approach to valuation is a subject in its own right, which will not be fleshed out here.[87] Suffice it to say that the Court has maintained that the compensation must reflect the value of the property at the date on which ownership was lost, as any other approach could open the door to uncertainty or arbitrariness.[88] A lower amount may occasionally be justified where the market value cannot be objectively determined, in which case the Court considers other expressions of the property's value, for example, the value used by the State as a basis for calculating land tax.[89]

Furthermore, the compensation must reflect all the applicant's losses resulting from the interference. Otherwise, the deprivation measure can upset the 'fair balance' principle. In *Bistrović v. Croatia*, for example, the construction of a public road in the vicinity of the applicant's property had contributed directly to the substantial depreciation of the value of the remaining property. This fact was not reflected in the compensation awarded. The State's failure to take account of the fact that expropriation of one part of the applicant's property affected the value or amenities of another, non-expropriated part resulted in a violation of Protocol 1 Article 1.[90]

5.3 *Public Interests Justifying Compensation below Market Value*

As noted, Protocol 1 Article 1 does not guarantee a right to full compensation in all circumstances. The Court maintained in *James* that legitimate objectives of public interest may justify compensation below market value, such as those pursued in measures of economic reform or measures designed to

---

87 Discrepancies between the amount of compensation offered by the State and the amount of compensation ultimately awarded by the Court pursuant to Article 41 in the case of violation raise particular questions in this respect. See e.g. M Frigo, 'Peaceful Enjoyment of Possessions, Expropriation and Control of the Use of Property in the System of the European Convention on Human Rights' (2000) *Italian Yearbook of International Law* 66, and A R Çoban, *Protection of Private Property Rights within the European Convention of Human Rights* (Ashgate 2004) 229.

88 See e.g. *Guiso-Gallisay v. Italy* (58858/00) judgment [GC] 22 December 2009, para. 103.

89 See e.g. *Vistiņš and Perepjolkins v. Latvia* (n 52), para. 118.

90 *Bistrović v. Croatia* (25774/05) judgment 31 May 2007, paras. 42–44. See also *Kozacıoğlu v. Turkey* (2334/03) judgment [GC] 19 February 2009, where Turkish law prevented the applicant from being compensated for the historical importance of his building; as a result the level of compensation was unfair and the applicant had suffered a breach of Protocol 1 Article 1. See also *Arsovski v. The Former Republic of Macedonia* (30206/06) judgment 7 February 2019, where the Court emphasised that the possibility of exploiting mineral water on the applicants' land had not been sufficiently reflected in the compensation awarded by the domestic courts.

achieve greater social justice.[91] There is therefore a direct link between the importance of the aim pursued and the compensation which should be provided in order for the 'fair balance' principle to be observed. Protocol 1 Article 1 requires that there be a reasonable relationship between the two.[92]

The Court has not defined which public interests may call for compensation below reimbursement of market value.[93] Fundamental changes to a country's constitutional system, such as the transition from a monarchy to a republic,[94] the incorporation of one state into another[95] as well as the transition towards a democratic regime[96] have justified departures from the market-value standard. In particular, the Court has considered a number of complaints where property rights have been affected by the transition from a socialist to a market-based economic system.[97]

There is no set of general principles tying these categories together, and the Court is sometimes divided over the issue of compensation. This is aptly illustrated by the judgment in *Vistiņš and Perepjolkins v. Latvia*. The case concerned properties in the port of Riga, which the applicants had inherited following Latvia's restoration of independence. The Grand Chamber noted that Latvian authorities were justified in offering less than market value for the land for three reasons: Firstly, because the market value of the land could not be objectively determined; secondly, because the property was subject to statutory servitude for the benefit of the port; and thirdly because the applicants had not invested in development of the land or paid any land tax. However, the 'extreme disproportion' between the official cadastral values and the amount of compensation paid to the applicants was

---

91 *James and Others v. the United Kingdom* (n 17), para. 54. See also *The Holy Monasteries v. Greece* (n 86), paras. 70–71, *Pye v. the United Kingdom* (44302/02) judgment [GC] 30 August 2007, para. 54, and *Urbárska obec Trenčianske Biskupice v. Slovakia* (n 56), para. 115.

92 See e.g. *Urbárska obec Trenčianske Biskupice v. Slovakia* (n 56), para. 126, where the Court introduced the idea of a 'sliding scale … balancing the scope and degree of importance of the public interest against the nature and amount of compensation provided to the persons concerned'.

93 See D Popović, *Protecting Property in European Human Rights Law* (Eleven International Publishing 2009) 59–64.

94 See e.g. *The Former King of Greece and Others v. Greece* (25701/94) judgment [GC] 23 November 2000, para. 88.

95 See e.g. *Forrer-Niedenthal v. Germany* (47316/99) judgment 20 February 2003, para. 48.

96 See e.g. *Broniowski v. Poland* (31443/96) judgment [GC] 22 June 2004, para. 182, and *Velikovi and Others v. Bulgaria* (43278/98 et al.) judgment 15 March 2007, para. 172.

97 See e.g. *Jahn and Others v. Germany* (46720/99; 72203/01; 72552/01) judgment [GC] 30 June 2005.

tantamount to a complete lack of compensation, contrary to Protocol 1 Article 1.[98] The minority took the view that the process of trial-and-error inherent in the economic transition warranted a wider margin of appreciation for the State, and that the State had fulfilled its obligations under the Convention.[99]

5.4 *The Reference to 'General Principles of International Law'*

The reference to the 'general principles of international law' in the second sentence of Protocol 1 Article 1 has historically been the subject of some debate. Public international law requires prompt, appropriate and effective compensation for all forms of property deprivation, but this applies only to the benefit of aliens, that is non-nationals of the State.[100]

The Court in *James* addressed the implications of the reference to 'general principles of international law'. The applicants argued that treating nationals differently from non-nationals would violate the principle of non-discrimination enshrined in the ECHR.[101] The Court responded that nationals and non-nationals generally enjoy the same protection under the Convention, but this does not exclude exceptions if any may be indicated in the text of a particular right.[102] It went on to hold that:

> Especially as regards a taking of property effected in the context of a social reform, there may well be good grounds for drawing a distinction between nationals and non-nationals as far as compensation is concerned. To begin with, non-nationals are more vulnerable to domestic legislation: unlike nationals, they will generally have played no

98 *Vistiņš and Perepjolkins v. Latvia* (n 52), paras. 118–119.

99 Ibid., joint partly dissenting opinion of Judges Bratza, Garlicki, Lorenzen, Tsotsoria and Pardalos.

100 See e.g. Article 13 of the Energy Charter Treaty, which provides that expropriation must be for a purpose which is in the public interest, not discriminatory, carried out under due process of law and accompanied by payment of prompt, adequate and effective compensation. See generally R Dolzer and C Schreuer, *Principles of International Investment Law* (Oxford University Press 2012) 296, and M Shaw, *International Law* (8th edn, Cambridge University Press 2017) 632.

101 Differentiation on the ground of nationality would, in the applicants' view, be incompatible with two provisions that are incorporated in Protocol 1 by virtue of Article 5: Article 1 of the Convention which obliges the Contracting States to secure to 'everyone' within their jurisdiction the rights and freedoms guaranteed, and Article 14 of the Convention which enshrines the principle of non-discrimination.

102 See e.g. Article 4 para. 3 (b), Article 5 para. 1 (f) and Article 16 of the Convention, and Protocol 4 Articles 3 and 4.

> part in the election or designation of its authors nor have been consulted on its adoption. Secondly, although a taking of property must always be effected in the public interest, different considerations may apply to nationals and non-nationals and there may well be legitimate reason for requiring nationals to bear a greater burden in the public interest than non-nationals.[103]

The Court's examination of the *travaux préparatoires* revealed that the 'general principles of international law' entail the obligation to pay compensation to non-nationals in cases of expropriation. The sole purpose of including the reference in the text of Protocol 1 Article 1 was to underline that principles of customary international law requiring States to compensate foreigners for the taking of their property would remain in force.[104] On this basis, the Court concluded that any requirements that follow from the general principles of international law do not apply to a taking of property belonging to the State's own nationals.[105]

This interpretation was strongly criticised by the minority in *James* as well as by many observers of the Court. In the first place, it seemed to conflict with the literal meaning of Article 1 of the Convention, which commits the States to secure the Convention rights and freedoms for 'everyone'. Secondly, the majority's interpretation stood in the way of systematic interpretation, since it had no objective or reasonable basis.[106] Thirdly, it clashed with a teleological interpretation of the Convention, which aims, in the long term, to eliminate distinctions between nationals and non-nationals. Lastly, the Court relied on a historical interpretation of the *travaux préparatoires,* which it generally does not consider to be authoritative.[107]

---

103 *James and Others v. the United Kingdom* (n 17), para. 63.

104 'Resolution 52' by the Committee of Ministers, 19 March 1952, *Travaux Préparatoires,* vol VIII, 204.

105 See generally H Ruiz Fabri, 'The Approach Taken by the European Court of Human Rights to the Assessment of Compensation for "Regulatory Expropriations" of the Property of Foreign Investors' (2002) 11 *New York University Environmental Law Journal* 162–163.

106 See e.g. F Matscher, 'Methods of Interpretation of the Convention' in R St J Macdonald et al. (eds), *The European System for the Protection of Human Rights* (Martinus Nijhoff Publishers 1993) 69, who describes the case of *James* as an example of a restrictive interpretation of rights protected by the Convention.

107 L Sermet, 'The European Convention on Human Rights and Property Rights' 11 *Human Rights Files* (Council of Europe Publishing 1998) 42.

For these reasons, it is doubtful whether the Court's interpretation in *James* remains valid on this point. The essential holding has not been revisited in any subsequent case, since practically all of the jurisprudence concerns the property of nationals. In any event, as Pellonpää has argued, disregarding the elements inherent in the 'prompt, adequate and effective' standard under international law is likely to upset the 'fair balance' required under Protocol 1 Article 1.[108]

5.5 *Compensation for Interference Not Constituting Deprivation*

Whenever the State does not expropriate property, but only subjects it to a form of regulatory power, compensation is a controversial issue indeed. In *Pennsylvania Coal v. Mahon*, the Supreme Court of the United States recognised that a statute which restricts or regulates the use of property can in some circumstances amount to a taking. Yet as Justice Oliver Wendell Holmes famously observed, 'Government hardly could go on if to some extent values incident to property could not be diminished without paying for every such change in the general law. As long recognized, some values are enjoyed under an implied limitation, and must yield to the police power'.[109]

A similar attitude can be discerned in the early case law of the Convention institutions. The Commission established that the second paragraph of Protocol 1 Article 1 does not, as a rule, contain any right to compensation, but that it is relevant to the proportionality assessment to what extent a concrete economic loss was caused by the legislation and whether compensation based on the market value of the property was made available.[110] That result may also be said to flow from the Court's interpretation of Protocol 1 Article 1: Since the three sentences are part of an integrated whole reflecting the 'fair balance' requirement, the availability of compensation is

108 See M Pellonpää, 'Does the European Convention on Human Rights require "prompt, adequate and effective" compensation for deprivation of possessions?' in M Tupamäki (ed), *Liber Amicorum Bengt Broms* (Finnish Branch of the International Law Association 1999) 394. See also E Bjørge, 'The Convention as a Living Instrument Rooted in the Past, Looking to the Future' (2016) *Human Rights Law Review* 248–250.

109 *Pennsylvania Coal Co. v. Mahon* 260 U.S. 393 (1922), 413. See generally R A Epstein, *Takings: Private Property and the Power of Eminent Domain* (Harvard University Press 1985).

110 See e.g. *Banér v. Sweden* (11763/85) decision [EComHR] 9 March 1989, *Pinnacle Meat Processors Company and 8 others v. the United Kingdom* (33298/96) decision [EComHR] 21 October 1998, and *Beyeler v. Italy* (33202/96) judgment [GC] 5 January 2000, para. 114. See also P De Sena, 'Economic and Non-Economic Values in the Case Law of the European Court of Human Rights' in P-M Dupuy et al. (eds), *Human Rights in International Investment Law and Arbitration* (Oxford University Press 2009) 215.

also relevant to the assessment of interference not amounting to deprivation. Unlike in the case of deprivation, however, the absence of compensatory measures has normally not been sufficient to lead the Court to conclude that the 'fair balance' has been upset.[111]

Combined with its heightened level of scrutiny with respect to the economic effects of regulatory measures, the Court appears increasingly inclined to require the State to offer compensation, especially where the measure has severe economic consequences for the applicant. To what extent and in what form compensation must be offered depends, of course, on the type of interference.[112] In cases involving rent control, the statutory rent should be reasonably related to the market value of the property.[113] In cases where national authorities have revoked a licence in commercial use, the Court has required a transition period to mitigate harmful consequences for the applicants' interests.[114]

6 The Applicant's Legitimate Expectations and Acceptance of Risk

6.1 *A Relative Standard of Legal Certainty*

The analysis thus far has focused on the Court's assessment of proportionality in the strict sense – the importance of the aim pursued relative to the effects of the interference on the applicant. The 'fair balance' test has facilitated an increasing level of scrutiny with respect to both these elements, with the aim of ensuring that the right to property is practical and effective. In the broader assessment of 'fair balance', the Court has come to take account of other legal and factual circumstances as well. The impetus behind this development appears to be not only to ensure that the right to property is effective, but also to protect the individual against arbitrariness at the domestic level.

As explained in Chapter 4, legitimate expectations have a function in the 'fair balance' test in terms of strengthening or weakening the applicant's position in the eyes of the Court. In this context, the relevant question is

111 See e.g. *Anonymos Touristiki Etairia Xenodocheia Kritis v. Greece* (35332/05) judgment 21 February 2008, para. 45, and *Depalle v. France* (34044/02) judgment [GC] 29 March 2010, para. 91.

112 See e.g. *Islamic Republic of Iran Shipping Lines v. Turkey* (n 53), para. 99.

113 See Section 4 above.

114 See *Vékony v. Hungary* (65681/13) judgment 13 January 2015, paras. 34–35, *Werra Naturstein Gmbh & Co KG v. Germany* (32377/12) judgment 19 January 2017, para. 45, and *Könyv-Tár Kft and Others v. Hungary* (n 51), paras. 56–58.

whether the applicant knew or should reasonably have known about existing restrictions on the property or the possibility of future restrictions.[115] Measures interfering with the applicant's legitimate expectations concerning the future use of his or her property require a stronger justification by the State.[116] Conversely, any risk assumed on acquisition of the property is held against the applicant.[117]

The Court's rationale for protecting legitimate expectations is to uphold the principle of legal certainty – an element of the rule of law. As the Court has put it, those who act in good faith on the basis of law should not be frustrated in their statute-based expectations without specific and compelling reasons.[118] Consequently, protecting legitimate expectations is a means for the Court to take action against arbitrariness.[119]

The case law reflects that the standard of legal certainty is relative to the applicant's concrete situation. In other words, the level of precision required of domestic legislation depends to a considerable degree on the content of the law in question, the field it is designed to cover and the number and status of those to whom it is addressed.[120]

A line of cases concerning regulation of commercial enterprise can serve to illustrate the role of legitimate expectations and acceptance of risk in

115 See e.g. *Matczyński v. Poland* (32794/07) judgment 15 December 2015, para. 106.

116 See e.g. *Potomska and Potomski v. Poland* (33949/05) judgment 29 March 2011, para. 80, where the Court concluded that the interference in the applicants' property rights failed to satisfy the 'fair balance' principle, *inter alia* on the grounds that they could not have known about the restrictions at the time of their purchase. See also M Sigron, *Legitimate Expectations under Article 1 of Protocol No. 1 to the European Convention on Human Rights* (Intersentia 2014) 198.

117 See e.g. *Allan Jacobsson v. Sweden no. 1* (10842/84) judgment 25 October 1989, para. 61, where the municipal authorities had repeatedly declined the applicant's application to build on his property. This was not a disproportionate interference, according to the Court, because the applicant could not reasonably have been unaware of the building restrictions when he bought the land.

118 See e.g. *N.K.M. v. Hungary* (n 62), para. 75. See also *Lindheim and Others v. Norway* (n 56), para. 133, where the Court held that the applicants could entertain a legitimate expectation that the relevant lease contracts would expire as agreed according to their terms, independently of the intervening discussions on, and adoption of, legislative measures.

119 P Popelier, 'Legitimate Expectations and the Law Maker in the Case Law of the European Court of Human Rights' (2006) *European Human Rights Law Review* 19.

120 See e.g. *O'Sullivan McCarthy Mussel Development Ltd v. Ireland* (44460/16) judgment 7 June 2018, para. 107, and *Vistiņš and Perepjolkins v. Latvia* (n 52), paras. 95–99.

the 'fair balance' assessment.[121] When faced with corporate applicants, the Court often reverts to its statement in *Pine Valley Developments Ltd.* that commercial ventures by their very nature involve an element of risk.[122] The same cannot be said about all individuals invoking Protocol 1 Article 1 in defence of their personal property rights. For example, recipients of social benefits cannot be expected to take account of the risk of future changes to the same degree.[123]

Thus, the case law shows that property interests held by commercial entities generally enjoy a lower level of protection under the 'fair balance' assessment than does property used in the service of other private interests, because commercial actors are expected to take greater care in assessing the legal risks that their activities entail.[124] This goes some way in explaining the observation made by Harris et al. that the Strasbourg Court has been notably unsympathetic towards those who have taken development risks and who have failed to make gains as a result of action or inaction by the State.[125]

6.2 *The Problem of Retroactive Laws*

A common feature in cases involving legitimate expectations is that the applicants have relied on an instrument of domestic law which has been retrospectively invalidated to their detriment. Retroactive legislation poses a fundamental challenge to the principle of legal certainty, which requires that the law must be foreseeable so as to allow legal subjects to regulate their conduct. Pleas for protection of legitimate expectations in the face of perceived retroactive laws typically arise when new legislation is introduced

---

121 See e.g. *Fredin v. Sweden (no. 1)* (12033/86) judgment 18 February 1991, para. 54, *Pine Valley Developments Ltd and Others v. Ireland* (12742/87) judgment 29 November 1991, para. 59, *Stretch v. the United Kingdom* (44277/98) judgment 24 June 2003, *Nobel and Others v. the Netherlands* (27126/11 et al.) decision 2 July 2013, para. 39, *Kristiana Ltd. v. Lithuania* (36184/13) judgment 6 February 2018, para. 110, and *O'Sullivan McCarthy Mussel Development Ltd v. Ireland* (44460/16) judgment 7 June 2018, para. 117.

122 *Pine Valley Developments Ltd and Others v. Ireland* (12742/87) judgment 29 November 1991, para. 59. See also *Stretch v. the United Kingdom* (44277/98) judgment 24 June 2003.

123 See e.g. *Béláné Nagy v. Hungary* (53080/13) judgment [GC] 13 December 2016, paras. 123–125.

124 See by comparison *Vékony v. Hungary* (n 114), paras. 36–37, where the Court emphasised the fact that the applicant depended on the continued sale of tobacco products for his livelihood.

125 D J Harris et al. (n 52) 884.

which extinguishes the applicant's claim against the State. Such interference generally requires a strong justification.[126]

One prominent illustration is *Pressos Campania Naviera SA and Others v. Belgium*. The case concerned an act which, with retroactive effect and without compensation, extinguished the liability of private and public operators of pilot services for seagoing vessels. The Court decided that the aim of protecting the State's financial interests could not justify the act's retroactive effect. Thus, extinguishing the claims without compensation was 'a fundamental interference with the applicants' rights [which] is inconsistent with preserving a fair balance between the interests at stake'.[127]

A similar situation arose in *Kamoy Radyo Televizyon Yayincilik ve Organizasyon A.S. v. Turkey*, where the State's legislative intervention definitively settled the substance of a dispute between the applicant company and the rival media group before the domestic courts. The Court noted that the retroactivity had not been 'justified by any grounds of general interest, as required, in particular, by the principle of the rule of law'.[128]

7 The Conduct of the Parties

The aim of ensuring effective rights and safeguarding legal subjects against arbitrariness commits the Court to take into account all relevant factual and legal circumstances in the case at hand. In line with this, the conduct of the parties is pertinent to its substantive review under Protocol 1 Article 1. However, the role that this element plays in practice varies with the nature of the interference and the circumstances as a whole.

In cases concerning confiscation of property used for or derived from criminal activities, for example, the Court considers the relationship between the degree of culpability or negligence on the part of the applicant

126 See e.g. *National & Provincial Building Society, the Leeds Permanent Building Society and the Yorkshire Building Society v. the United Kingdom* ('*National & Provincial Building Society v. the United Kingdom*') (21319/93; 21449/93; 21675/93) judgment 23 October 1997, where the Court held that there is a compelling public interest in the enactment of legislation imposing liability to pay tax with retrospective effect and without compensation where it is done to ensure that private entities do not enjoy the benefit of a windfall in a transition to a new tax payment regime.

127 *Pressos Compania Naviera S.A. and Others v. Belgium* (17849/91) judgment 20 November 1995, paras. 43–44.

128 *Kamoy Radyo Televizyon Yayıncılık ve Organizasyon A.Ş. v. Turkey* (19965/06) judgment 16 April 2019, paras. 50–51.

and the offence in question.[129] In tax cases, the Court has attached weight to the fact that the applicant has deliberately attempted to take advantage of a weakness or a loophole in the system.[130] Both action and inaction of the applicant are relevant in this context.[131]

Conversely, the Court has used as an argument against the respondent State the fact that the applicant has been forced to live in uncertainty about the property's legal status for an unnecessarily long time. Uncertainty – be it legislative, administrative or arising from practices applied by the authorities – is a factor to be taken into account when assessing the State's conduct.[132] Yet while it is fundamental to the Court that the protection of property rights take place in an effective manner, the Court recognises that requirements of efficiency in public administration must correspond to the complexity of the task at hand and the overall circumstances.[133]

Inactivity on the part of the authorities may also lead to questions about whether the State has fulfilled its positive obligations. In *Broniowski v. Poland*, for example, the Court established that in order to maintain citizens' confidence in the State and the law, the authorities were required to eliminate the dysfunctional provisions from the legal system and to rectify extra-legal practises. It held that 'where an issue in the general interest is at stake,

129 *G.I.E.M. S.r.l. and Others v. Italy* (n 29), para. 301.

130 *National & Provincial Building Society v. the United Kingdom* (n 126), para. 109. See also *OGIS-Institut Stanislas, OGEC St. Pie X and Blanche de Castille and Others v. France* (42219/98 54563/00) judgment 27 May 2004, paras. 69 and 71.

131 See also *Pye v. the United Kingdom* (n 91), para. 78, where the Court emphasised that very little was required on the part of the applicant companies to stop time running and to prevent the extinguishment of their title to the land. It went on to note that: '[t]he evidence was that if the applicant companies had asked for rent, or some other form of payment, in respect of the Grahams' occupation of the land, it would have been forthcoming, and the possession would no longer have been "adverse". Even in the unlikely event that the Grahams had refused to leave and refused to agree to conditions for their occupation, the applicant companies need only have commenced an action for recovery, and time would have stopped running against them'.

132 See e.g. *Almeida Garrett, Mascarenhas Falcão and Others v. Portugal* (29813/96; 30229/96) judgment 11 January 2000, para. 54, and *Broniowski v. Poland* (n 47), para. 151.

133 See e.g. *Allan Jacobsson v. Sweden* (n 117), para. 63. See also *Zelenchuk and Tsytsyura v. Ukraine* (n 41), paras. 146–147, and *Kurban v. Turkey* (n 42), para. 85, where the Court concluded that the authorities had acted negligently in communicating crucial information that affected the qualification of participants in the procurement process in which the applicant company took part.

it is incumbent on the public authorities to act in good time, in an appropriate and consistent manner'.[134]

The Court occasionally emphasises norms of 'good governance' as a guideline for the authorities' conduct, especially in cases where there is a question whether the authorities' handling of the case has been sufficiently effective. It is not clear what role such norms play in the 'fair balance' assessment. The expectation of timely action is inherent in the State's positive obligations, and the need to prevent arbitrary interference in property is largely consumed by the lawfulness principle and the requirements of proceedings complying with the rule of law.[135] If anything, this shows that there is a considerable degree of overlap between the substantive and procedural elements of the 'fair balance' assessment.

8 Conclusion

This chapter has explored developments in the substantive dimension of the justification assessment under Protocol 1 Article 1, where the Court's overriding concern is to ensure that the right to property is practical and effective, and not theoretical and illusory. The Court's primary means to that end is the 'fair balance' requirement. It is worth recalling that in the early years, the Court did not consider the proportionality of measures interfering with the right to property, but restricted itself to supervising the lawfulness and the purpose of interference. Following *Sporrong and Lönnroth*, the Court has come to review all forms of interference with the right to property under the heading of 'fair balance'.

In the context of Protocol 1 Article 1, the 'fair balance' functions as a test whereby the interference is unjustified when the applicant has been forced to bear an 'individual and excessive burden'. Developments in the case law reflect a heightened level of scrutiny with regard to the substantive elements of the case.

The Court generally does not subscribe to a theoretical model of proportionality; issues of suitability, necessity, and proportionality in the strict

134 *Broniowski v. Poland* (n 47), para. 151. See also *Jokela v. Finland* (28856/95) judgment 21 May 2002, para. 65, where the Court held that property owners being subjected to expropriation are entitled to expect 'a reasonably consistent approach' from the authorities, and *Beinarovič and Others v. Lithuania* (70520/10; 21920/10; 41876/11) judgment 12 June 2018, para. 140, where the Court required that the authorities rectify their own errors in an effective manner without prejudice to the applicant's legal position.

135 See Chapter 10 below.

sense are integrated into the premises of the Court's judgments as arguments, rather than as prescriptive requirements. But while the Court initially rejected a strict necessity test under Protocol 1 Article 1, it appears to place increasing emphasis on the existence of less intrusive means in the 'fair balance' assessment.

The core of the 'fair balance' test is to weigh the public interest against the effects of the interference on the applicant. Since Protocol 1 Article 1 primarily protects economic interests, economic effects are at the heart of the assessment. The case law shows that the Court conducts a careful review of how the interference affects the applicant in economic terms. This is particularly evident in the Court's approach to compensation. Although the text is silent on the issue, the States' obligation to offer compensation has been integrated as an element of the 'fair balance' test.

In cases concerning regulation of property, the Court appears to view compensation as increasingly relevant as a means of 'softening the blow' to the applicant's interests, especially where the measure has significant economic consequences. This explains why the Court is more inclined to conclude that measures deemed to 'control' the use of property violate Protocol 1 Article 1, whereas earlier it rarely found that the economic impact on the applicant was too severe.[136]

Finally, the Court has gone beyond an isolated analysis of ends and means to look more broadly at the legal and factual circumstances in the case. For one thing, it takes account of the applicant's legitimate expectations and acceptance of risk. The standard of legal certainty is higher for commercial companies than for private individuals because companies are expected to take greater care in assessing and mitigating the legal risks that their activities entail. Furthermore, the Court has come to place emphasis on the conduct of the parties – a result of the Court's effort to protect legal subjects against arbitrariness at the domestic level.

The Court's increasing scrutiny of Protocol 1 Article 1 complaints has been made possible by the 'fair balance' assessment. Since both ensuring effective rights and upholding the rule of law are part of the ECHR's object and purpose, the developments in the substantive dimension are evidence of the Court's teleological method of interpretation. However, the Court's adjudicatory role in this and other controversial areas of ECHR law has attracted criticism, which is bringing about changes in the nature and intensity of its review.

136 T Allen, *Property and the Human Rights Act 1998* (Oxford University Press 2005) 119.

CHAPTER 9

Institutional Dimension: Towards 'Deeper Subsidiarity'?

1 Introduction: The Two Functions of the 'Legitimate Aim' Test

The Strasbourg Court's review of alleged Convention violations has always been affected by the institutional setting in which it operates. There is a tension running through the history of the ECHR between effective protection of human rights and fundamental freedoms on the one hand, and respect for the sovereignty of the Member States on the other.

The institutional dimension of the justification assessment is premised on the recognition that the Court has an obligation to safeguard the interests of the States as well as the rights of the individuals. From the very beginning, the margin of appreciation has been the Court's primary tool for doing so. It is a manifestation of the principle of subsidiarity, according to which the Court's responsibility to secure the ECHR rights is subsidiary to that of the Contracting States.

The Court has traditionally adopted a wide margin of appreciation in cases concerning Protocol 1 Article 1. In recent years, it has increasingly sought to take account of the quality of the assessments made at the domestic level which led to an interference with the right to property when applying the margin of appreciation. Thus, the Court has begun to engage with the States' observance of Protocol 1 Article 1 in a novel way. This chapter will analyse the rationale for the Court's traditionally deferential stance and account for the developments in the direction of 'deeper subsidiarity'.

At the outset, a few words should be said about the nature of the 'legitimate aim' test. Protocol 1 Article 1 requires that deprivation of property must be carried out in the 'public interest', and that control of the use of property must take place in the 'general interest'.[1] It is not clear from the *travaux préparatoires* why the text refers to both the 'public' and the

1 The integrated structure of Protocol 1 Article 1 implies that an interference subsumed under the first sentence must also pursue an aim in the public or general interest, even though it does not follow from the wording, see e.g. *Arišić and Others v. Bosnia and Herzegovina, Croatia, Serbia, Slovenia and the former Yugoslav Republic of Macedonia* (60642/08) judgment [GC] 16 July 2014, para. 105. The principle of 'fair balance', discussed in

 | DOI:10.1163/9789004735088_010

'general' interest. The French version speaks of 'utilité publique' and 'l'intérêt général', which suggests that these terms were chosen to convey different meanings.

The Court addressed the discrepancy in *James and Others v. the United Kingdom*. The applicants argued that the 'public interest' is satisfied in cases of deprivation only if the property is taken for a purpose which benefits the general community. Deprivation of property effected for no reason other than to confer a benefit on a private party cannot be in the 'public interest', they submitted, with reference to the French text.

The Court agreed in principle, but noted that the compulsory transfer of property may constitute a legitimate means for promoting the public interest if it is effected in pursuance of legitimate social policies. It went on to hold that:

> ... the fairness of a system of law governing the contractual or property rights of private parties is a matter of public concern and therefore legislative measures intended to bring about such fairness are capable of being 'in the public interest', even if they involve the compulsory transfer of property from one individual to another.[2]

The Court thus adopted a wide, autonomous interpretation of the 'public interest' in Protocol 1 Article 1. As a result, it laid to rest any potential differences in meaning between the 'public' and 'general' interest.[3]

To understand how the Court's review under Protocol 1 Article 1 has evolved, it is necessary to distinguish between two functions of the 'legitimate aim' test at the justification stage. In its first function, the Court requires that interference by a public authority with the peaceful enjoyment of 'possessions' serve a legitimate public interest.

Chapter 8 above, also presupposes the existence of a general interest of the community, see *Beyeler v. Italy* (33202/96) judgment [GC] 5 January 2000, para. 111.

2 *James and Others v. the United Kingdom* (8793/79) judgment 21 February 1986, para. 41. See also *Bäck v. Finland* (37598/97) judgment 20 July 2004, para. 60, where the Court recognised that rules on debt sanitation were in the 'public interest' even though they benefited only private parties.

3 See Ibid, para. 43, where the Court noted that at the 'point under consideration no fundamental distinction of the kind contended for by the applicants can be drawn between them'. See also D Rook, *Property Law and Human Rights* (Blackstone 2001), 78 and 92, who concludes that it is unclear whether there is any difference between 'public' and 'general' interest; the Court's interpretation in *James and Others* hardly left any doubts about this matter, however. This chapter will mainly refer to the public interest when referring to the aim of interference in the right to property.

Most of the qualified rights in the Convention define which aims are legitimate. The second paragraph of Article 8, for example, stipulates that the State may restrict the right to respect for family and private life in 'the interests of national security, public safety or the economic well-being of the country, for the prevention of disorder or crime, for the protection of health or morals, or for the protection of the rights and freedoms of others'. The second paragraphs of Articles 9–11 contain similar lists. The Court has made clear that the aims there are exhaustively enumerated; in other words, a restriction of rights which does not pursue an aim falling into one of these categories will automatically constitute a violation of the right in question.[4] By comparison, the wording of Protocol 1 Article 1 is entirely open-ended in this respect.

The Court has often observed that the notion of the 'public' or 'general' interest is necessarily extensive.[5] In the case law, a wide range of aims restricting the right to property has been deemed to be compatible with the Convention – social and economic policy aims in the field of housing and town planning, restrictions on alcohol consumption, protection of the environment, the need to combat international drug trafficking, the need to preserve evidence of offences and prevent aggravation of offences, to name a few.[6] The Court has also recognised aims which do not figure elsewhere in the Convention, such as the cultural and artistic inheritance of the State and the need to avoid unregulated hunting and encourage rational management of game stocks.[7]

Despite the open-ended wording of Protocol 1 Article 1, it would be a mistake to assume that the range of permissible aims is unlimited. The Court's position with respect to the right to free elections under Article 3 of the same protocol can provide some guidance in this respect:

> [g]iven that Article 3 of Protocol No. 1 is not limited by a specific list of 'legitimate aims' such as those enumerated in Articles 8 to 11 of the Convention, the Contracting States are … free to rely on an aim not

---

4 See, in relation to Article 8, *Aliyev v. Azerbaijan* (68762/14; 71200/14) judgment 20 September 2018, para. 182.

5 See e.g. *Hentrich v. France* (13616/88) judgment 22 September 1994, para. 39.

6 For further examples of relevant objectives held to be legitimate by the Court, see A R Çoban, *Protection of Private Property Rights within the European Convention of Human Rights* (Ashgate 2004) 202, and P van Dijk et al. (eds), *Theory and Practice of the European Convention on Human Rights* (Intersentia 2018) 889–890.

7 See, respectively, *Beyeler v. Italy* (33202/96) judgment [GC] 5 January 2000, and *Chassagnou and Others v. France* (25088/94; 28331/95; 28443/95) judgment [GC] 29 April 1999.

> contained in that list to justify a restriction, provided that the compatibility of that aim with the principle of the rule of law and the general objectives of the Convention is proved in the particular circumstances of a case.[8]

There is evidence in the case law that the same holds true for restrictions in the right to property.[9] Aims which directly contradict the object and purpose of the Convention cannot be deemed legitimate in the context of Protocol 1 Article 1. In most cases, however, the respondent State is able to invoke a *prima facie* legitimate purpose to justify the impugned interference. In certain instances, the Court has even identified the purpose of its own motion.[10]

The Court accepts the purported aim unless it is 'manifestly without reasonable foundation'.[11] This low standard of scrutiny has applied from the outset. The drafters recognised the inherent challenges linked to 'evaluat[ing] the legitimacy of the charges and restrictions of various kinds which, according to the economic or social conditions of a country, might be imposed on private property, on account of its social function or general utility'.[12] The Commission observed early on that 'in assessing the necessity of a measure under [Protocol 1] Article 1 the Commission retains a limited review of the legitimacy of the aim of the legislation and a fuller review of the proportionality of the actual interference with the applicant's rights'.[13] As the case law has developed, however, the Court has applied an heightened level of scrutiny, *inter alia* by looking more closely at the State's justification for the interference, as discussed in Chapter 8 above.

This leads us to the second and more important function of the 'legitimate aim'. In the 'fair balance' assessment the aim is a reference point against which the Court weighs the effects of the interference and other

8 *Ždanoka v. Latvia* (58278/00) judgment [GC] 16 March 2006, para. 115 (b).

9 See e.g. *Kamoy Radyo Televizyon Yayıncılık ve Organizasyon A.Ş. v. Turkey* (19965/06) judgment 16 April 2019, para. 50, where the Court concluded that the State's legislative intervention, which definitively settled – in a retroactive manner – the dispute between the applicant company and its rival media group was not justified by any grounds of general interest, 'as required, in particular, by the principle of the rule of law'.

10 See e.g. *Ambruosi v. Italy* (31227/96) judgment 19 October 2000, para. 28.

11 See e.g. *James and Others v. the United Kingdom* (n 2), para. 46. See also T Allen, *Property and the Human Rights Act 1998* (Oxford University Press 2005) 133, who calls this standard 'a test of good faith'. It is probably correct to see the Court's approach to the legitimate aim test as a case of implementation freedom, see Section 2 below.

12 *Travaux Préparatoires*, vol I, 198.

13 *Gillow v. the United Kingdom* (9063/80) report [EComHR] 3 October 1984, para. 147.

relevant substantive elements.[14] In this context, the public interest also defines the margin of appreciation afforded to the State.

The remainder of this chapter is devoted to the jurisprudential developments in the institutional dimension, specifically in the Court's application of the margin of appreciation in cases concerning Protocol 1 Article 1. Section 2 analyses the legal basis and functions of the margin of appreciation to illuminate the topic of discussion. Section 3 then examines the arguments used by the Court to justify a traditionally deferential stance with regard to the right to property. Finally, Section 4 looks at the developments in the case law in the direction of 'deeper subsidiarity'.

2 The Margin of Appreciation, Its Legal Basis and Functions

A core tenet of the Court's case law is that the rights in the Convention must not be applied in such a way as to undermine the role of the democratically elected organs of the State to make decisions on behalf of their communities. Promoting democratic ideals is, after all, also a part of the ECHR's object and purpose.[15] Accordingly, a degree of freedom should be granted to national authorities in the Court's determination of whether the Convention rights have been secured in an adequate manner.

Historically, neither the Convention text nor the *travaux préparatoires* made any mention of the States' margin of appreciation. With Protocol 15's entry into force, a direct reference has been included in the Preamble:

> Affirming that the High Contracting Parties, in accordance with the principle of subsidiarity, have the primary responsibility to secure the rights and freedoms defined in this Convention and the Protocols thereto, and that in doing so they enjoy a margin of appreciation, subject to the supervisory jurisdiction of the European Court of Human Rights established by this Convention.

The added recital is intended to codify the Court's margin of appreciation doctrine as it has been developed in the case law primarily in the context of the qualified rights.[16] However, because the Court has never elaborated on

---

14 See Chapter 8 Section 3 above.

15 See Chapter 3 above.

16 Council of Europe, *Explanatory Report to Protocol No. 15 Amending the Convention for the Protection of Human Rights and Fundamental Freedoms* (Council of Europe Treaty

the margin of appreciation doctrine, its scope, legal basis and function remain amenable to various interpretations. The term itself is a direct translation of 'marge d'appréciation', a term used in French administrative law, and the Court's approach has been widely understood to be inspired by national doctrines concerning judicial control by the executive branch of government.[17]

The margin of appreciation and its role in relation to the 'fair balance' requirement has been analysed at length in the literature.[18] Frowein has observed that '[t]he way necessity is established cannot be understood without discussing the difficult issue of the margin of appreciation'.[19] In the words of Arai-Takahashi, the margin of appreciation is 'an inevitable spin-off of the notion of balancing inherent in the Convention'.[20] The Court's former vice president John Cremona described the interaction thus:

> In practice the principle of proportionality goes hand in hand with the recognition to the States, as having the initial responsibility for securing the Convention rights and freedoms, of a margin of appreciation,

---

Series No. 213), para. 7. The margin of appreciation is virtually nonexistent when it comes to the Convention's non-derogable rights – the right to life under Article 2, the prohibition of torture under Article 3, the prohibition of slavery and forced labour under Article 4, and the prohibition of retroactive legislation in criminal cases under Article 7. See generally D J Harris et al., *Law of the European Convention on Human Rights* (4th edn, Oxford University Press 2018) 17, and D Spielmann, 'Allowing the Right Margin: The European Court of Human Rights and The National Margin of Appreciation Doctrine: Waiver or Subsidiarity of European Review?' (2012) 14 *Cambridge Yearbook of European Legal Studies* 381–418.

17 See e.g. R St J Macdonald, 'The Margin of Appreciation' in R St J Macdonald et al. (eds), *The European System for the Protection of Human Rights* (Martinus Nijhoff Publishers 1993) 83.

18 See in particular Y Arai-Takahashi, *The Margin of Appreciation Doctrine and the Principle of Proportionality in the Jurisprudence of the ECHR* (Intersentia 2002), G Letsas, 'Two Concepts of the Margin of Appreciation' (2006) 26 (4) *Oxford Journal of Legal Studies* 705–732, J Christoffersen, *Fair Balance: Proportionality, Subsidiarity and Primarity in the European Convention on Human Rights* (Martinus Nijhoff Publishers 2009), A Legg, *The Margin of Appreciation in International Human Rights Law – Deference and Proportionality* (Oxford University Press 2012), and O M Arnardóttir 'Rethinking the Two Margins of Appreciation' (2016) 12 *European Constitutional Law Review* 27–53.

19 J Frowein, 'The European Convention on Human Rights as the Public Order of Europe' (1990) 1(2) *Collected Courses of the Academy of European Law* 345.

20 Y Arai-Takahashi, 'The Margin of Appreciation Doctrine: A Theoretical Analysis of Strasbourg's Variable Geometry' in A Føllesdal et al. (eds), *Constituting Europe: The European Court of Human Rights in a National, European and Global Context* (Cambridge University Press 2013) 86.

> which … is not unlimited and is subject to the supervision of the Court, which in fact gives the final ruling.[21]

If anything is gained by these and similar observations it must be that there is a close, intricate relationship between the margin of appreciation and 'fair balance'. But a closer analysis is called for if we are to understand how the doctrine has impacted the Court's justification assessment generally, and the interpretation of Protocol 1 Article 1 specifically.

Harris et al. have defined the margin of appreciation as 'the vehicle relied upon to give a certain degree of deference to the judgment of national authorities when they weigh public and individual interests in view of their local knowledge and the principle of subsidiarity'.[22] In the same vein, Arai-Takahashi has described the margin of appreciation as 'the measure of discretion allowed the member states in the manner in which they implement the Convention's standards, taking into account their own particular national circumstances and conditions'.[23] Similarly, Letsas has understood the margin of appreciation as 'the latitude a government enjoys in evaluating factual situations and in applying the provisions enumerated in international human rights treaties'.[24]

Words like 'deference', 'discretion' and 'latitude' express the recognition that the Court has a tendency to shy away from applying the ECHR in a manner which infringes on the sovereignty of the Member States. This connotation may impart something about the effect of the margin of appreciation, but it leaves unclear what, exactly, is its function. Legal doctrine appears to have offered as many views on this crucial question as there have been contributions. Navigating through the various abstractions is indeed a challenge unto itself. Christoffersen has made a laudable effort to bring order to the semantic chaos. In his analysis, it is necessary to distinguish conceptually between the States' implementation freedom and the Court's subsidiary review.[25]

---

21 See e.g. J J Cremona, 'The Proportionality Principle in the Jurisprudence of the European Court of Human Rights' in U Beyerlin et al. (eds), *Recht zwischen Umbruch und Bewahrung – Festschrift für Rudolf Bernhardt* (Springer Verlag 1995) 328. See also *Handyside v. the United Kingdom* (5493/72) judgment 7 December 1976, paras. 48–49.

22 D J Harris et al. (n 16) 16.

23 Y Arai-Takahashi (n 18) 1.

24 G Letsas (n 18) 705.

25 J Christoffersen (n 18) 233.

States always have a degree of freedom to implement obligations they assume under international law.[26] In the specific context of the ECHR, States are to an extent free to choose how to implement the rights and freedoms in the Convention within the boundaries of interpretation established by the Court.[27] Indeed, it was assumed during the drafting of the Convention that the States should have a certain 'freedom of action'.[28] The implementation freedom has sometimes been mistaken for a margin of appreciation, but clearly, the States' obligation under international law to implement the ECHR in good faith would have existed irrespective of the current enforcement machinery, and absent a court of human rights such as the Strasbourg Court.[29]

The freedom enjoyed by the States when implementing their obligations under the ECHR is distinct from any self-restraint exercised by the Court in its adjudication of alleged violations. In the latter sense, the margin of appreciation should be understood as a manifestation of the principle of subsidiarity, the essence of which is that the Court's role in securing the rights and freedoms in the ECHR is subsidiary to the primary role of the Contracting States. Like the margin of appreciation, the subsidiarity principle has not had a direct textual basis in the Convention until the entry into force of Protocol 15.[30]

---

26 See Article 31 para. 1 VCLT, which states that a treaty shall be interpreted 'in good faith'.

27 This is particularly evident in respect of the execution of the Court's judgments pursuant to Article 41. See e.g. *Papamichalopoulos and Others v. Greece* (14556/89) judgment (just satisfaction) 31 October 1995, para. 34, where the Court held that '[t]he Contracting States ... are in principle free to choose the means whereby they will comply with a judgment', and that this choice attaches to their primary obligation of the States to secure the rights and freedoms guaranteed under the Convention pursuant to Article 1.

28 *Collected Edition of the Travaux Préparatoires*, Council of Europe, Doc H(61)4, vol I, 130.

29 See e.g. L Crema, 'Disappearance and New Sightings of Restrictive Interpretation(s)' (2010) 21 *European Journal of International Law* 699, who has described the concept of margin of appreciation as an expression of the principle of 'good faith' within the meaning of Article 31 VCLT.

30 In the past, the subsidiarity principle was seen to derive primarily from the States' obligation to 'secure' the Convention rights and freedoms under Article 1, the right to an effective national remedy in Article 13, establishment of the Court in Article 19, and the requirement of exhaustion of domestic remedies in Article 35 para. 1, see e.g. A Mowbray, 'Subsidiarity and the European Convention on Human Rights' (2015) 15 *Human Rights Law Review* 319. With the entry into force of Protocol 15, a reference to

Subsidiarity is a broad political principle found *inter alia* in the law of the European Union and in the canonical law of the Catholic Church. It was introduced and developed in the ECHR system in the *Belgian Linguistic case* and *Handyside*, where the Court made clear that the principle of subsidiarity is a reflection first and foremost of the position of the Court relative to the domestic authorities of the Member States.[31] In line with this, the principle of subsidiarity has been described as a norm of power distribution between the Court and the States with the ultimate aim of securing Convention rights.[32]

As Arnardóttir has shown, the principle of subsidiarity has a two-fold rationale encompassing functional as well as normative aspects. The functional rationale is concerned with efficiency and competence. Subsidiarity recognises that small, local units are better equipped to deal with events than an international tribunal with limited resources at its disposal. Furthermore, the principle acknowledges the States' consent as the foundation of Convention obligations and the corresponding, relatively weak enforcement mechanism upon which the ECHR system rests.

Normatively, the rationale behind the principle of subsidiarity is that it respects the self-determination of individuals or groups through democratic processes, as alluded to in the introduction. As such, subsidiarity facilitates the pluralism and diversity associated with democratic society, and recognises that there may exist different, but equally valid, ways of ensuring the same Convention rights. Together, these factors call for a certain amount of respect for, or deference to, the States.[33]

The margin of appreciation should be viewed as an operative manifestation of the principle of subsidiarity encompassing these functional and normative justifications. In a way, the subsidiarity principle authorises the Court to take a deferential stance with regard to the factual and legal elements of a case.[34] This is something of a paradox, since what would

---

the principle of subsidiarity has been added to the Preamble, rendering it a valid source of Convention interpretation, see Article 31 para. 2 VCLT.

31 *Belgian Linguistic case* (1474/62 et al.) judgment 23 July 1968, and *Handyside v. the United Kingdom* (5493/72) judgment 7 December 1976.

32 R Spano, 'The Future of the European Court of Human Rights – Subsidiarity, Process-based Review and the Rule of Law' (2018) *Human Rights Law Review* 20.

33 See O M Arnardóttir (n 18) 27–53. See also R St J Macdonald (n 17) 123.

34 As demonstrated by Arai-Takahashi, the margin of appreciation operates at five stages of the Court's review: fact-finding and ascertainment of fact; interpreting and applying national laws; evaluating the parameters of a specific ECHR right and applying them in relation to a specific issue; balancing between an individual person's right and a

presumably be required under international law is a legal basis for scrutiny, not deference. Be that as it may; the point is that deference is a choice for the Court. At a fundamental level, the Court's self-restraint is a reflection of the role it chooses to take *vis-à-vis* the Member States. Later this chapter will examine the arguments the Court has used to justify a deferential stance in cases concerning Protocol 1 Article 1.

At this stage, a few more observations should be made about the operative function of the margin of appreciation. The Court established in *James* that the State enjoys a wide margin of appreciation with respect to interference in the right to property. This recognition, which has had a lasting significance, helps explain why most complaints regarding Protocol 1 Article 1 have not resulted in a violation.[35] The Court in *James* also articulated the basic effect of the margin of appreciation: That it will respect the State's assessment as to the existence of a problem of public concern and the remedial action to be taken, and not substitute its own assessment for that of the national authorities.[36] In this manner, the margin of appreciation serves to qualify the Court's own substantive assessment under the 'fair balance' test.

The margin of appreciation is variable and alters the intensity of the Court's review in the 'fair balance' assessment.[37] In practice, the Court applies a 'sliding scale model of intensity of review', distinguishing between a 'wide', 'certain', 'narrow' and 'zero' margin of appreciation. When applied under the 'fair balance' test, these labels can be said to correspond to a lenient standard of proportionality, *via* a moderate to an intense or even full proportionality review, respectively.[38] Even where the margin is wide, the Court is not barred from finding breaches of Protocol 1 Article 1, but in these situations, it has historically confined itself to verifying whether the measure was 'manifestly without reasonable foundation'.[39]

---

public interest, including the evaluation of the means to achieve the ends sought; and weighing two competing rights against each other, see Y Arai-Takahashi (n 20) 69.

35 As of 31 December 2022, 3 810 violations of Protocol 1 Article 1 were recorded in the HUDOC database, see <https://www.echr.coe.int/Documents/Stats_violation_1959_2022_ENG.pdf> accessed 30 May 2025. By comparison, the Convention organs have rendered more than 25,000 judgments and decisions in response to Protocol 1 Article 1 complaints as of 30 May 2025.

36 *James and Others v. the United Kingdom* (n 2), para. 46. See also *Hutten-Czapska v. Poland* (35014/97) judgment [GC] 19 June 2006, para. 166.

37 A Mowbray, 'A Study of the Principle of Fair Balance in the Jurisprudence of the European Court of Human Rights' (2010) 10(2) *Human Rights Law Review* 316–317.

38 Y Arai-Takahashi (n 18) 236.

39 See e.g. *Immobiliare Saffi v. Italy* (22774/93) judgment [GC] 28 July 1999, para. 49.

The scope of the margin afforded to the State in a given case is influenced by several factors. As the Court has explained, the margin will 'vary according to the nature of the Convention right in issue, its importance for the individual and the nature of the activities restricted, as well as the nature of the aim pursued by the restrictions'.[40] The Convention right is given for the purposes of the present discussion. The remaining factors can be categorised in two groups which will be referred to here to as substantive and structural arguments.[41]

Substantive arguments relate to the intensity of the interference and its impact on the applicant. The more intense the interference, the greater scrutiny is called for on the part of the Court. In cases concerning Protocol 1 Article 1, it is natural that the margin is narrowest in cases involving deprivation of property. Interference which does not amount to deprivation has normally justified a correspondingly wider margin, but other substantive elements may play a role as well.

In practice, many of the factors influencing the margin of appreciation are identical to the substantive elements in the 'fair balance' assessment discussed in Chapter 8. For this reason, it is sometimes difficult to know whether the Court, by awarding the State a margin of appreciation, has found that the State has acted within the margin, or has reviewed the interference and concluded that the 'fair balance' requirement has been satisfied.[42]

Structural arguments concern the division of responsibility between the Court and the Member States. These arguments can be labelled in various ways, but will be referred to here as the 'proximity' argument, the 'consensus' argument and the 'legitimacy' argument. The next section explores how the Court has employed these arguments to justify a deferential standard of review in cases concerning the right to property.

Admittedly, it is often difficult to distinguish between substantive and structural arguments in practice. Structural arguments generally serve to justify a more lenient review of the substantive issues, and the two groups of arguments often interact in a way which results in partial deference. A more serious issue is that these two groups of arguments fail to

40 See e.g. *Chapman v. the United Kingdom* (27238/95) judgment [GC] 18 January 2001, para. 91, and *Gillow v. the United Kingdom* (n 13), para. 55.

41 See G Letsas (n 18). See also A Legg (n 18) 8–9, who refers to these arguments as merits reasons and non-merits reasons for deference.

42 See e.g. R St J Macdonald (n 17) 85. See also J Christoffersen (n 18) 232, who calls this tendency 'frustrating to observe'.

accommodate a clear trend in the jurisprudence, namely the Court's tendency to refrain from substituting its own view for that of the national authorities where the latter have carefully assessed and decided the case at the domestic level.[43] The development towards 'deeper subsidiarity' will be discussed at the end of the chapter.

3 Arguments for Deferential Review in Cases concerning the Right to Property

3.1 *Structural Arguments: Proximity, Consensus and Legitimacy*

Having analysed the legal basis and function of the margin of appreciation, the discussions now proceed to its role in the Court's application of Protocol 1 Article 1. In *James and Others v. the United Kingdom* the Court justified the margin of appreciation under Protocol 1 Article 1 in the following way:

> Because of their direct knowledge of their society and its needs, the national authorities are in principle better placed than the international judge to appreciate what is 'in the public interest'. Under the system of protection established by the Convention, it is thus for the national authorities to make the initial assessment both of the existence of a problem of public concern warranting measures of deprivation of property and of the remedial action to be taken … Here, as in other fields to which the safeguards of the Convention extend, the national authorities accordingly enjoy a certain margin of appreciation.
>
> Furthermore, the notion of 'public interest' is necessarily extensive. In particular … the decision to enact laws expropriating property will

43 See, in particular, *M.A. v. Denmark* (6697/18) judgment [GC] 9 July 2021, para. 149 where the Grand Chamber phrased the relevant test thus: 'domestic courts must put forward specific reasons in the light of the circumstances of the case, not least to enable the Court to carry out the European supervision entrusted to it. Where the reasoning of domestic decisions is insufficient, and the interests in issue have not been weighed in the balance, there will be a breach of the requirements of Article 8 of the Convention … Where, on the other hand, the domestic courts have carefully examined the facts, applied the relevant human rights standards consistently with the Convention and the Court's case-law, and have adequately weighed up the individual interests against the public interest in a case, the Court would require strong reasons to substitute its own view for that of the domestic courts'. See also *Animal Defenders International v. the United Kingdom* (48876/08) judgment [GC] 22 April 2013, para. 108.

> commonly involve consideration of political, economic and social issues on which opinions within a democratic society may reasonably differ widely.[44]

Three arguments can be derived from these paragraphs. Firstly, the Court maintained that by reason of their direct and continuous contact with the vital forces of their countries, domestic authorities are in principle better placed than an international court to evaluate local needs and conditions (the 'proximity' argument). This argument emphasises the State's factual knowledge and respect for different local needs and conditions. The Court often leaves a wide margin of appreciation to the States because they are in a better position to assess the necessity, suitability and overall reasonableness of a limitation of rights.

Secondly, the Court noted that opinions within a democratic society may reasonably differ widely with respect to the political, economic and social issues at stake. It might have added that opinions on these issues differ among democratic societies as well. A lenient standard of review in cases concerning the right to property can therefore be explained by the existence of plurality of opinion in and among the Member States.

On the face of it, there appear to be few common standards which could justify a common approach to the protection of the right to property. In many jurisdictions, property protection is based on deeply embedded thinking about the relationship between private property rights and State power.[45] Domestic legislation in this area is often organic and characterised by formalistic and tradition-bound concepts. In *Pye*, the Court recognised as much when it described as 'a characteristic of property that different countries regulate its use and transfer in a variety of ways. The relevant rules reflect social policies against the background of the local conception of the importance and role of property'.[46]

Moreover, in recent decades, the Council of Europe has been expanded to incorporate a number of Central and Eastern European States with legal cultures that differ significantly from those of the original Member States in Western Europe. Following the eastward expansion, the diversity and lack of consensus among the current Member States with respect to the right to

44 *James and Others v. the United Kingdom* (n 2), para. 46.

45 See e.g. R Schlatter, *Property – the History of an Idea* (Rutgers University Press 1951) and P Garnsey, *Thinking About Property: From Antiquity to the Age of Revolution* (Cambridge University Press 2007).

46 See *Pye v. the United Kingdom* (44302/02) judgment [GC] 30 August 2007, para. 74.

property clearly mandate a degree of deference on the part of the Court with regard to the interpretation and application of Protocol 1 Article 1. The consensus argument can therefore be expected to play a minor role in the premises of the Court's judgments.

Thirdly, the Court reasoned that the legislature should have a wide margin of appreciation 'in implementing social and economic policies', and that the role of the domestic policy-maker should be given special weight.[47] Implicitly, domestic authorities should be given a wide margin of appreciation because decisions made by democratically accountable organs enjoy more legitimacy than those made by the Court (the 'legitimacy argument'). As Mowbray has argued, the Court's propensity for a deferential approach is enhanced where decisions entail complex political issues that are closely bound up not merely with the demand of sovereignty, but also with that of the legitimacy of the national or local community.[48]

The three structural arguments may be distinguishable on a conceptual level, but they are interdependent and mutually reinforcing in practice. This is aptly illustrated by the following passage from *Hatton and Others v. the United Kingdom*:

> [N]ational authorities have direct *democratic legitimation* and are … in principle *better placed* than an international court to evaluate local needs and conditions … In matters of general policy, on which *opinions within a democratic society may reasonably differ widely*, the role of the domestic policy-maker should be given special weight.[49]

It is often noted that the margin of appreciation in cases concerning interference with the right to property is wide compared with, for example, cases involving interference with the individual's autonomy or physical freedom.[50] But while the margin may generally be wide, the structural arguments described above manifest themselves in different ways depending on the aim of the interference and the factual circumstances of the case. Put differently, the Court's rationale for not substituting its own assessment for

47 See e.g. *Maurice v. France* (11810/03) judgment [GC] 6 October 2005, para. 117.

48 A Mowbray (n 37) 316.

49 *Hatton and Others v. the United Kingdom* (36022/97) judgment [GC] 8 July 2003, para. 97 (emphasis added).

50 See e.g. *Stretch v. the United Kingdom* (44277/98) judgment 24 June 2003, para. 37. See also Y Winisdoerffer, 'Margin of Appreciation and Article 1 of Protocol No. 1' (1998) *Human Rights Law Journal* 18.

that made by the domestic authorities varies with the public interest at issue. To illustrate this point, the remainder of this chapter will analyse the Court's approach to some public aims which typically motivate interference in private property. At this point the case law is worth studying in detail because the Court's reasoning essentially explains why most complaints regarding Protocol 1 Article 1 ultimately have not resulted in a violation.

3.2 *The Nature of the Public Interest*

3.2.1 Land and Housing Regulation

When considering the various public interests which can justify restrictions of private property rights, it is worth bearing in mind that property is a scarce resource to which human beings need access for their subsistence. Unlike most other objects of human rights, property has an intrinsic social function in the sense that private ownership comes with an obligation to use property in ways that contribute to the collective or common good. The drafters recognised early on that the State has a role in ensuring that the allocation of property conforms to ideals of justice and fairness, and in *James*, the Court acknowledged that '[e]liminating what are judged to be social injustices is an example of the functions of a democratic legislature'.[51]

In a line of judgments concerning regulation of land and housing, the Court has acknowledged that shortages of property are an almost universal problem of modern society. Legislative measures such as rent control are often motivated by a concern for the interests of third parties, typically members of vulnerable categories of the population. The Court's reasoning in these cases suggests that a wide margin of appreciation is justified primarily by virtue of the legitimacy argument, and that in the Court's view, only the legislative organs of the State can legitimately determine what is a just distribution of property.

An intriguing illustration is found in the case of *Hutten-Czapska v. Poland*.[52] The Court took as its point of departure that some form of regulation is called for in the sphere of housing, which modern societies consider a prime social need and which plays a central role in the welfare and economic policies of the State. Decisions as to whether housing may fully be left to the play of free-market forces or whether it should be subject to State control involve consideration of complex social, economic and political questions. The exceptionally difficult housing situation in Poland, the inevitably serious social consequences involved in the reform of the lease

51 *James and Others v. the United Kingdom* (n 2), para. 47.

52 See Chapters 4 and 8 above.

market, and the impact that that reform had on economic and other rights all led the Court to conclude that the margin of appreciation available to the authorities should be wide.[53]

In light of the need for legitimate regulation of property, the Polish Parliament's decision to introduce laws restricting levels of rent in privately owned flats in order to protect tenants was generally justified, in the Grand Chamber's view. However, the statutory rent level was not sufficient to cover the landlords' costs of maintaining the properties, let alone provide a minimum level of profit from the lease of the flats. Despite the State's wide margin of appreciation, and even in a situation where the tenants were generally deemed to be vulnerable and deserving of legal protection, the Court intervened in favour of the landlords. *Hutten-Czapska* thus serves to demonstrate how the social function of property can be outweighed by the economic effects of the interference, despite the State's wide margin of appreciation in this area.[54]

3.2.2 Area Planning and Expropriation

Restrictions resulting from area planning are among the classic instances of control of the use of property.[55] The Court has maintained that regional planning policies, where the community's general interest is preeminent, confer a margin of appreciation on the State that is greater than when exclusively civil rights are at stake.[56] The authorities are therefore free to choose both regulatory purposes and areas for regulation without prejudice to the owners' right to the peaceful enjoyment of property under the ECHR.

In *Sporrong and Lönnroth v. Sweden*, the Court stated that 'in an area as complex and difficult as that of the development of large cities, the Contracting States should enjoy a wide margin of appreciation in order to implement their town-planning policy'.[57] By emphasising the complexity of area planning, the Court relied on the argument that domestic authorities

53 *Hutten-Czapska v. Poland* (n 36), para. 166.

54 See also *Urbárska Obec Trenčianske Biskupice v. Slovakia* (74258/01) judgment 27 November 2007, para. 131, where the Court found that the compulsory letting of the land owned by the members of the applicant association and the subsequent transfer of that land to the tenants breached Protocol 1 Article 1, with emphasis on the fact that the supposed beneficiaries of those measures did not belong to a socially weak or particularly vulnerable part of the population.

55 See Chapter 6 above.

56 See e.g. *Depalle v. France* (34044/02) judgment [GC] 29 March 2010, para. 84.

57 *Sporrong and Lönnroth v. Sweden* (7151/75; 7152/75) judgment 23 September 1982, para. 69.

are generally better placed than the international judge in order to justify a wide margin of appreciation. Still, the Court does not abdicate its role of ensuring the observance of the obligations undertaken by the States. This was demonstrated by the Court's conclusion that the combination of a building ban and the threat of expropriation over an extended period of time had upset the 'fair balance'.

Expropriation is a powerful instrument of area planning policy. The Court has recognised that domestic authorities are generally in a better position to determine whether it is necessary to resort to expropriation and, if so, which level of compensation is fair. The States therefore enjoy a wide margin of appreciation in deciding the compensation terms.

The Court's judgment in *Lithgow and Others v. the United Kingdom* illustrates the practical implications. The case concerned the nationalisation of industries under the Aircraft and Shipbuilding Industries Act 1977. The applicant companies maintained that the compensation which they had received was grossly inadequate. The Court acknowledged that nationalisation by its very nature involves consideration of a large number of competing interests which the national authorities are better placed to consider than an international judge is. Emphasising the State's wide margin of appreciation in deciding the terms of compensation, the Court stated that it would respect the legislature's judgment in this connection unless that judgment was 'manifestly without reasonable foundation'.[58] Having found a sufficient rationale for the compensation formula, the Court concluded that the decision to adopt it was one which the State was entitled to make in the exercise of its margin of appreciation.[59]

In recent practice, the Court has tended to emphasise the existence of procedural safeguards ensuring that the State meets its obligation to pay compensation.[60] In particular, the process of paying out compensation must be expeditious, since a delay in the payment of compensation aggravates the applicant's financial loss and places him or her in an uncertain

58 *Lithgow and Others v. the United Kingdom* (9006/80 et al.) judgment 8 July 1986, para. 122.

59 See Ibid., para. 121, where the Court also held that a wide margin of appreciation was particularly necessary in cases of nationalisation, because '[t]he valuation of major industrial enterprises for the purpose of nationalising a whole industry is in itself a far more complex operation than, for instance, the valuation of land compulsorily acquired and normally calls for specific legislation which can be applied across the board to all the undertakings involved'.

60 See e.g. *Svitlana Ilchenko v. Ukraine* (47166/09) judgment 4 July 2019, para. 73.

situation.[61] On that basis, the Court has ruled against the State in cases where the public authorities failed to take account of the fact that many years had elapsed and the applicant had not yet received any compensation.[62] As will be seen in the next chapter, the Court has generally emphasised that expropriation measures must be accompanied by a procedure allowing for an overall assessment of the measure.[63]

3.2.3 Protection of the Environment

The public's interest in preserving the natural environment is commonly recognised in all States which are parties to the ECHR.[64] The framing and administration of such policies offer the authorities a wide array of possible measures, some of which necessitate interfering with the right to property. In granting the State a wide margin of appreciation in the choice between available measures, the Court has relied on the argument that domestic authorities are generally better placed to evaluate local needs and conditions to determine which measures are necessary. In cases where the State interferes with private property to protect the environment, the Court has further observed that the State has a special responsibility to respond in a timely manner. The importance of intervening in time to prevent detriment to the environment calls for a wider margin of appreciation.

In the case of *Depalle v. France*, the applicant had been forced to move from a beach property where he had lived for more than 30 years, because the local authorities wished to make the area available to the public. The Court held that 'environmental conservation, which in today's society is an increasingly important consideration … has become a cause whose defence arouses the constant and sustained interest of the public, and consequently

61 See e.g. *Almeida Garrett, Mascarenhas Falcão and Others v. Portugal* (29813/96; 30229/96) judgment 11 January 2000, para. 54.

62 See e.g. *Schembri and Others v. Malta* (42583/06) judgment 10 November 2009, para. 43. See also *Guiso-Gallisay v. Italy* (58858/00) judgment [GC] 22 December 2009, paras. 103–105, where the Court held that the market value of property at the time of taking should be converted to current value to offset the effects of inflation, and a simple statutory interest should be applied to offset the period during which the applicant has been deprived of the property.

63 See e.g. *Bistrović v. Croatia* (25774/05) judgment 31 May 2007, para. 37.

64 See e.g. *G.I.E.M., S.r.l. and Others v. Italy* (1828/06; 34163/07; 19029/11) judgment [GC] 28 June 2018, para. 295, where the Grand Chamber noted that the legitimacy of State policies in favour of environmental protection cannot be called into question because the well-being and health of individuals are thereby also guaranteed and defended.

the public authorities'.[65] In the assessment of 'fair balance' the Court noted that it is first and foremost for the national authorities to decide which type of measures should be imposed to protect coastal areas due to their proximity to events. In the Court's analysis, however, the applicant had not been severely affected by the measure: he had known that the residence permit could be changed or withdrawn, and that he had a duty to demolish the house without compensation if the authorities demanded it. On this basis, the majority in the Grand Chamber concluded that the State had acted within its margin of appreciation.

3.2.4 Protection of Public Health and Morality

Among the aims listed in the second paragraphs of Articles 8-11, the protection of public health and morality has been a consistent feature in the case law concerning the right to property. One of the very first judgments that dealt with Protocol 1 Article 1, *Handyside v. the United Kingdom*, concerned the seizure of an obscene schoolbook. The Court invoked both the argument that views on what is moral may be subject to reasonable disagreement – thus creating a lack of consensus – and the argument that domestic authorities are generally better placed than the Court to consider which restrictions are necessary. It concluded that the interference was justified by the second paragraph of Protocol 1 Article 1, according to which items whose use has been adjudged illicit and dangerous to the general interest are forfeited with a view to destruction.[66]

The Court has applied a wide margin of appreciation on similar grounds with respect to measures implemented to protect public health. In *Vékony v. Hungary*, a new governmental policy to limit the access of minors to tobacco products had led to the applicant's licence being withdrawn. The Court would not call into question the government's argument that the measure served the purpose of combating underage smoking, in accordance with the general interest. Despite the State's wide margin of appreciation, however, the new licencing policy had been implemented in a disproportionate and arbitrary manner, leading the Court to conclude that the applicant had had to bear an excessive individual burden contrary to Protocol 1 Article 1.[67]

---

65 *Depalle v. France* (n 56), para. 81.

66 *Handyside v. the United Kingdom* (n 21), para. 63.

67 *Vékony v. Hungary* (65681/13) judgment 13 January 2015, paras. 35–36.

3.2.5 Prevention of Disorder and Crime

Prevention of disorder and crime is another public policy aim recognised as legitimate by the Convention.[68] The Court has in a number of cases dealt with interference with the right to property for the purpose of preventing disorder and crime. In *Raimondo v. Italy*, for example, which concerned measures taken against the mafia whose income from drug-trafficking had been invested in the property sector, the Court described confiscation as 'an effective and necessary weapon in the combat against this cancer'.[69] In the Court's view, the preventive purpose of confiscation justified its immediate application notwithstanding any appeal.

As already noted, the Court has introduced procedural safeguards attached to the right to property as a check on assessments which the authorities are generally deemed better placed to perform. An important illustration is found in *G.I.E.M. S.r.l. and Others v. Italy*, which concerned confiscation of constructions erected in violation of area plans. The Court held that even though Protocol 1 Article 1 contains no explicit procedural requirements, judicial proceedings concerning the right to the peaceful enjoyment of one's possessions must afford the individual a reasonable opportunity of putting his or her case to the competent authorities for the purpose of effectively challenging the measures interfering with his or her right to property. Indeed, the Court held that an interference with Protocol 1 Article 1 'cannot ... have any legitimacy' in the absence of adversarial proceedings. In the Grand Chamber's view, the automatic application of confiscation in cases of unlawful site development, provided for by Italian legislation, was ill-suited to these principles. In any event, since the applicant companies were not parties to the impugned proceedings, they did not have the benefit of any of the procedural safeguards.[70] This was sufficient for the Court to find a violation of Protocol 1 Article 1.

3.2.6 'To Secure the Payment of Taxes or Other Contributions or Penalties'

Pursuant to the second paragraph of Protocol 1 Article 1, States have the right to pass such laws as they may deem necessary to 'secure the payment of taxes or other contributions or penalties'. Taxation is widely regarded as legitimate since it is required for society to function. This truth is not lost on the Court, of course, which has described taxation as 'part of the hard

---

68 See Articles 8–11 para. 2.

69 *Raimondo v. Italy* (12954/87) judgment 22 February 1994, para. 30.

70 *G.I.E.M., S.r.l. and Others v. Italy* (n 64), paras. 302–304.

core of public-authority prerogatives' where the public nature of the relationship between the taxpayer and the community remains predominant.[71] Taxation raises particular questions in relation to the right to property; indeed, it has remained a matter of controversy whether there is any scope at all under the ECHR for international supervision of domestic taxation rules.[72]

As Chapter 2 showed, some members of the Consultative Assembly were concerned about whether the draft of Protocol 1 Article 1 could make taxation laws subject to the jurisdiction of the Convention organs. Yet even at a stage when the proposed text did not contain any explicit reference to taxes, the right to property was understood to reserve the States' power to pass whatever fiscal laws they considered desirable, provided that measures in this field did not amount to arbitrary confiscation.[73] Ultimately, the second paragraph was expanded to make it clear that Protocol 1 Article 1 does not prevent the State from collecting taxes, or other penalties such as fines, even though they might constitute the whole value of the property in question.[74]

Initially, the Commission seemed to read this element of Protocol 1 Article 1 as not placing any particular limits on national measures in the area of taxation. It later accepted that the State's taxation schemes did not escape its powers of review if the scheme places 'an excessive burden on the person concerned or fundamentally interferes with his financial position'.[75] The Court presently recognises that the States have a right to frame and organise their fiscal policies and make necessary arrangements to ensure that taxes are paid.[76] It respects the legislature's assessment in such matters unless it

71 See, in relation to Article 6, *Ferrazzini v. Italy* (44759/98) judgment [GC] 12 July 2001, para. 29.

72 See e.g. C Endresen, 'Taxation and the European Convention for the Protection of Human Rights: Substantive Issues' (2017) 45(8/9) *InterTax* 508–526.

73 See e.g. remarks by Sir David Maxwell-Fyfe in the Consultative Assembly's session on 25 August 1950, *Travaux Préparatoires*, vol VI, 138–140. See also A R Çoban, *Protection of Private Property Rights within the European Convention of Human Rights* (Ashgate 2004) 133.

74 'Commentary by the Secretariat General on the draft Protocol' 18 September 1951, *Travaux Préparatoires*, vol VIII, 10.

75 See e.g. *Svenska Managementgruppen AB v. Sweden* (11036/84) decision [EComHR] 1 December 1985, *Wasa Liv Omsesidigt v. Sweden* (13013/87) decision [EComHR] 14 December 1988 and *Ferretti v. Italy* (25083/94) decision [EComHR] 26 February 1997. See also *Buffalo S.r.l. in liquidation v. Italy* (38746/97) judgment 3 July 2003, para. 32.

76 See e.g. *Hentrich v. France* (n 5), para. 39, where the Court recognised the prevention of tax evasion as a legitimate objective in the public interest.

is devoid of reasonable foundation, based on the rationale that decisions in the area of taxation normally involve an assessment of political, economic and social problems, which domestic authorities are clearly better placed to assess.[77]

As a result of the wide margin of appreciation, most applications which have invited the Court to review the level of tax imposed have been dismissed as manifestly ill-founded.[78] The majority of judgments on the merits related to taxation concern enforcement proceedings. In the case of *OAO Neftyanaya Kompaniya Yukos v. Russia*, for example, the applicant company had been presented with exorbitant tax obligations, which had the result of forcing it into liquidation. The Court accepted that the enforcement proceedings against the applicant company had the legitimate aim of securing the payment of taxes.[79] In the assessment of 'fair balance', it noted that the authorities had acted very swiftly and constantly refused to concede to the applicant company's demands for additional time. Given the pace of the enforcement proceedings, the obligation to pay the exorbitant enforcement fee and the authorities' failure to take proper account of the consequences of their actions, the domestic authorities had failed to strike a 'fair balance' between the legitimate aims sought and the measures employed.[80] Thus, despite the State's wide margin of appreciation in the tax sphere, there had been a violation of Protocol 1 Article 1.

3.2.7 Compliance with Obligations under International Law

Measures implemented to fulfil the State's obligations under international law are normally deemed to be in the public interest, but they do not require justification by force of the structural arguments relating to proximity, consensus and legitimacy discussed thus far. Rather, the justification for the Court's deferential review is found on a different plane.

---

77 See e.g. *Azienda Agricola Silverfunghi S.a.s. and Others v. Italy* (48357/07 et al.) judgment 24 June 2014, para. 103, and *Cacciato v. Italy* (60633/16) decision 16 January 2018, para. 25.

78 See e.g. *Imbert de Trémiolles v. France* (25834/05; 27815/05) decision 4 January 2008.

79 See, by comparison, *Hulley Enterprises Limited (Cyprus) v. The Russian Federation* (PCA Case No AA 226), *Yukos Universal Limited (Isle of Man) v. The Russian Federation* (PCA Case No AA 227) and *Veteran Petroleum Limited (Cyprus) v. The Russian Federation* (PCA Case No AA 228), 756, where the Permanent Court of Arbitration (PCA) held that 'the primary objective of the Russian Federation was not to collect taxes but rather to bankrupt Yukos and appropriate its valuable assets'.

80 *OAO Neftyanaya Kompaniya Yukos v. Russia* (14902/04) judgment 20 September 2011, para. 657.

The Court maintains that the Convention cannot be interpreted in a vacuum, but must be read in light of relevant rules of international law applicable in relations between the Member States.[81] A basic principle of international law is that of *pacta sunt servanda*, which dictates that the Convention should as far as possible be interpreted in conformity with the States' other international legal obligations.[82] In practice, this suggests that the State should enjoy a wide margin of appreciation when interfering with private property rights out of respect for its obligations under public international law.

Obligations flowing from membership in international organisations to which the State has transferred sovereignty give rise to particular issues in this context. The traditional view has been that States which are members of international organisations cannot be held responsible for the acts or omissions of these organisations because they enjoy legal personality distinct from that of their member states. Thus, the Strasbourg Court is barred from reviewing acts by, for example, the organs of the European Union (EU), as long as those organs are not parties to the ECHR.

The question is, essentially, to what extent the Strasbourg Court may exercise a form of indirect control of EU law by reviewing measures taken by States which are parties to both organisations.[83] From the perspective of ECHR law, a degree of control is necessary in order to ensure that the rights and freedoms in the Convention are effectively protected. On the other hand, such supervision invariably results in some form of assessment on the part of national authorities of whether the legal act in question is compatible with the State's obligations under the Convention. From the perspective of EU law, independent assessments by national authorities carry the risk of undermining the supremacy and direct effect of EU law, and threaten the uniform application of law in the EU Member States.

In early case law, the Strasbourg organs rejected applications challenging the conventionality of EU law as incompatible *ratione materiae* with the ECHR. As long as EU law was deemed to provide adequate protection, the Strasbourg Court would refrain from considering alleged Convention

81 See, in relation to Article 6, *Al-Dulimi and Montana Management Inc. v. Switzerland* (5809/08) judgment [GC] 21 June 2016, para. 134.

82 See Article 31 para. 3 (c) VCLT.

83 As of May 2025, all 27 EU Member States are parties to the European Convention on Human Rights (Austria, Belgium, Bulgaria, Croatia, Republic of Cyprus, Czech Republic, Denmark, Estonia, Finland, France, Germany, Greece, Hungary, Ireland, Italy, Latvia, Lithuania, Luxembourg, Malta, Netherlands, Poland, Portugal, Romania, Slovakia, Slovenia, Spain and Sweden).

violations in the individual case.[84] In *Bosphorus v. Ireland*, however, the Grand Chamber dismissed the preliminary objections regarding incompatibility. Instead, it took the view that the scope of the respondent State's responsibility was a matter to be examined under the merits of Protocol 1 Article 1.[85]

The applicant company, an airline charter company, had leased two aircraft from the national airline of former Yugoslavia. In response to human rights violations in that country, the United Nations Security Council adopted sanctions against 'all aircraft in which a majority or controlling interest is held by a person or undertaking in or operating from [the Former Republic of Yugoslavia]'.[86] In January 1993, the applicant company contracted maintenance with a service company, which was a subsidiary of two airline companies wholly owned by the State of Ireland. One of the applicant company's aircraft was detained at the airport in Dublin, in conformity with the UN sanctions.

The Strasbourg Court determined that the seizure of the aircraft undoubtedly amounted to interference with the right to property under Protocol 1 Article 1, and that it was lawful under both EU and Irish law. Under the legitimate aim test, the Court recognised that a State's compliance with its obligations under EU law is a general-interest objective of considerable weight.[87] The Court also recognised the growing importance of international cooperation and the need to secure the proper functioning of international organisations. The remaining question was whether Ireland's legitimate interest in complying with its international obligations under EU law could justify the interference with the applicant company's right to property under the ECHR.

The Grand Chamber began by recognising that the Convention does not prohibit States from transferring sovereign power to an international organisation in order to pursue cooperation in certain fields of activity. On the other hand, a State is responsible under Article 1 of the Convention for all acts and omissions of its organs regardless of whether the act or omission in question was a consequence of domestic law or of the necessity to comply

84 See e.g. *M. & Co. v. Germany* (13258/87) decision [EComHR] 9 February 1990. Among the pre-*Bosphorus* rulings, see also *Matthews v. the United Kingdom* (24833/94) judgment [GC] 18 February 1999, which heralded a more scrutinising approach.

85 *Bosphorus v. Ireland* (45036/98) judgment [GC] 30 June 2005, paras. 137–138.

86 This resolution was implemented by Regulation (EEC) no. 990/93.

87 *Bosphorus v. Ireland* (n 85), paras. 150–151. See also *Michaud v. France* (12323/11) judgment 6 December 2012, para. 100, and *Lohuis and Others v. the Netherlands* (37265/10) decision 30 April 2013, para. 54.

with international legal obligations. Article 1 makes no distinction as to the type of rule or measure concerned and does not exclude any part of a State's 'jurisdiction' from scrutiny under the Convention.[88]

In reconciling these positions, the Court recognised that absolving States completely from their Convention responsibility in the areas covered by a transfer of sovereignty would be incompatible with the Convention's object and purpose. This would mean that the Convention's guarantees could be limited or excluded at will, thereby depriving it of its peremptory character and undermining the practical and effective nature of its safeguards. In an attempt to establish the extent to which a State's action can be justified by obligations flowing from its membership in an international organisation to which it has transferred part of its sovereignty, the Grand Chamber held:

> In the Court's view, State action taken in compliance with such legal obligations is justified as long as the relevant organisation is considered to protect fundamental rights, as regards both the substantive guarantees offered and the mechanisms controlling their observance, in a manner which can be considered at least equivalent to that for which the Convention provides ...[89]

If such equivalent protection is provided by the organisation in question, there is a presumption that a State has not departed from the requirements of the Convention when it does no more than implement legal obligations flowing from its membership in the organisation. Having clarified that the word 'equivalent' should be read as 'comparable', because any requirement that the organisation's protection be identical could run counter to the interest of international cooperation pursued, the Grand Chamber went on to establish the following exception:

> However, any such presumption can be rebutted if, in the circumstances of a particular case, it is considered that the protection of Convention rights was manifestly deficient. In such cases, the interest of international cooperation would be outweighed by the Convention's role as a 'constitutional instrument of European public order' in the field of human rights ...[90]

88 See also *United Communist Party of Turkey and Others v. Turkey* (19392/92) judgment [GC] 30 January 1998, para. 29.

89 *Bosphorus v. Ireland* (n 85), para. 155.

90 Ibid., para. 156.

According to these principles, there would be a presumption of Convention compliance in the case of *Bosphorus* if the protection of fundamental rights in the EU was considered comparable to that of the ECHR, since Ireland had only complied with its obligations under EU law by seizing the aircraft. Having reviewed the substantive and procedural level of rights protection in EU law, the Court concluded that the EU protects human rights on par with the ECHR system and effectively established a general presumption that interference which complies with EU rules also complies with the ECHR.[91]

This presumption could be rebutted only if the applicant company could show that the protection of its Convention rights was 'manifestly deficient' in the circumstances. In view of the nature of the interference, the legitimate interests pursued by the seizure and by the sanctions regime, and the ruling of the European Court of Justice in the matter, the Grand Chamber concluded that the presumption of Convention compliance had not been rebutted in the case.[92] In conclusion, there had been no violation of the applicant company's rights under Protocol 1 Article 1.

Bosphorus v. Ireland is a landmark case because it established the principles governing the relationship between ECHR law and EU law from the perspective of the Strasbourg Court. Yet at several points, the limits of the so-called *Bosphorus* doctrine remain blurry.

The Court in *Bosphorus* held that the legal order of the EU offers protection equivalent to the substantive Convention guarantees, but the Court came to this conclusion without really engaging with the substance of EU law.[93] The substance of ECHR law is made up of a large corpus of judgments and decisions rendered by the Strasbourg Court, which are not automatically transferable to the EU context.

Furthermore, the Court concluded that EU law protects human rights in a manner equivalent to the ECHR also as regards 'the mechanisms controlling their observance'. But the EU system does not guarantee the right of access to court in the same way as Article 34 of the ECHR does. As Judge Ress pointed out in his separate opinion, a more concrete standard of review would have been more in harmony with the right of individual application

91 Ibid., para. 155. The Court held that EU law provides 'equivalent protection' of human rights 'as regards both the substantive guarantees offered and the mechanisms controlling their observance'.

92 *Bosphorus v. Ireland* (n 85), para. 166.

93 The equivalence of EU law is presumed to be safeguarded by Article 52 (3) of the EU's Charter of Fundamental Rights, which states that insofar as the rights contained in the Charter correspond to rights guaranteed by the Convention, their meaning and scope are the same.

to the Court.[94] Given this ambiguity, the *Bosphorus* doctrine makes it difficult to say whether other international organisations provide equivalent rights protection – for instance the organs set up by the European Economic Area (EEA) Agreement, a question which the Court has deliberately left unanswered.[95]

The *Bosphorus* doctrine is also ambiguous with respect to which types of legal instruments the Court considers as conferring a margin of manoeuvre on the State and which it considers to be binding under international law. The EU regulation in *Bosphorus* was binding, leaving the respondent State with no margin of discretion.[96] The opposite was the case in *O'Sullivan McCarthy*, which involved an EU directive.[97] But it remains an open question whether, for example, a State is required to obtain a preliminary ruling from the European Court of Justice clarifying the extent of its obligations under EU law.

On a final note, the scope for rebutting the *Bosphorus* presumption where the rights protection offered by international law is 'manifestly deficient' is not clear. Following *Avotiņš v. Latvia*, there are indications that the *Bosphorus* doctrine will be applied more strictly in the context of EU law in the future.[98] On this point in particular, there is an ongoing dialogue between the Strasbourg Court on one hand, and the Luxembourg Court on the other.[99]

4 Conclusion

Pursuant to Article 32 of the ECHR, the Strasbourg Court is empowered to decide 'all matters concerning the interpretation and application of the

94 See *Bosphorus v. Ireland* (n 85), concurring opinion of Judge Ress.

95 See *Norwegian Confederation of Trade Unions (LO) and Norwegian Transport Workers' Union (NTF) v. Norway* (45487/17) judgment 10 June 2021, paras. 104–108.

96 *Bosphorus v. Ireland* (n 85), paras. 143-148. In European Union (EU) Member States in particular, regulations become part of domestic law without any need for implementing legislation. In this situation, the interference does not result from an exercise of discretion, but from the State's compliance with its legal obligations flowing from Community law.

97 See also *Michaud v. France* (12323/11) judgment 6 December 2012, para. 113.

98 See *Avotiņš v. Latvia* (17502/07) judgment [GC] 23 May 2016, para. 111. See also C Costello, 'The Bosphorus Ruling of the European Court of Human Rights: Fundamental Rights and Blurred Boundaries in Europe' (2006) 6 *Human Rights Law Review* 87.

99 See e.g. P Gragl, 'An Olive Branch from Strasbourg? Interpreting the European Court of Human Rights' Resurrection of *Bosphorus* and reaction to *Opinion 2/13* in the *Avotiņš* Case' (2017) 13 *European Constitutional Law Review* 551–567.

Convention and the Protocols thereto'. The Court's mandate commits it to perform a full substantive review of the applicant's complaint and adjudicate on the merits of the case before it. In the context of the right to property under Protocol 1 Article 1, the Court has qualified its review by reference to the margin of appreciation, based on the reasoning that its responsibility for securing the rights and freedoms in the Convention is subsidiary to that of the Member States. This chapter has explained why the margin of appreciation in property cases has historically been wide. The Court's use of structural arguments related to proximity, consensus and legitimacy varies with the nature of the public interest and interacts with substantive arguments in a way which has resulted in deference to the national authorities.

It is possible to view the Court's deferential stance as recognising a right for States to regulate private property.[100] Emberland has argued that through the Court's application of the margin of appreciation doctrine, national authorities are effectively authorised to regulate property in pursuit of the common good. In his view, the Convention's acknowledgment of the regulatory state's rightful and necessary place in society is a 'significant justificatory factor' underlying the Court's lenient standards of review in the case law concerning Protocol 1 Article 1.[101]

That analysis may be accurate insofar as the Court has generally recognised the State's role in ensuring a fair allocation of property. But as discussed in the previous chapter, the case law has evolved to reflect a heightened level of scrutiny with regard to the substantive elements of the interference, in particular the State's justification and the economic effects on the applicant's interests. Thus, even though the Court has continued to maintain that States enjoy a wide margin of appreciation under Protocol 1 Article 1, it has also examined the interests involved in the case before it with increasing scrutiny. Adding to this, the Court is increasingly inclined to conclude that Protocol 1 Article 1 has been violated if the applicant has been denied basic procedural rights in the decision-making process, as will be shown in the next chapter.

More fundamental changes are also taking place in the Court's review. Many observers have noted the tendency in the case law that the Court's focus is shifting away from its own assessment of whether the State's

100 See e.g. F Sudre '"Le Droit au Respect de ses Biens" au Sens de la Convention Européenne des Droits de l'Homme' (2005) 3 *Cahiers du GRIDAUH* 67–80.

101 M Emberland, *The Human Rights of Companies – Exploring the Structure of ECHR Protection* (Oxford University Press 2006) 192–193.

interference adheres to the 'fair balance' requirement, towards the question of whether the domestic authorities have assessed the interests impacted by a given measure in an adequate manner.[102] The so-called 'process-based review' is directed at the quality of the assessments undertaken at the domestic level – by legislative, executive and judicial branches of government – and implies that the Court draws substantive inferences from whether or not such assessments have been adequately conducted by the national authorities.[103]

Process-based review is closely linked to the State's margin of appreciation. The effect is that the Court exhibits more deference when it is satisfied that the 'fair balance' assessment has been thoroughly carried out at the domestic level, and more scrutiny when the opposite is the case. If the assessment at the domestic level has been made in the light of the principles established in the case law, the Court requires strong reasons to substitute its own view for that of the domestic authorities, which consequently will enjoy a wide margin of appreciation.[104]

---

102 See J Gerards, 'Procedural Review by the ECtHR: A Typology' in J Gerards and E Brems (eds), *Procedural Review in European Fundamental Rights Cases* (Cambridge University Press 2017), P Popelier, 'The Court as Regulatory Watchdog: The Procedural Approach in the Case-Law of the European Court of Human Rights' in P Popelier et al. (eds), *The Role of Constitutional Courts in Multilevel Governance* (Intersentia 2012) 249–268, P Popelier and C Van de Heyning, 'Procedural Rationality: Giving Teeth to the Proportionality Analysis' (2013) 9(2) *European Constitutional Law Review* 230–262, E Brems and L Lavrysen, 'Procedural Justice in Human Rights Adjudication: The European Court of Human Rights' (2013) 35 *Human Rights Quarterly* 176-200, E Brems, 'Procedural Protection – an Examination of Procedural Safeguards Read into Substantive Convention Rights' in J Gerards and E Brems (eds), *Shaping Rights in the ECHR – The Role of the European Court of Human Rights in Determining the Scope of Human Rights* (Cambridge University Press 2013) 137–161, J P Rui, 'The Interlaken, Izmir and Brighton Declarations: Towards a Paradigm Shift in the Strasbourg Court's Interpretation of the European Convention on Human Rights' (2013) 31(1) *Nordic Journal of Human Rights* 28–54, M Saul, 'The European Court of Human Rights' Margin of Appreciation and the Processes of National Parliaments' (2015) 15 *Human Rights Law Review* 745–774, and D J Harris et al. (n 16) 13.

103 See e.g. *Hirst v. the United Kingdom (No. 2)* (74025/01) judgment [GC] 6 October 2005, para. 79, where the Grand Chamber found a violation of Protocol 1 Article 3 *inter alia* because 'there [was] no evidence that Parliament has ever sought to weigh the competing interests or to assess the proportionality of a blanket ban on the right of a convicted prisoner to vote'.

104 See e.g. *Axel Springer AG v. Germany* (39954/08) judgment [GC] 7 February 2012, para. 88. See T Kleinlein, 'The Procedural Approach of the European Court of Human Rights: Between Subsidiarity and Dynamic Evolution' (2019) 68 *International & Comparative Law Quarterly* 96–97, who notes that the focus of the Court's review is moving from

Thus, while the Court retains the last word on the legitimacy of the interference, evidence that the relevant national authorities have considered in substance the 'fair balance' issue will be an argument for the State in demonstrating that it has acted within its margin of appreciation. In fact, as Arnardóttir has argued, this situation effectively creates a presumption of complete deference with respect to the substantive proportionality assessments, which resembles the presumption of Convention compliance established for EU law in the *Bosphorus* judgment.[105]

The notion of process-based review is not altogether novel in the context of Protocol 1 Article 1. In *James*, the Court referred to the quality and extensiveness of parliamentary debates leading up to the adoption of the impugned legislation.[106] The Court used this as an argument for finding the result of that decision-making process – the interference with the applicants' property rights – compatible with the Convention.

Yet while thorough assessments at the national level have occasionally served as an argument in the Court's 'fair balance' test in the past, the Court now links its own application of the margin of appreciation doctrine explicitly to the quality of these assessments. In particular, it relies on the absence of assessments as an argument in favour of a narrow margin.[107] For example, in *Lindheim and Others v. Norway*, the Court stressed that no specific assessment had been made by the national legislature of whether the statute achieved a 'fair balance' between the respective interests of the lessors and the lessees. This was an important argument for concluding that the lessors' right to property under the Convention had been violated, notwithstanding the State's wide margin of appreciation in this area.[108]

---

assessing the effects of general measures on individuals *in concreto* to a more lenient review of the justification provided by the national authorities *in abstracto*.

105 See O M Arnardóttir (n 18) 48–49.

106 See *James and Others v. the United Kingdom* (n 2), para. 69. See also *Sporrong and Lönnroth v. Sweden* (n 57), para. 69, where the Court suggested that the manner in which national authorities have struck the balance may be a factor in deciding whether the balance is 'fair' in accordance with the Convention's requirements.

107 See e.g. *Skibińscy v. Poland* (52589/99) judgment 14 November 2006, para. 96, *Megadat.com SRL v. Moldova* (21151/04) judgment 8 April 2008, para. 74, *OAO Neftyanaya Kompaniya Yukos v. Russia* (n 80) paras. 651–653, and *Kurban v. Turkey* (75414/10) judgment 24 November 2020, para. 84.

108 *Lindheim and Others v. Norway* (13221/08; 2139/10) judgment 12 June 2012, paras. 134–136. See also *The Karibu Foundation v. Norway* (2317/20) judgment 10 November 2022, where the Court was invited to check the legislative work undertaken by the Norwegian authorities following *Lindheim*. Since the legislature had carried out extensive work with the aim of bringing the relevant legislation into line with the Convention's

The Court applies its own case law as the yardstick for evaluating the assessments carried out at the domestic level. In other words, the failure by domestic authorities to conduct a 'fair balance' analysis in line with the Court's case law will be an argument in favour of more intense review under Protocol 1 Article 1.[109] To facilitate the work of domestic organs, the Court has begun to formulate operative, interpretational criteria applicable to specific forms of property interference.[110] This development reflects the core purpose of the Court's process-based review: to enable national judges, in particular, to engage with established principles of ECHR law when undertaking assessments of legality, legitimate aims and 'fair balance' under the limitation clauses of qualified Convention provisions.[111]

Focusing on national decision-making processes prevents the Court from dealing with the substance of cases in which national authorities have greater legitimacy or are better placed to make decisions than the Court itself. But the Court's deference is based on the assumption that domestic institutions and procedures are working as they should, allowing for participation of affected rights-holders and under conditions that are capable of generating reasonable outcomes. Process-based review thus lays the foundations for an embedded international regime of human rights.[112] As Spano has put it, it is a means for the Court to develop a more robust and coherent concept of subsidiarity in its case law – hence the term 'deeper subsidiarity'.[113] At the same time, it is hoped that these developments may strengthen the Court's role in distinctly political areas of ECHR law.

So far, there is a degree of inconsistency in the Court's reliance on process-based arguments. It is not always clear why the Court sometimes embarks on its own review of proportionality, and why it sometimes defers to

---

requirements, the Court decided to 'focus primarily on the national parliamentary and judicial reviews of the Convention issues' (para. 79).

109 See e.g. *Paulet v. the United Kingdom* (6219/08) judgment 13 May 2014, para. 68, where the Court concluded that 'the scope of the review carried out by the domestic courts was too narrow to satisfy the requirement of seeking the "fair balance" inherent in the second paragraph of [Protocol 1 Article 1]'.

110 See e.g. *G.I.E.M. S.r.l. and Others v. Italy* (n 64), para. 301, where the Court listed factors to be taken into account when assessing whether confiscation of property is proportionate. See also *Könyv-Tár Kft and Others v. Hungary* (21623/13) judgment 16 October 2018, para. 49, where the Court noted which factors are relevant for considering cases concerning loss of clientele and the practice of a profession.

111 R Spano (n 32) 15–16.

112 T Kleinlein (n 104) 101–102.

113 R Spano, 'Universality or Diversity of Human Rights? Strasbourg in the Age of Subsidiarity' (2014) 14(3) *Human Rights Law Review* 491.

the State's judgment. Some cases concerning deprivation of property, for example, have been fully reviewed on substantive grounds, without the Court making any real reference to the quality of the national judicial procedure or to the national court's review.[114] It is difficult to find a coherent method to the Court's choice to either rely on process-based arguments to a greater or lesser degree, or to leave them completely out of consideration.[115]

The Court's process-based review has yet to take a comprehensive form in the case law, and it is still too early to tell exactly how it will influence the protection of the right to property and the evolution of ECHR law more broadly in the future. Process-based review may ultimately amount to a reform of the Court's supervisory function as it enables the Court to engage with the States' observance of Protocol 1 Article 1 in a new way.[116] Nonetheless, it should be a supplement to – and not a substitute for – the Court's own assessment of the interference. The principle of effective rights, which was discussed in Chapter 8, and the rule of law, to which the book will now turn, require an independent examination on the part of the Court of whether the interference is justified.

---

114 See e.g. *Pyrantienė v. Lithuania* (45092/07) judgment 12 November 2013.

115 J Gerards (n 102) 159.

116 See R Spano (n 32) 20, who notes that the overarching aim of process-based review is to increase the level of Convention protection at the domestic level, subsidiarity-based deference being based on good faith engagement with Convention principles.

CHAPTER 10

Procedural Dimension: Protocol 1 Article 1 as a Safeguard against Arbitrary Interference

1 Introduction

The Court's justification assessment under Protocol 1 Article 1 has always been a matter of finding the appropriate balance between ensuring effective protection of the right to property and respecting the sovereignty of the Member States. How such a balance should be struck has been a contentious issue since the right to property was conceived and has remained so throughout the Court's history. Yet from the outset, the assessment under Protocol 1 Article 1 has also contained a third and, in a way, less controversial dimension: that States must observe the rule of law whenever they interfere with the right to property.

The principle of the rule of law presupposes the existence of a legal basis for interfering with individual rights. The requirement that interference with the right to property must be lawful follows from the text of Protocol 1 Article 1, and will be briefly discussed in Section 2. However, the mere existence of a law does not suffice to make the interference compatible with the rule of law. The law must also conform to standards of legal certainty, in particular accessibility and foreseeability, which are discussed in Section 3. More importantly, the Court has come to understand the rule of law as requiring a measure of legal protection in the form of procedural safeguards against arbitrary interference by public authorities. Section 4 examines the extent of the States' obligation to provide legal subjects with access to effective adversarial proceedings, while Section 5 explores the requirement that those proceedings must afford a minimum of fairness.

2 The Principle of Lawfulness

The principle of lawfulness is a primordial element of any system based on the rule of law. That the executive or judicial branches of government cannot exercise authority without prior approval by the legislature is crucial for preserving the separation of powers. When laws are the outcome of a transparent, democratic process – 'publicly made', in Lord Bingham's

 | DOI:10.1163/9789004735088_011

words – the principle of lawfulness also serves to uphold the principle of democracy, a fundamental Convention value.[1]

The lawfulness principle permeates the Convention, as evidenced by the numerous references to 'law' in the text: The second paragraphs of Articles 2 and 8-11 require that interference must be either 'lawful', 'in accordance with a procedure prescribed by law', 'in accordance with the law' or 'prescribed by law'. Despite the differences in the wording, the Court has made clear that the concept is to be understood in a uniform manner.[2]

The second sentence of Protocol 1 Article 1 makes clear that deprivation of property must be 'subject to the conditions provided for by law'. Measures amounting to control of the use of property within the meaning of the third sentence must be authorised by 'such laws as [the State] deems necessary'. There is no direct reference to law in the first sentence, but because of the article's integrated structure the lawfulness requirement applies to all forms of interference with the peaceful enjoyment of property.[3] In fact, the Court has declared that 'the first and most important requirement of Article 1 of Protocol No. 1 is that any interference by a public authority with the peaceful enjoyment of possessions should be lawful'.[4]

As a human right, the right to property is fundamentally different from, for example, the right to protection from torture or respect for one's private life. All natural persons have a body requiring protection from torture and a private life, but not everyone owns property. The right to property exists only by virtue of the protection that the law provides. As Underkuffler has put it, unprotected speech is still speech, but property not protected by law is not property. Thus, property does not exist, as a coherent idea, apart from the idea of legal protection.[5] This rationale explains the central place held by the lawfulness requirement in the Court's justification assessment.

The text of Protocol 1 Article 1 implies that interference in the right to property must be provided for by a legal instrument accepted as 'law' within

1 T Bingham, *The Rule of Law* (Allen Lane 2010) 8.

2 See e.g. *Špaček, s.r.o., v. the Czech Republic* (26449/95) judgment 9 November 1999, para. 54.

3 See *Vistiņš and Perepjolkins v. Latvia* (71243/01) judgment [GC] 25 October 2012, para. 95, and *Béláné Nagy v. Hungary* (53080/13) judgment [GC] 13 December 2016, para. 112.

4 *Iatridis v. Greece* (31107/96) judgment [GC] 25 March 1999, para. 58.

5 See L Underkuffler, 'Property and Change: The Constitutional Conundrum' (2015) 91 *Texas Law Review* 2030.

the meaning of the Convention.[6] Thus, in situations where the interference lacks a legal basis altogether, the Court has been content to find a violation of Protocol 1 Article 1 on that basis alone.[7]

At the same time, it is not the Court's task to decide whether national law has been applied correctly.[8] In its subsidiary role, the Court has limited power to review compliance with domestic law, and is called to intervene only in situations where the national assessment is regarded as 'manifestly unreasonable or arbitrary', 'manifestly without reasonable foundation' or inconsistent with the principles underlying the Convention.[9] To Sermet, such supervision is at once cautious and bold: cautious because few laws are likely to be manifestly unreasonable, and bold because the Court nonetheless assumes the power to review the acceptability of national legislation in light of the Convention's requirements.[10]

3 Legal Certainty

The mere existence of a domestic legal basis does not suffice to satisfy the requirement that interference in the right to property must be lawful. Since their early jurisprudence, the Convention organs have maintained that the principle of lawfulness does not only refer back to domestic law; it also requires that domestic law be compatible with the rule of law.[11] In the Court's view, a degree of legal certainty is essential for maintaining confidence in the judicial system and in the rule of law. While this development is not

---

6 The Court has confirmed that the term denotes an autonomous concept which covers not only statute but also unwritten law, see e.g. *Špaček, s.r.o. v. the Czech Republic* (n 2) para. 57.

7 See e.g. *Frizen v. Russia* (58254/00) judgment 24 March 2005, para. 36, and *R & L, s.r.o. and Others v. the Czech Republic* (37926/05 et al.) judgment 3 July 2014, paras. 113–127, where the States' measures lacked a legal basis completely.

8 See e.g. *Winterwerp v. the Netherlands* (6301/73) judgment 24 October 1979, para. 46, where the Court established that '[i]t is in the first place for the national authorities, notably the courts, to interpret and apply the domestic law'.

9 See e.g. *Håkansson and Sturesson v. Sweden* (11855/85) judgment of 21 February 1990, para. 47, *Tre Traktörer Aktiebolag v. Sweden* (10873/84) judgment 7 July 1989, para. 58, and *Pye v. the United Kingdom* (44302/02) judgment [GC] 30 August 2007, para. 75.

10 L Sermet, 'The European Convention on Human Rights and Property Rights' 11 *Human Rights Files* (Council of Europe Publishing 1998) 34.

11 See e.g. *Golder v. the United Kingdom* (4451/70) judgment 21 February 1975, para. 34, and *Silver and Others v. the United Kingdom* (5947/72 et al.) judgment 25 March 1983, para. 90.

unique to Protocol 1 Article 1, it serves to illustrate how the Court's understanding of the rule of law has evolved over time.

In *The Sunday Times v. the United Kingdom*, the Court held that two requirements follow from the principle of legal certainty.[12] Firstly, the law must be adequately accessible – the citizen must be able to have an indication that is adequate in the circumstances of the legal rules applicable to a given case. The Court generally requires that the law providing the basis for the interference has been published at the time of the interference, but given that the term 'law' is to be understood in its substantive sense and not in its formal one, it holds no opinion of the appropriateness of the methods by which national authorities choose to make laws public.[13] The Court's primary concern is the applicant's ability to access and understand the applicable laws.[14]

Secondly, the principle of legal certainty presupposes that the applicable provisions have a certain quality. Laws must be clear and not excessively vague and open to abuse. As the Court put it in *The Sunday Times* case, 'a norm cannot be regarded as a "law" unless it is formulated with sufficient precision to enable the citizen to regulate his conduct'.[15] At the same time, the Court recognises that such consequences need not be foreseeable with absolute certainty, since excessive rigidity is undesirable. Many laws are more or less vague and their interpretation and application are questions of practice. To the Court, a norm is 'foreseeable' when it affords a measure of protection against arbitrary interference by the public authorities.[16]

The domestic legal provisions must not only be precisely formulated; they must also be foreseeable in their application.[17] Thus, the foreseeability

12 *The Sunday Times v. the United Kingdom (No. 1)* (6538/74) judgment 26 April 1979, para. 49.

13 See e.g. *Silver and Others v. the United Kingdom* (5947/72 et al.) judgment 25 March 1983.

14 See *Špaček, s.r.o. v. the Czech Republic* (n 2), paras. 57–60, where the fact that regulations pertaining to the exercise of rights protected by Protocol 1 Article 1 were not published in official gazettes in the appropriate form did not prevent such regulations from being considered 'law', since the Court was satisfied that they were made known to the public by way of other means.

15 *The Sunday Times v. the United Kingdom* (n 12), para. 49.

16 See e.g. *Centro Europa 7 S.r.l. and Di Stefano v. Italy* (38433/09) judgment [GC] 7 June 2012, paras. 141–143, where the legislative framework had not been sufficiently clear to enable the applicant company to foresee when it might be allocated frequencies in order to start broadcasting.

17 See e.g. *Beyeler v. Italy* (33202/96) judgment [GC] 5 January 2000, para. 109, and *Lekić v. Slovenia* (36480/07) judgment [GC] 11 December 2018, para. 95.

requirement applies to the domestic courts and executive organs as well as to the domestic legislature. In the case of *OAO Neftyanaya Kompaniya Yukos v. Russia*, the Court held that the Convention does not prevent the gradual development of domestic case law as long as it is compatible with the requirement of foreseeability. The Court concluded that the change in domestic courts' interpretation of the rules pertaining to the applicant company's tax assessment, and the effect of this change, violated the lawfulness requirement in Protocol 1 Article 1.[18]

Importantly, the Court in *Yukos* reaffirmed that the foreseeability of a law must be considered in the light of the applicant's specific situation: The level of precision required of domestic legislation depends to a considerable degree on the content of the law in question, the field it is designed to cover and the number and status of those to whom it is addressed.[19] In the tax sphere, States may be afforded additional deference and latitude under the lawfulness test.[20] Furthermore, in view of the complexity of tax law, corporate entities – as opposed to individual taxpayers – are required to act with additional caution and diligence by consulting competent specialists.[21] These actors are expected to proceed with a high degree of caution when pursuing their activity, and to take special care in assessing and mitigating the legal risks that such activity entails.

The Court's relative standard of legal certainty was introduced in Chapter 8 above in relation to the applicant's legitimate expectations and acceptance of risk.[22] At this particular point, the Court's assessments of 'fair balance' and lawfulness converge in the sense that the same facts are subsumed under both or either of these requirements. Even where the lawfulness requirements have been complied with, elements of uncertainty in do-

---

18 *OAO Neftyanaya Kompaniya Yukos v. Russia* (14902/04) judgment 20 September 2011, paras. 571–575.

19 Ibid. See also *O'Sullivan McCarthy Mussel Development Ltd v. Ireland* (44460/16) judgment 7 June 2018, para. 107, and *Vistiņš and Perepjolkins v. Latvia* (71243/01) judgment [GC] 25 October 2012, paras. 95–99. See also P van Dijk et al. (eds), *Theory and Practice of the European Convention on Human Rights* (5th edn, Intersentia 2018) 875–876.

20 See e.g. *National & Provincial Building Society, the Leeds Permanent Building Society and the Yorkshire Building Society v. the United Kingdom* (21319/93; 21449/93; 21675/93) judgment 23 October 1997, paras. 75–83.

21 See *Špaček, s.r.o., v. the Czech Republic* (n 2) para. 59.

22 See Section 6. See also D Maxwell, 'The Human Right to Property: A Practical Approach to Article 1 of Protocol No. 1 to the ECHR' (Hart Publishing 2022) 111–116.

mestic law are material considerations to be taken into account in determining whether the interference struck a 'fair balance'.[23]

The problem of retroactive laws furnishes another example. Retroactive legislation impacting the applicant's property rights has generally been deemed to conform to the lawfulness requirement, but the retroactivity of the legislation has been relevant to the Court's 'fair balance' assessment.[24] Overall, the identification of a legal basis of interference and compliance with the standards of legal certainty have only occasionally posed difficulties in the case law. Uncertainty in the legal basis which is insufficient to violate the lawfulness requirement has instead been used as an argument by the Court in determining whether the 'fair balance' has been upset.

4 Access to Effective Proceedings

4.1 *The Basis and Rationale for Protocol 1 Article 1's Procedural Safeguards*

Chapter 2 demonstrated that the drafters' primary concern was to protect against arbitrary interference in the right to property. However, the word 'arbitrary' was thought to be too imprecise in a legal text and capable of varying interpretations. It was therefore replaced by the phrase 'subject to the conditions provided for by law', which was believed to be more precise and to adequately cover the object in mind.[25] Thus, the drafters probably never intended Protocol 1 Article 1 to do more than provide an international guarantee that States would adhere to the rule of law when exercising their powers over property.[26]

---

23 *Beyeler v. Italy* (33202/96) judgment [GC] 5 January 2000, para. 110. See also, in relation to Article 8, *Roman Zakharov v. Russia* (47143/06) judgment [GC] 4 December 2015, para. 236, where the Court noted that 'the lawfulness of the interference is closely related to the question whether the "necessity" test has been complied with and it is therefore appropriate for the Court to address jointly the "in accordance with the law" and "necessity" requirements'.

24 See e.g. *Azienda Agricola Silverfunghi S.a.s. and Others v. Italy* (48357/07 et al.) judgment 24 June 2014, para. 104, *Maggio and Others v. Italy* (46286/09 et al.) judgment 31 May 2011, para. 60, and *Arras and Others v. Italy* (17972/07) judgment 14 February 2012, para. 81.

25 *Travaux Préparatoires*, vol VIII, 8–10.

26 T Allen, 'Compensation for Property under the European Convention on Human Rights' (2007) *Michigan Journal of International Law* 289.

The rule of law can be defined as the absence of, or the antithesis to, arbitrariness.[27] Spano has defined the rule of law as 'a set of legal rules and standards that provide for a framework of laws that pay due respect [to] the rational autonomy of human beings and precludes the arbitrary use of governmental power'.[28]

In ordinary usage, arbitrariness carries at least two different connotations. In a substantive sense, it can be understood to refer to a (manifestly) disproportionate relationship between the measure and aim pursued. Conceived in this way, arbitrariness is consumed by the substantive dimension of the justification assessment, as discussed in Chapter 8. What we are concerned with here is arbitrariness in the procedural sense.

The principles of lawfulness and standards of legal certainty reflected in the case law offer protection against procedural arbitrariness in so far as they require the law to enable the applicant to foresee the consequences of his or her actions. It does not follow logically that proceedings for reviewing those consequences should be available, let alone that such proceedings should comply with any particular standards of effectiveness or fairness. This may explain why the existence of procedural safeguards is sometimes viewed as part of the lawfulness requirement and sometimes subsumed under the 'fair balance' assessment. Occasionally, the Court has even combined these questions into a single general test.[29]

In any event, even though Protocol 1 Article 1 does not contain requirements of a procedural nature, the Court has interpreted it to mean that anyone affected by measures interfering with the right to property must be given a reasonable opportunity of putting his or her case to the competent authorities for the purpose of effectively challenging those measures.[30] This interpretation follows from the Court's understanding of the rule of law.

---

27 See, in relation to Article 6, *Al-Dulimi and Montana Management Inc. v. Switzerland* (5809/08) judgment [GC] 21 June 2016, para. 145, where the Court held that '[o]ne of the fundamental components of European public order is the principle of the rule of law, and arbitrariness constitutes the negation of that principle'.

28 R Spano, 'The Rule of Law as the Lodestar of the European Convention on Human Rights: The Strasbourg Court and the Independence of the Judiciary' (2021) *European Law Journal* 5.

29 See e.g. *Lekić v. Slovenia* (n 17), para. 95.

30 See e.g. *Sovtransavto Holding v. Ukraine* (48553/99) judgment 25 July 2002, para. 96, *Capital Bank AD v. Bulgaria* (49429/99) judgment 24 November 2005, para. 134, *Anheuser-Busch Inc. v. Portugal* (73049/01) judgment [GC] 11 January 2007, para. 83, and *Pye v. the United Kingdom* (n 9), para. 57.

Many legal systems recognise that procedural safeguards must be in place to protect against arbitrary interference with property. For example, the Fifth Amendment to the United States Constitution states that '[n]o person shall be deprived of life, liberty or property without due process of law'. As noted above, the right to property exists solely by virtue of the law, and can be granted and taken away by the State through the mere exercise of legislative authority. Thus, in many legal systems it is regarded as important that the right to property be attended by certain minimum procedural rights.

Procedural review by courts is also a well-known concept to national administrative lawyers. In many jurisdictions, ideals of democracy and the rule of law have given rise to a set of predominantly procedural principles – the right of affected persons to be heard before a decision is made, the right to be heard by an impartial decision-maker, the requirement that the decision-maker give reasons for their decision, the requirement of transparency as to information relied upon, and so on.[31]

At a fundamental level, procedural guarantees uphold the legitimacy of the legal system, because the absence of due process in the determination of private interests inevitably taints outcomes and results as illegitimate. In line with this, the theory of procedural justice emphasises the fundamental importance of procedural fairness in shaping citizens' satisfaction and compliance with the outcome of a legal process and, ultimately, in strengthening the legitimacy of legal institutions.[32]

4.2 *Availability of Proceedings*

That Protocol 1 Article 1 contains rights of a procedural nature is now firmly established in the case law. Judging from the Court's reasoning, the absence of procedural guarantees appears to have become an increasingly important factor in the assessment of whether interference with the right to property is justified, sometimes taking the form of absolute requirements.[33] This section will take a closer look at how this tendency of 'proceduralisation' has manifested itself in the case law.

---

31 See e.g. A Nussberger, 'Procedural Review by the ECHR: View from the Court' in J Gerards and E Brems (eds), *Procedural Review in European Fundamental Rights Cases* (Cambridge University Press 2017) 161–176.

32 E Brems and L Lavrysen, 'Procedural Justice in Human Rights Adjudication: The European Court of Human Rights' (2013) 35 *Human Rights Quarterly* 176–200.

33 See e.g. P De Sena, 'Economic and Non-Economic Values in the Case Law of the European Court of Human Rights' in P-M Dupuy et al. (eds), *Human Rights in International Investment Law and Arbitration* (Oxford University Press 2009), 215.

It is natural to begin with the requirement that proceedings must be available to anyone subjected to interference with the right to property. The basic idea is that everyone should be able to challenge governmental actions and decisions adverse to their economic rights or interests. In order for that possibility to be real and effective, the body responsible for reviewing those actions or decisions must be competent to rule on the lawfulness and conventionality of those decisions with binding effect and in accordance with a procedure prescribed by law.[34]

Access to justice is one of the basic elements of the rule of law in the ECHR system. It has been regarded as an implied right in Article 6 para. 1 since *Golder v. the United Kingdom*, where the Court famously proclaimed that 'in civil matters one can scarcely conceive of the rule of law without there being a possibility of having access to the courts'.[35] A similar rationale appears to have motivated the emergence of this requirement in the case law under Protocol 1 Article 1.

In *Fredin v. Sweden*, the applicants argued that as a result of the absence of any judicial review, the Swedish system did not contain adequate safeguards against abuse to meet the procedural requirements embodied in Protocol 1 Article 1 and that the decision had been unlawful and arbitrary. The Court did not share these views. Rather, the matter fell to be considered under Article 6 of the Convention.[36]

A few years later, in *Hentrich v. France*, the Court found that the applicant's ability to effectively challenge the interference in question was relevant to the 'fair balance' requirement under Protocol 1 Article 1. The law gave the State a right of preemption when properties were transferred at a price which, in the opinion of the tax authorities, was lower than the market price. In the applicant's case, the State had exercised its right of first refusal in an arbitrary and unpredictable manner. The Court concluded that the burden borne by the applicant 'could have been rendered legitimate only if she had had the possibility ... of effectively challenging the measure taken against her'.[37]

The Court ruled in line with the same principles in *Capital Bank AD v. Bulgaria*, but here the lack of procedural safeguards was subsumed under the lawfulness requirement. The applicant company's banking licence had

34 See, in relation to Article 6, *Benthem v. the Netherlands* (8848/80) judgment 23 October 1985.

35 *Golder v. the United Kingdom* (n 11), para. 34 *in fine*.

36 *Fredin v. Sweden (no. 1)* (12033/86) judgment 18 February 1991, para. 50.

37 *Hentrich v. France* (13616/88) judgment 22 September 1994, para. 49.

been revoked by the national bank on the ground of insolvency, as a result of which the bank was put into compulsory liquidation. The applicant company had been notified of the national bank's decision only after it had been taken, the national bank had no legal obligation to take the applicant bank's submissions into account, and there was no subsequent possibility for an administrative or judicial review of the decision.

The Court accepted that in certain situations there may be a need to act expeditiously and without advance notice in order to avoid irreparable harm to the banking system. Yet the circumstances did not give rise to such urgency that any delay occasioned by some sort of formal procedure would have been unduly prejudicial. A number of options existed to safeguard the interests of the bank's depositors and other creditors while maintaining the stability of the banking system. The law in force opted for the drastic solution of dispensing with any sort of proceedings, and this solution made the interference unlawful within the meaning of Protocol 1 Article 1.[38]

4.3 *Effectiveness of Proceedings*

Inherent in the notion of access to justice is the expectation that proceedings must be sufficiently effective – hence the maxim: 'Justice delayed is justice denied'. The right to a determination within a reasonable time has played a prominent role in the Court's case law under Article 6, but the Court acknowledges that requirements of effectiveness must necessarily reflect the complexity and importance of the case. As under Article 6, the proceedings applicable to interference in the right to property under Protocol 1 Article 1 must strike a balance between safeguards on one hand, and efficiency and economy on the other.[39]

The Court has taken the view that ineffective proceedings may effectively hamper the peaceful enjoyment of property contrary to the principle of 'fair balance'. In this connection, it has taken into consideration the length of time it took to challenge the measures restricting the applicant's rights.[40]

---

38 *Capital Bank AD v. Bulgaria* (49429/99) judgment 24 November 2005, paras. 138–139. See also *Družstevní Záložna Pria and Others v. the Czech Republic* (72034/01) judgment 31 July 2008, para. 95, and *Project-Trade d.o.o. v. Croatia* (1920/14) judgment 19 November 2020, paras. 84–86.

39 See generally O J Settem, *Applications of the 'Fair Hearing' Norm in ECHR Article 6 (1) to Civil Proceedings – With Special Emphasis on the Balance between Procedural Safeguards and Efficiency* (Springer Verlag 2016) 65.

40 In the case of *Sporrong and Lönnroth*, for example, the enjoyment of the right of property was impeded for a total period of 25 years in the case of one applicant, and of 12 years in the case of the other, see *Sporrong and Lönnroth v. Sweden* (7151/75; 7152/75)

Effective proceedings further presuppose that the relevant organs have jurisdiction. In *Immobiliare Saffi v. Italy*, the Court concluded that no domestic court had jurisdiction to rule on the impact which the delay in enforcing eviction orders might have in a particular landlord's situation. There were no other safeguards in place to ensure that the operation of the system and its impact on a landlord's property rights were neither arbitrary nor unforeseeable. The absence of procedural safeguards imposed an excessive burden on the landlords in terms of their ability to dispose of their property.[41]

Conversely, the fact that judicial remedies were available to the applicant but left unused has been held against the applicant in the 'fair balance' assessment.[42] In the case of *Gasus Dosier- und Fördertechnik GmbH*, for example, the Court observed that, under Dutch law, third parties whose goods are seized could have the seizure reviewed by a tribunal under a procedure which satisfied the requirements of Article 6 para. 1 ECHR. In view of the fact that the applicant company had not availed itself of that opportunity, the 'fair balance' requirement under Protocol 1 Article 1 was not upset, in the Court's view.[43]

5 Safeguards against Arbitrariness at the Domestic Level

5.1 *Fairness in Proceedings*

If the Court is satisfied that proceedings have been available and reasonably effective, the question becomes whether they provided the applicant a fair opportunity of defending his or her interests.[44] Procedural fairness as an ideal is central to Article 6 and to the Convention as a whole. As Bårdsen has observed, securing fairness in proceedings is imperative not only in its own right, but 'as a foundation stone for protection against the abuse of

---

judgment 23 September 1982, para. 72. See also *Matos e Silva, Lda., and Others v. Portugal* (15777/89) judgment 16 September 1996, para. 79, and *Uzan and Others v. Turkey* (19620/05; 41487/05; 17613/08; 19316/08) judgment 5 March 2019, para. 207.

41 *Immobiliare Saffi v. Italy* (22774/93) judgment [GC] 28 July 1999, para. 54.

42 See e.g. *Air Canada v. the United Kingdom* (18465/91) judgment 5 May 1995, para. 46.

43 *Gasus Dosier – und Fördertechnik GmbH v. the Netherlands* (15375/89) judgment 23 February 1995, para. 73.

44 See e.g. *Bäck v. Finland* (37598/97) judgment 20 July 2004, para. 63, *Wittek v. Germany* (37290/97) judgment 12 December 2002, para. 55, and *Forrer-Niedenthal v. Germany* (47316/99) judgment 20 February 2003, paras. 44–45.

power, it is even decisive in order to establish and preserve the rule of law as a societal, democratic credo'.[45]

The essence of the fairness standard in Protocol 1 Article 1 is that the procedure must be adversarial, comply with the principle of equality of arms, and allow for a real discussion of aspects that are important for the outcome of the case.[46] In ascertaining whether proceedings are fair, the Court has come to take a comprehensive view of the applicable procedures.[47]

In this particular context, the applicant's case must be subjected to an individual assessment.[48] The Court has generally reacted negatively to the blanket and inflexible nature of restrictions in property which are not subject to any individual review or exception.[49] The question is whether the procedure applied provided the applicant a fair possibility of defending his or her interests, and this question must necessarily be answered in the light of the concrete circumstances.[50] The nature of the fairness standard is best illustrated through examples from different branches of the case law.

5.1.1 Expropriation

When property is subject to expropriation the Court requires that a procedure be in place which ensures an adequate assessment of the consequences – that compensation granted is reasonable in relation to the value of the expropriated property, that the holders of the right to compensation are identified correctly, and that any other issue relating to the expropriation is settled.[51] In *Bistrović v. Croatia*, for example, expropriation meant that the

---

45 A Bårdsen, 'Reflections on "Fair Trial" in Civil Proceedings According to Article 6 para. 1 of the European Convention on Human Rights' (2007) 51 *Scandinavian Studies in Law* 100.

46 See e.g. *G.I.E.M., S.r.l. and Others v. Italy* (1828/06; 34163/07; 19029/11) judgment [GC] 28 June 2018, para. 302. See also *Družstevni Záložna Pria and Others v. the Czech Republic* (n 38), paras. 94–95, where the Court found a violation on account of a refusal by the receiver of a credit union to grant its directors access to the union's accounting documents, which would have enabled them to show that it was financially sound.

47 See e.g. *Jokela v. Finland* (28856/95) judgment 21 May 2002, para. 45.

48 See e.g. *Spadea and Scalabrino v. Italy* (12868/87) judgment 28 September 1995, paras. 37–40. See also *Lohuis and Others v. the Netherlands* (37265/10) decision 30 April 2013, paras. 59–60, and *Plaisier B.V. and Others v. the Netherlands* (46184/16; 47789/16; 19958/17) decision 14 November 2017, para. 91.

49 *Zelenchuk and Tsytsyura v. Ukraine* (846/16; 1075/16) judgment 22 May 2018, para. 144.

50 See e.g. *Microintelect OOD v. Bulgaria* (34129/03) judgment 4 March 2014, paras. 38–50.

51 See e.g. *Efstathiou and Michailidis & Co. Motel Amerika v. Greece* (55794/00) judgment 10 July 2003, para. 29, and *Alfa Glass Anonymi Emboriki Etairia Yalopinakon v. Greece* (74515/13) judgment 28 January 2021, para. 36.

applicants could no longer continue farming on the remaining part of the land where their home was located. The Court observed that proceedings before domestic courts must conform to the rule of law, and that the rights guaranteed by the Convention would be illusory and theoretical in the absence of any obligation for a judicial authority to give reasons for their decisions. Without requiring a detailed response to each argument presented before a court, this obligation nevertheless presupposes the right of a party to the proceedings to have his or her essential contentions carefully examined with respect to the consequences of the expropriation.[52]

5.1.2 Regulation of Licensed Business

In cases concerning the regulation of licensed businesses, the Court expects domestic authorities to follow a genuine and consistent policy. The case of *Megadat.com* SRL *v. Moldova* concerned a company which had lost its licence to provide internet services due to its failure to inform the authorities about a change in its street address. It had not had an opportunity to appear and explain its position before the national regulatory agency, and the domestic court of appeal had decided the ensuing case – which concerned the applicant company's economic survival – in its absence. Importantly, the Court noted that no balancing exercise appeared to have been carried out at the domestic level between the general issue at stake and the sanction applied to the applicant company.[53] This failure resulted in a violation of Protocol 1 Article 1.

5.1.3 Tax Enforcement Proceedings

Enforcement proceedings aimed at securing the payment of taxes or other contributions must allow the legal subject a fair opportunity to comply. In OAO *Neftyanaya Kompaniya Yukos v. Russia*, the authorities had been unyielding as to the pace of the enforcement proceedings, acting very swiftly and constantly refusing to concede to the applicant company's demands for additional time. In addition, the applicant company had been subjected to a seven per cent enforcement fee calculated on the basis of its entire tax-related liability and unrelated to the actual amount of the enforcement

52 See *Bistrović v. Croatia* (25774/05) judgment 31 May 2007, para. 37. See also *Katikaridis and Others v. Greece* (19385/92) judgment 15 November 1996, para. 49, *Papachelas v. Greece* (31423/96) judgment [GC] 25 March 1999, paras. 53–54, and *Efstathiou and Michailidis & Co. Motel Amerika v. Greece* (n 51), para. 33.

53 *Megadat.com* SRL *v. Moldova* (21151/04) judgment 8 April 2008, paras. 73–74. See also *Vékony v. Hungary* (65681/13) judgment 13 January 2015, paras. 32–36.

expenses borne by the bailiffs. Payment of the enforcement fee – which amounted to more than EUR 1.16 billion – could not be suspended or rescheduled, and because of its rigid application, it contributed significantly to the applicant company's demise. Given the pace of the enforcement proceedings, the obligation to pay the full enforcement fee and the authorities' failure to take proper account of the consequences of their actions, the Court concluded that the domestic authorities failed to strike a 'fair balance' between the legitimate aims sought and the measures employed.[54]

5.1.4 Confiscation Measures

Confiscation measures are often subject to compulsory judicial review, which invites the Court to consider the quality of the domestic legal proceedings. In *Air Canada v. the United Kingdom*, the applicant company complained of arbitrary confiscation when one of its aeroplanes, onto which cannabis resin had been brought without its knowledge, was temporarily seized. The Court was satisfied that the measures complained of were designed to combat international drug-trafficking and justified in the public interest.[55] However, no reasons were given by the authorities for the seizure, and the applicant company was effectively penalised for a crime committed by a person unknown to it. The Court noted that since the judicial review procedure available in domestic law was not an appeal on the merits, it was sufficient to satisfy the requirements of the second paragraph of Protocol 1 Article 1.[56] Bearing in mind the State's margin of appreciation in this area, the Court was satisfied that a 'fair balance' had been achieved.

It transpires from these examples that the Court's assessment of whether the applicant has had a reasonable opportunity of putting his or her case to the competent authorities is not strictly procedural in nature. When examining whether the proceedings were 'fair' in the context of the specific interference, the Court is called to evaluate substantive elements such as presumptions in domestic legislation, the transparency of domestic policies, the conduct of proceedings and the quality of domestic review.

---

54 *OAO Neftyanaya Kompaniya Yukos v. Russia* (n 18), paras. 656–657.

55 *Air Canada v. the United Kingdom* (18465/91) judgment 5 May 1995, para. 42.

56 Ibid. para. 46. See also *AGOSI v. the United Kingdom* (9118/80) judgment 24 October 1986, para. 55.

5.2 *The Quality of the Assessments Made by Domestic Authorities – Revisiting the Court's Process-Based Review*

At this point, we venture beyond the blurry boundaries of the procedural dimension to revisit a novel aspect of the Court's supervisory function. As discussed in Chapter 9, many observers have noted the Court's tendency to emphasise the quality of national decision-making in its justification assessment. In one sense, the Court's process-based review can be seen as an extension of the tendency of proceduralisation discussed in the present chapter. After all, it is only a small step from ensuring that domestic procedures are fair to ascertaining that the domestic organs have accounted for and balanced the relevant interests in the case.

Proceduralisation of substantive rights and process-based review must be considered separately, however.[57] Process-based review is never absolute in the sense that inadequate assessments at the domestic level *per se* lead to a violation. Nor is its normative justification found in the rule of law, as the case is for the procedural requirements. There is also an important difference in principle between reviewing the process leading up to the interference on procedural grounds and reviewing the rationale on which the interference was based. It is more accurate to view the Court's process-based review as a hybrid between procedural and substantive review, linked to the States' margin of appreciation and the principle of subsidiarity.[58]

6 Conclusion

This chapter has traced the emergence of the procedural dimension of the Court's justification assessment, which has rendered Protocol 1 Article 1 a safeguard against procedural arbitrariness at the domestic level. The

57 The literature discusses two aspects of what may be generally referred to as Strasbourg Court's 'procedural turn': On one hand, the Court's tendency to interpret substantive rights as implying obligations of a procedural nature (proceduralisation), and on the other, the Court's tendency to rely on the quality of national decision-making in the assessment of justification of interference with Convention rights (process-based review). See e.g. R Spano 'The Future of the European Court of Human Rights – Subsidiarity, Process-based Review and the Rule of Law' (2018) 18(3) *Human Rights Law Review* 8.

58 See, in relation to Article 10, *Animal Defenders International v. the United Kingdom* (48876/08) judgment [GC] 22 April 2013, para. 108, where the Court held that '[t]he quality of the parliamentary and judicial review of the necessity of the measure is of particular importance … to the operation of the relevant margin of appreciation'.

principle that interference in the right to property must be lawful is expressed in the text itself. When interpreted in the light of the principle of the rule of law, lawfulness also implies a degree of legal certainty. In line with the basic tenets formulated in *The Sunday Times*, the Court requires the legal basis for interference in the right to property to be accessible and foreseeable.

More importantly, even though Protocol 1 Article 1 contains no explicit procedural requirements, the rule of law demands a measure of protection in domestic law in the form of procedural safeguards. Anyone subjected to interference in the right to property must be given access to effective proceedings which afford a minimum of fairness. Increasingly, the Court appears to find interference to be unlawful solely due to the absence of procedural safeguards. In this way, the 'proceduralisation' of Protocol 1 Article 1 has contributed notably to the development of the right to property in the Convention.[59]

The procedural requirements in Protocol 1 Article 1 appear to be inspired by the guarantees in Article 6 para. 1 of the Convention. The requirement that procedural remedies must be available and effective derives from the principle of access to justice, which is inherent in the right to a fair trial.[60] Furthermore, the Court has incorporated the most important elements of the 'fairness' standard applicable to civil cases, in particular the expectation that proceedings in property cases must be adversarial and comply with the principle of equality of arms.

That being said, Article 6 para. 1 retains an independent function in cases involving the right to property, irrespective of any procedural rights that may follow from Protocol 1 Article 1. A violation of Article 6 of the Convention does not automatically lead to a violation of Protocol 1 Article 1 in cases where both articles are applicable.[61] Conversely, when a case involving a 'possession' is heard before a national tribunal, the applicant is always entitled to a fair hearing under Article 6. In order for the Court to find a

---

59 See J Christoffersen, *Fair Balance: Proportionality, Subsidiarity and Primarity in the European Convention on Human Rights* (Martinus Nijhoff Publishers 2009) 498, who shows that Protocol 1 Article 1 and Article 8 are the qualified provisions in the Convention most affected by the tendency of 'proceduralisation' of substantive rights. The procedural aspect of Articles 2 and 3 has evolved into a separate and autonomous duty and is nowadays taken for granted, see e.g. *Calvelli and Ciglio v. Italy* (32967/96) judgment [GC] 17 January 2002, and *Šilih v. Slovenia* (71463/01 judgment [GC] 9 April 2009, para. 159.

60 See e.g. O J Settem (n 39) 60–66.

61 See e.g. *Ukraine-Tyumen v. Ukraine* (22603/02) judgment 22 November 2007, para. 52.

violation of Protocol 1 Article 1 in overlapping cases, the unfairness established under Article 6 must have a 'direct impact' on the applicant's property rights.[62]

In *G.I.E.M., S.r.l. and Others v. Italy*, the Court held that:

> An interference with the rights provided for by Article 1 of Protocol No. 1 cannot ... have any legitimacy in the absence of adversarial proceedings that comply with the principle of equality of arms, allowing discussion of aspects that are important for the outcome of the case.[63]

This statement suggests that the procedural guarantees inherent in Protocol 1 Article 1 constitute absolute limits – in other words, that the State's failure to comply with basic procedural guarantees cannot be 'balanced out' by important public interests. Such an application would render the procedural requirements qualitatively different from the substantive elements of 'fair balance', which the Court views in a holistic perspective, allowing one factor to outweigh another. Equally, the application of procedural requirements under Protocol 1 Article 1 appears to be unqualified by any margin of appreciation.

In practice, the Court attaches different weight to procedural arguments – as the exclusive or decisive factor in some cases, and as a supporting element in others.[64] It is difficult to draw firm conclusions from the case law, but the normative impetus provided by Article 6 and the rule of law justifies the view that procedural guarantees in Protocol 1 Article 1 are different in nature from the substantive elements of 'fair balance'.[65] Rather than factors which can be balanced out by public interests, they establish absolute thresholds for justified interference. In this way, the rule of law sets firm boundaries for the exercise of balancing effective protection of the right to property against respect for the sovereignty of the Member States.

---

62 See e.g. *Sovtransavto Holding v. Ukraine* (n 31), para. 97, and *Zagrebačka banka d.d. v. Croatia* (39544/05) judgment 12 December 2013, para. 269.

63 *G.I.E.M., S.r.l. and Others v. Italy* (1828/06; 34163/07; 19029/11) judgment [GC] 28 June 2018, para. 302 (emphasis added).

64 L M Huijbers, 'The European Court of Human Rights' Procedural Approach in the Age of Subsidiarity' (2017) 6(2) *Cambridge Journal of International and Comparative Law* 193.

65 See by comparison Case C-584/10 P, *Commission and Others v. Kadi*, 18 July 2013, para. 66, where the Court of Justice of the European Union (CJEU) explained the importance of procedural obligations on the basis of the principle of the rule of law. The absolute character of procedural requirements is also reflected in the Court's famous statement in *Golder* above, see *Golder* (n 35) para. 34 *in fine*.

PART 4

CHAPTER 11

The Evolving Scope and Justification of the Right to Property in the ECHR

1 The Court's Expansive Approach to Protocol 1 Article 1's Scope of Protection

It is time to bring this book to a close. The aim has been to account for developments in the case law concerning Protocol 1 Article 1 and explain them in light of the Court's teleological method of interpretation.

With respect to the scope of the right to property, the Court has generally taken an expansive approach, as demonstrated in Part 2. Chapter 4 showed how it has developed an autonomous property concept which largely reflects the notion of property in many European jurisdictions. The Court has made clear that the term 'possessions' is not limited to ownership of physical goods, but covers various forms of limited rights in property and virtually all existing assets with economic value. In some cases, the Court has tested the limits of traditional understandings of property, particularly in the context of a human rights treaty, for example by including the right to profit among the elements of ownership.

Importantly, the Court has not limited the material scope of Protocol 1 Article 1 to interests protected as property under national law. It has expanded the property concept to positions based on 'legitimate expectations' to prevent outcomes which are at odds with the Convention's object and purpose. As might be expected, the doctrine on legitimate expectations has attracted criticism from within the Court as well as from outside observers, and it remains to be seen how far the Court will go in this direction. Nonetheless, this development shows that the rule of law, in addition to being concerned with the quality of domestic laws and the existence of judicial safeguards, sets limitations on their substantive content by requiring the law to protect citizens' legitimate expectations.

Protocol 1 Article 1 bestows the right to property on legal persons and human beings alike. The personal scope of the right to property is therefore easily established. But as discussed in Chapter 5, whose property rights are protected by the Convention is also limited by the articles governing the Court's jurisdiction and the Convention's enforcement machinery.

 | DOI:10.1163/9789004735088_012

Complaints related to Protocol 1 Article 1 has provided the Court with an opportunity to clarify the principles used to define the sphere of persons protected by the Convention. As a result of these developments, entities indirectly affected by the alleged violation, such as shareholders in a company, can in some situations achieve 'victim' status. Also, it is clearly established that the ECHR only protects property rights held by private, non-governmental entities.

The drafters' overriding concern was that the Convention should provide protection against the arbitrary deprivation of property. That intention is reflected in the *travaux préparatoires* and follows from a natural reading of the text of Protocol 1 Article 1. It is also how the article's scope and function were first understood by the Convention organs. However, the Court has ventured far beyond the drafters' original intention in its jurisprudence, as Chapter 6 showed. The 'three rules' approach represents a radical enlargement of the scope of Protocol 1 Article 1, as it has effectively empowered the Court to review all forms of interference in the right to property.

As is often the case whenever new law is formulated, the 'three rules' approach raises as many problems as it resolves. The choice of the applicable rule depends primarily on the effects of the interference on the applicant's property interests, but the purpose of the interference, the asset in question and the specific circumstances of the case also have a role to play. The criteria defining deprivation of property remain elusive. As a consequence, the Court has in some cases subsumed analogous facts under different rules and allowed the judges' subjective views to prevail.

It is problematic that the Court has failed to formulate a doctrinal test to distinguish between different forms of interference in the right to property. As long as that remains the case, the choice of the applicable 'rule' is vulnerable to arbitrary outcomes. Such concerns may be alleviated by the fact that requirements for justification have evolved to become more or less uniform. Yet for States and legal subjects alike it is paramount to know how the principles apply to the facts before them – in particular in which circumstances the owner is entitled to compensation. More transparency is needed for making that determination. It remains for the Court, therefore, to live up to its own ideals and make Protocol 1 Article 1 fully operational.

2 The Dynamics of the Court's Justification Assessment

The Court's justification assessment under Protocol 1 Article 1 is normally framed in terms of three questions, but it is more fruitful to view it as consisting of a substantive, institutional and procedural dimension. This conceptual model has at least brought out the dynamics of the Court's assessment at the justification stage. As Part 3 demonstrated, there have been developments within these dimensions, as well as in the interaction between them.

In the substantive dimension, the Court's aim is to ensure that the right to property is practical and effective, not theoretical and illusory. The 'fair balance' requirement is the Court's primary means to that end. Since *Sporrong and Lönnroth v. Sweden*, the Court has reviewed the proportionality of all forms of interference with the right to property under the heading of 'fair balance'. It has established an obligation for States to pay compensation in situations where the applicant has been deprived of their property, and in recent years narrowed the circumstances in which just compensation amounts to less than full market value.

As discussed in Chapter 8, the Court has subjected interference in the right to property to a heightened level of substantive scrutiny. This development is evident in at least three ways. Firstly, the 'least intrusive measure' test – although initially rejected as irrelevant to the interpretation of Protocol 1 Article 1 – has gradually become a more prominent factor in the 'fair balance' assessment.

Secondly, the Court now conducts more thorough analysis of how the interference affects the applicant in economic terms, in some situations requiring that any losses sustained be offset by compensation reflecting the value of the property. This tendency reflects Protocol 1 Article 1's primary purpose, which is to protect economic interests. The Court is increasingly inclined to find a violation when faced with measures deemed to 'control' the use of property or interfering with the general principle, and no longer allows such questions to be resolved with reference to the States' margin of appreciation.

Thirdly, in order to ensure that the right to property is effective, the Court has gone beyond a strict analysis of ends and means to look more broadly at the legal and factual circumstances in the case. The applicant's legitimate expectations and acceptance of risk are relevant, as is the conduct of the parties. In this respect, the Court's main concern appears to be to safeguard legal subjects against arbitrary treatment at the domestic level.

As discussed in Chapter 9, the Court has fielded three arguments to justify a deferential stance with regard to the right to property. Firstly, that due to their direct knowledge of their society, domestic authorities are generally better placed than the international judge to evaluate local needs and conditions. Secondly, that regulation of property involves consideration of political, economic and social issues on which opinions within democratic societies may reasonably differ widely. And thirdly, that domestic authorities should have a wide margin of appreciation in implementing social and economic policies, because decisions made by democratically accountable domestic organs enjoy more legitimacy than do those made by the Court.

These three structural arguments manifest themselves in different ways in the Court's reasoning depending on the nature of the public interest at stake. Traditionally, they have interacted with substantive arguments in ways which result in a wide margin of appreciation, with the Court's substantive review becoming more intense over time. In recent years, the Court has begun to emphasise the quality of the domestic assessments leading up to an interference with the right to property when applying the margin of appreciation. Process-based review has important implications for the Court's assessment under Protocol 1 Article 1, because it allows for an examination which can give greater effect to the principle of subsidiarity. It remains to be seen how this development will influence the protection of property rights and ECHR law more broadly in the future.

Protocol 1 Article 1 has always been an instrument for securing the rule of law in the sense that it requires that interference in the right to property must be lawful. But as Chapter 10 made clear, the Court's understanding of the rule of law has evolved over time as well. The emergence of a procedural dimension is a significant development in the Court's justification assessment.

In line with the basic tenets of *The Sunday Times*, the Court has understood the principle of legal certainty as giving rise to requirements that the legal basis for interference must be accessible and foreseeable. More importantly, even though Protocol 1 Article 1 contains no explicit procedural rights, the rule of law implies that there must be a measure of protection from arbitrariness in domestic law in the form of access to effective and fair proceedings. The procedural requirements in Protocol 1 Article 1 are different from the substantive elements in the 'fair balance' assessment in that they cannot be outweighed by important public interests and are unqualified by any margin of appreciation granted to the State. As such, the rule of law sets clear limits for the Court's balancing exercise at the justification stage.

CHAPTER 12

The Right to Property and the Rule of Law in the ECHR System

1 Contextualising the Legal Developments

The starting point for this book was observations made both by the Court itself and by outside observers that the protection of the right to property in the ECHR has undergone developments in the case law. By means of conclusion, it is worthwhile to try to offer some historical context to the developments accounted for in this book.

Traditional legal analyses of the Court's jurisprudence continue to dominate in the literature, but in recent years there has been a growing interest in the political and sociological factors that affect the operation, effectiveness and evolution of the ECHR system. Christoffersen and Rask Madsen have argued that:

> … an understanding of the rise of the European Court [of Human Rights] necessitates an analysis of the interdependency between the evolution of European human rights law and the changing socio-political and institutional contexts in which this development is embedded. However… it is imperative that the analysis does not diverge from the legal core of the ECHR system…[1]

This statement recognises, first, that an evolution of European human rights law is taking place and secondly, that the law is evolving both within a socio-political and an institutional context. The main point is that there is an interaction between the changes taking place in the law and changes in the socio-political and institutional contexts, and that the role of the Court cannot be fully understood without analysing that interaction.

In seeking to identify the forces behind jurisprudential developments related to the right to property, this book has stayed in the legal realm – what Christoffersen and Rask Madsen refer to as the 'legal core' of the ECHR

1 J Christoffersen and M Rask Madsen, 'Introduction: The European Court of Human Rights Between Law and Politics' in J Christoffersen and M Rask Madsen (eds), *The European Court of Human Rights Between Law and Politics* (Oxford University Press 2011) 2.

 | DOI:10.1163/9789004735088_013

system. It has studied judgments and decisions to see how the Court has interpreted and applied Protocol 1 Article 1. The method for analysing the developments has relied on the text, the preparatory works, legal doctrine and other legal sources.

The question, then, is whether there are factors other than sources of law that can explain the development of the right to property. In line with the cited passage, we can begin with the 'socio-political context' in which the Court operates and in which Strasbourg law develops.

At the outset, this presents us with an empirical question: Which socio-political changes have there been in the member states of the Council of Europe since 1952 that might have influenced the status of property rights? The answer, of course, will depend entirely on who is asked. Historians will probably focus on the political developments after the Second World War, the impact of the Cold War and the fall of the Berlin Wall, and the spread of democracy in Europe. Economists are likely to emphasize the birth of the European Union and the integration of a common European market. Sociologists might address the impact of technological developments. The list could go on.

Leaving aside this empirical question, there is no doubt that the law must be a reflection of the society in which it operates. As far as judge-made law is concerned, this is true for all courts of law. Unlike most other courts, however, the Strasbourg Court cannot leave the task of lawmaking to a legislator. This is one reason why it maintains that the rights in the ECHR must be practical and effective, and an important aspect of the effectiveness principle is the idea that the Convention is a 'living instrument' to be interpreted in the light of present-day conditions.

The living instrument doctrine is premised on the existence of a European consensus with regard to particular human rights issues. However, as discussed above, there are few common standards which can justify a European approach to the protection of the right to property. The Court has recognised as much, and the divergence of opinions explains why the Court has traditionally allowed a wide margin of appreciation for the States.

Chapter 8 showed how the Court has applied a heightened level of scrutiny with respect to the 'fair balance' between the individual and the general interest. In other words, it now conducts a closer examination of the effects of the interference on the individual held up against the purpose served by the interference than it did in earlier case law. Yet it is difficult to ascribe this development to an emerging or actual consensus about the importance of securing legal protection for property rights. Rather, it is the result of the Court's broader effort to ensure that the protection offered by the

Convention is effective. In the absence of any clear indications to that effect, there is little basis for establishing a causal link between the Court's heightened level of scrutiny and socio-political changes taking place in Europe. Instead, there are other factors which better explain the developments in the Court's justification assessment.

This brings us to the institutional context. The Council of Europe has undergone profound institutional changes over the past decades. After the fall of the Berlin Wall, some 20 former Communist states ratified the ECHR.[2] The influx of new countries coincided with a major reform which abolished the Commission and turned the Court into a permanent institution as of 1 January 1998. The expansion eastwards led to a great increase in the number of applications, which in turn generated new reforms of the ECHR system – in particular the 14th additional protocol, which aimed at streamlining the system for handling applications, and the 15th protocol, which emphasized the principle of subsidiarity. As a result, calls for reform have been a constant feature in discussions about the institutions in the ECHR system over the past three decades.

This book is premised on the view that the Court's interpretation and application of Protocol 1 Article 1 depends to a great degree on the institutional setting in which the Court operates. For example, the movement towards so called 'deeper subsidiarity' discussed in Chapter 9 should be seen as a result of the Council of Europe conferences on the future of the Court in Interlaken (2010), Izmir (2011), Brighton (2012) and Brussels (2015) as well as the adoption of the 15th additional protocol. The message from these conferences was that the primary responsibility for securing ECHR rights should remain with the States, where it belongs. Thus, process-based review is a means for the States and the Court of giving full effect to the subsidiarity principle.

The ultimate goal for the Court is that its interpretation and application of the Convention is legitimate. Legitimacy is ensured mainly through legal and doctrinal development which remains the crucial line of communication

2 After the fall of the Berlin Wall, the following States ratified the ECHR: Hungary (1990), Poland (1991), Bulgaria (1992), Estonia (1993), Lithuania (1993), Slovenia (1993), the Czech Republic (1993), Slovakia (1993), Romania (1993), Latvia (1995), Moldova (1995), Albania (1995), Ukraine (1995), the former Yugoslav Republic of Macedonia (1995) (later renamed North Macedonia), Russia (1996, expelled 2022), Croatia (1996), Georgia (1999), Armenia (2001), Azerbaijan (2001), Bosnia and Herzegovina (2002) and Serbia and Montenegro (later Serbia) (2003).

between the Court on one hand and the Member States and the legal subjects on the other.

The Court must maintain legitimacy in both these relations: It must maintain political legitimacy *vis-à-vis* the States. That form of legitimacy is threatened if the Court goes too far in the direction of an expansionist or activist approach to the rights and freedoms in the ECHR. Equally, the Court must maintain social legitimacy *vis-à-vis* the legal subjects. That form of legitimacy comes under pressure whenever the Convention fails to offer redress for issues which affect the wellbeing of individuals in modern-day society. But there are limits to how far the Court can go in extending protection under the ECHR. When that limit is reached, it is generally up to the institutions of the Council of Europe, rather than the Court itself, to ensure the continued legitimacy of the system.

2 The Court's Search for Legitimacy in Cases concerning the Right to Property

The right to property in the ECHR has been controversial from the outset. When the foreign ministers gathered in Rome in November 1950 to sign the European Convention on Human Rights, the text was silent on the right to property. The first attempt to include it foundered because of disagreements about the nature of the right to property as a human right which survive to this day. The debates in the Council of Europe which culminated in the adoption of the First Protocol in 1952 reflect that the drafters were preoccupied with the excesses of the totalitarian regimes seen at the time. They also recognised that the liberty and autonomy of the individual depend on the security of possessions. Like the Convention itself, Protocol 1 Article 1 was an ambivalent text, containing both a pact against totalitarian rule and the seeds of constitutional protection of the right to property at the European level.[3]

---

3 E Bates, *The Evolution of the European Convention on Human Rights: From Its Inception to the Creation of a Permanent Court of Human Rights* (Oxford University Press 2010) 10–23. The ECHR is a 'constitutional' instrument in the sense that it contains a list of fundamental rights enjoyed by individuals against government; it sets out obligations for States which are independent of the performance by other parties and apply for an infinite duration; and it creates a judicial institution with the power to review whether rights have been violated. On the other hand, the ECHR differs from a national constitution *inter alia* in the sense that the enforcement of the rights and freedoms is conditional on State consent; if a state chooses to pull out, the Court has no jurisdiction to hear complaints in

The brief and broadly formulated text has left the Court with the same dilemmas as the drafters faced: What should be the scope of the right to property in the Convention, and what should be the limits for permissible restrictions? The Court has relied on the teleological method of interpretation when resolving these issues, as this book has shown.

The Court has always seen as its task to develop the rules instituted by the Convention.[4] As it established in the *Belgian Linguistic case*, the ECHR's overriding ambition is to create an effective instrument for the protection of human rights.[5] From the outset, this ambition has made a dynamic interpretation necessary, and the inverse proposition – that the Convention should generally be interpreted restrictively out of respect for the Contracting States – has long been dead and buried.[6] As the Court's former president Bernhardt has reflected, every step taken to ensure effective protection of individual rights and freedoms restricts State sovereignty, and it is by no means the latter that in case of doubt has had priority in ECHR law.[7]

Lord Sumption has observed that the Strasbourg Court generally does not allow the applicability of the right in question to bar applications. In his analysis, it adopts an expansive definition of rights in order to have the opportunity to review all interferences on the merits. The result is that most arguments about the ECHR are not about the existence of the rights in question

relation to that State. See generally D Rietiker, 'The Principle of "Effectiveness" in the Recent Jurisprudence of the European Court of Human Rights: Its Different Dimensions and its Consistency with Public International Law – No Need for the Concept of Treaty Sui Generis' (2010) 79 *Nordic Journal of International Law* 504, and G Letsas, 'The ECHR as a Living Instrument: Its Meaning and Legitimacy' in A Føllesdal, B Peters and G Ulfstein (eds), *Constituting Europe: The European Court of Human Rights in a National, European and Global Context* (Cambridge University Press 2013) 107.

4 *Ireland v. the United Kingdom* (5310/71) judgment 18 January 1978, para. 154.

5 *Belgian Linguistic case* (1474/62 et al.) judgment 23 July 1968, para. 5.

6 See E Bates (n 3) 375. See also R Bernhardt, 'Evolutive Treaty Interpretation, Especially of the European Convention of Human Rights' (1999) *German Yearbook of International Law* 14, who concludes that the traditional principle that treaties should be interpreted restrictively and in favour of State sovereignty (*in dubio mitius*) is no longer relevant in international human rights law.

7 R Bernhardt, 'Evolutive Treaty Interpretation, Especially of the European Convention of Human Rights' (1999) *German Yearbook of International Law* 14. See also R Bernhardt, 'Thoughts on the Interpretation of Human Rights Treaties' in F Matscher and H Petzold (eds), *Protecting Human Rights: The European Dimension. Studies in Honour of Gérard J Wiarda* (Heymann 1988) 65–66, who notes that while for some kinds of treaties the original meaning will be decisive, the position is otherwise for human rights treaties: interpretation of human rights treaties falls into a special category, since the distinct object and purpose of a human rights treaty take on a special importance.

but about the operation of the exceptions and qualifications.[8] The case law under Protocol 1 Article 1 generally corroborates this analysis.

A wide scope of rights leaves it to the Court to decide on the fairness of practically any action taken by the State. On the other hand, a generous interpretation in favour of the individual is bound to create controversy. The Court has been criticised for developing a justification assessment which highlights its own role in developing standards for the use of State power over property, and for effectively usurping the power of democratically elected parliaments.[9] Such criticism is part of a broader debate arising from the concern that the exercise of balancing competing interests imbues an unelected and unaccountable judiciary with excessive political power.[10]

The Court, for its part, has never made any secret about its own authority in this regard. In one of its first cases it conceded that several provisions in the ECHR 'are worded in such a way as to require what might be called political judgments', but affirmed that the Convention organs were empowered to make such judgments, because the international protection of human rights would otherwise lose its effectiveness and very meaning.[11]

The Court's manner of reasoning at the justification stage makes it difficult for observers to say with certainty whether any particular element was sufficient to upset the 'fair balance', and if so, which element ultimately did. Moreover, as Christoffersen has observed, the balancing exercise makes it impossible to demonstrate that a specific decision is uniquely correct: the assessment leads to different results in different contexts, because the weight of factors is different in different situations.[12]

Decision-making by judges is, of course, never a purely rational and deductive exercise. To a certain extent, the balancing of interests is vulnerable to subjective preferences and differential treatment of similar cases – a fact that the Court has itself recognised.[13] Again, the functioning of the ECHR

---

8 J Sumption, *Trials of the State: Law and the Decline of Politics* (Profile Books 2019) 62.

9 See e.g. A R Çoban, *Protection of Private Property Rights within the European Convention of Human Rights* (Ashgate 2004) 191.

10 See J Sumption (n 8) 62–63, where Lord Sumption addresses the role of judges in a democracy by asking: 'Who is to decide what is necessary in a democratic society? Or what purposes are legitimate? ... Or what is a fair balance between the individual and the community?'

11 *Belgian Linguistic case* (n 5), para. 4.

12 J Christoffersen, *Fair Balance: Proportionality, Subsidiarity and Primarity in the European Convention on Human Rights* (Martinus Nijhoff Publishers 2009) 32.

13 See e.g. *Broniowski v. Poland* (31443/96) judgment [GC] 22 June 2004, para. 182, where the Grand Chamber conceded that '(b)alancing the rights at stake ... is an

system depends on the extent to which the Court's judgments are perceived as legitimate by the Member States. In the long run, the Court is only able to maintain its important supervisory role if national authorities continue to accept its judgments as reflecting authoritative interpretation and application of the Convention.

The need to ensure legitimacy is an important reason why the Court has increasingly had recourse to the Convention's object and purpose – in particular, the rule of law – when interpreting and applying Protocol 1 Article 1. The book will end with a few reflections on the role and significance of the rule of law in the Court's jurisprudence.

3 The Convention's Preeminent Object and Purpose

The right to property has long been recognised as the only real economic right protected by the Convention.[14] Under this heading, the Court has been asked to resolve disputes which are far removed from what are traditionally viewed as human rights issues – for example the protection of a company's trademark or the protection of a minority shareholder against measures imposed by the majority.

It is no surprise, therefore, that Protocol 1 Article 1 has been invoked extensively by private companies in defence of their commercial interests.[15] Even outside Strasbourg, the Court's jurisprudence concerning Protocol 1 Article 1 has been perceived as 'business friendly' to such an extent that it is relied upon in international investment arbitration disputes.[16]

---

exceptionally difficult exercise'. See also *Chassagnou and Others v. France* (25088/94; 28331/95; 28443/95) judgment [GC] 29 April 1999, partly concurring and partly dissenting opinion of Judge Caflisch joined by Judge Panţîru: 'Quite obviously the criteria used by the Court to determine whether, in a given case, a State has infringed the freedom guaranteed by Article 1 of Protocol No. 1 – through a "manifestly unreasonable" judgment on the part of the legislature and the lack of a "fair balance" and a "reasonable relationship of proportionality" – involve a considerable degree of subjectivity; it could hardly be otherwise'.

14 J Frowein, 'The Protection of Property' in R St J Macdonald et al. (eds), *The European System for the Protection of Human Rights* (Martinus Nijhoff Publishers 1993) 515.

15 See B Rainey, P McCormick and C Ovey, *Jacobs, White and Ovey: The European Convention on Human Rights* (8th edn, Oxford University Press 2020) 559.

16 See e.g. U Kriebaum, 'Is the European Court of Human Rights an Alternative to Investor-State Arbitration?' in P-M Dupuy et al. (eds), *Human Rights in International Investment Law and Arbitration* (Oxford University Press 2009) 219–245, and S Steininger, 'What's Human Rights Got To Do With It? An Empirical Analysis of Human Rights

The first president of the current Court, Luzius Wildhaber, has observed that the role of the European Court of Human Rights as a protector of property and as an economic court has perhaps been underestimated.[17] Yet the development of the right to property in the ECHR should not primarily be understood as an expression of the Court's affinity for the right to property *per se*, but rather as a result of the Court's commitment to the fundamental values enshrined in the Convention and in particular its role as guardian of the rule of law.

The Court's former president Robert Spano has pointed out that the rule of law has had increasing normative impact in Strasbourg law, and that a broader development towards a more robust enforcement of the rule of law is now permeating the Court's jurisprudence.[18] This book has shown how the principle has manifested itself in the interpretation of Protocol 1 Article 1, but this development is not unique to the right to property. The Strasbourg Court uses the rule of law as an interpretative tool for the development of all the substantive guarantees set forth in the Convention.[19]

The normative impact of the rule of law is most evident in the Court's justification assessment, where its attitude has historically been one of self-imposed deference. As noted above, the balancing of interests under Protocol 1 Article 1 inevitably involves judgments of a political nature. The emergence of the procedural dimension shows how the Court has sought to ensure that, whatever balance is struck between the right to property and the public interest, the rule of law prevails.[20]

The Court's increasing reliance on the rule of law has historical as well as practical explanations. The Court has always had to adhere to a judicial discourse that is acceptable to all the Member States and is compatible with a variety of legal systems and traditions. It must search constantly for a

References in Investment Arbitration' (2018) 31(1) *Leiden Journal of International Law* 33–58.

17 I Wildhaber and L Wildhaber, 'Recent Case Law on the Protection of Property in the European Convention on Human Rights' in C Binder et al. (eds), *International Investment Law for the 21st Century, Essays in Honour of Christoph Schreuer* (Oxford University Press 2009) 677.

18 R Spano, 'The Rule of Law as the Lodestar of the European Convention on Human Rights: The Strasbourg Court and the Independence of the Judiciary' *European Law Journal* (2021) 17.

19 S O'Leary, 'The EU Charter Ten Years On: A View from Strasbourg' in M Bobek and J Prass (eds), *The EU Charter of Fundamental Rights in the Member States* (Hart Publishing 2020) 60.

20 *Vistiņš and Perepjolkins v. Latvia* (71243/01) judgment [GC] 25 October 2012, para. 99.

balance between the effective protection of fundamental rights and the need to respect national traditions and sensitivities.[21] Following ratification by a number of Central and Eastern European States after the fall of the Berlin Wall, the Court has had to find new common denominators for its interpretation of the ECHR's rights and freedoms. Emphasis on the rule of law has made it possible to respect cultural diversity and variation while upholding uniform minimum standards of protection.

Vis-á-vis the 'old' Member States in Western Europe, emphasis on the values embodied in the Convention text serves to ensure continuity and legitimacy, and to limit the permissible interpretations of open-ended clauses. In domestic jurisdictions, property protection is based on traditions of thought about the relationship between private property rights and State power.[22] For an international court, defending the basic guarantee of the rule of law is far less controversial than advocating for stronger protection of private property against State intervention. As Judge Nussberger has reflected, it is always easier for the Court to rely on procedural arguments than on substantive arguments – in practice, procedural arguments often help judges reach compromise solutions in controversial cases.[23]

Emphasis on the Convention's fundamental values also enables due protection to be given to rights such as the right to property at the domestic level, where the primary responsibility for securing them belongs.[24] When the principles underlying the development in Strasbourg case law are identified States have a better opportunity to develop their own laws regarding property rights by finding the best way of giving expression to those

---

21 J H Gerards and H C K Senden, 'The Structure of Fundamental Rights and the European Court of Human Rights' (2009) 7(4) *International Journal of Constitutional Law* 619.

22 See e.g. R Schlatter, *Property – The History of an Idea* (Rutgers University Press 1951) and P Garnsey, *Thinking about Property: From Antiquity to the Age of Revolution* (Cambridge University Press 2007).

23 A Nussberger, 'Procedural Review by the ECHR: View from the Court' in J Gerards and E Brems (eds), *Procedural Review in European Fundamental Rights Cases* (Cambridge University Press 2017) 176. See also J Christoffersen, *Fair Balance: Proportionality, Subsidiarity and Primarity in the European Convention on Human Rights* (Martinus Nijhoff Publishers 2009) 460.

24 See e.g. *OAO Neftyanaya Kompaniya Yukos v. Russia* (14902/04) decision 29 January 2009, para. 442, where the Court noted that the mission of the Convention is to raise 'the general standards of protection of human rights and extending human rights jurisprudence throughout the community of Convention States'.

principles.[25] In this way, the Court's reliance on the object and purpose of the Convention can help give effect to the crucial principle of subsidiarity.

As the European Convention on Human Rights continues to evolve into a constitutional instrument for Europe, the rule of law is emerging as its pre-eminent object and purpose. Obviously, the basic purpose of the ECHR is to protect human rights, but the Court's jurisprudence shows how upholding the rule of law has emerged as the primary means of doing so, as well as an objective in its own right.

In the case law, the rule of law takes the form of a precept, ensuring that the ideal of the law as an impartial, independent force is maintained.[26] It serves as a common European standard for new and old Member States alike. The Court's emphasis on the rule of law is an important reason why the Convention has truly become, in the words of Judge Mosler, the 'yardstick of our civilisation' during the seven decades of its existence.[27]

---

25 See R Spano, 'The Future of the European Court of Human Rights – Subsidiarity, Process-based Review and the Rule of Law' (2018) *Human Rights Law Review* 8, who notes that the process of 'embedding' human rights norms has moved from the substantive to the procedural phase.

26 P Mahoney, 'Judicial Activism and Judicial Self-Restraint in the European Court of Human Rights: Two Sides of the Same Coin' (1990) 11 *Human Rights Law Journal* 72.

27 H Mosler, 'Report on the Results of the Colloquy', in *Fifth ECHR Colloquy (Frankfurt, 1980)* 339–340, cited in E Bates, *The Evolution of the European Convention on Human Rights: From Its Inception to the Creation of a Permanent Court of Human Rights* (Oxford University Press 2010) 359. Judge Mosler of Germany was a judge at the Court between 1959 and 1980 and Vice-President of the Court between 1974 and 1977.

Case Law

The European Court of Human Rights and the European Commission of Human Rights

16 Austrian Communes and some of their Councillors v. Austria (5767/72 et al.) decision [EComHR] 31 May 1974

A. Association and H. v. Austria (9905/82) decision [EComHR] 15 March 1984

A, B and C v. Ireland (25579/05) judgment [GC] 16 December 2010

AGOSI v. the United Kingdom (9118/80) judgment 24 October 1986

Agrotexim and Others v. Greece (14807/89) judgment 24 October 1995

Air Canada v. the United Kingdom (18465/91) judgment 5 May 1995

Airey v. Ireland (6289/73) judgment 9 October 1979

Albert and Others v. Hungary (5294/14) judgment 29 January 2019

Albert and Others v. Hungary (5294/14) judgment [GC] 7 July 2020

Al-Dulimi and Montana Management Inc. v. Switzerland (5809/08) judgment [GC] 21 June 2016

Alfa Glass Anonymi Emboriki Etairia Yalopinakon v. Greece (74515/13) judgment 28 January 2021

Ališić and *Others v. Bosnia* and *Herzegovina, Croatia, Serbia, Slovenia and the former Yugoslav Republic of Macedonia* (60642/08) judgment [GC] 16 July 2014

Aliyev v. Azerbaijan (68762/14; 71200/14) judgment 20 September 2018

Allan Jacobsson v. Sweden (No 1) (10842/84) judgment 25 October 1989

Almeida Garrett, Mascarenhas Falcão and Others v. Portugal (29813/96; 30229/96) judgment 11 January 2000

Al-Skeini and Others v. the United Kingdom (55721/07) judgment [GC] 7 July 2011

Amat-G Ltd and Mebaghishvili v. Georgia (2507/03) judgment 27 September 2005

Amato Gauci v. Malta (47045/06) judgment 15 September 2009

Ambruosi v. Italy (31227/96) judgment 19 October 2000

Andrejeva v. Latvia (55707/00) judgment [GC] 18 February 2009

Anheuser-Busch Inc. v. Portugal (73049/01) judgment 11 October 2005

Anheuser-Busch Inc. v. Portugal (73049/01) judgment [GC] 11 January 2007

Animal Defenders International v. the United Kingdom (48876/08) judgment [GC] 22 April 2013

Anonymos Touristiki Etairia Xenodocheia Kritis v. Greece (35332/05) judgment 21 February 2008

Anttila v. Finland (16248/10) decision 19 November 2013

Arras and Others v. Italy (17972/07) judgment 14 February 2012

Arsovski v. The former Yugoslav Republic of Macedonia (30206/06) judgment 7 February 2019
Artico v. Italy (6694/74) judgment 13 May 1980
Autronic AG v. Switzerland (12726/87) judgment 22 May 1990
Avotiņš v. Latvia (17502/07) judgment [GC] 23 May 2016
Axel Springer AG v. Germany (39954/08) judgment [GC] 7 February 2012
Ayuntamiento de Mula v. Spain (55346/00) decision 1 February 2001
Azienda Agricola Silverfunghi S.a.s. and Others v. Italy (48357/07 et al.) judgment 24 June 2014
Balan v. Moldova (19247/03) judgment 29 January 2008
Banér v. Sweden (11763/85) decision [EComHR] 9 March 1989
Banković and Others v. Belgium and Others (52207/99) decision [GC] 12 December 2001
Bata v. the Czech Republic (43775/05) decision 24 June 2008
Bayatyan v. Armenia (23459/03) judgment [GC] 7 July 2011
Beinarovič and Others v. Lithuania (70520/10; 21920/10; 41876/11) judgment 12 June 2018
Béla Németh v. Hungary (73303/14) judgment 17 December 2020
Béláné Nagy v. Hungary (53080/13) judgment 10 February 2015
Béláné Nagy v Hungary (53080/13) judgment [GC] 13 December 2016
Benthem v. the Netherlands (8848/80) judgment 23 October 1985
Beyeler v. Italy (33202/96) judgment [GC] 5 January 2000
Bimer S.A. v. Moldova (15084/03) judgment 10 July 2007
Bistrović v. Croatia (25774/05) judgment 31 May 2007
Bittó and Others v. Slovakia (30255/09) judgment 28 January 2014
Bosphorus Hava Yolları Turizm ve Ticaret Anonim Şirketi v. Ireland (45036/98) judgment [GC] 30 June 2005
Bowler International Unit v. France (1946/06) judgment 23 July 2009
Bouyid v. Belgium (23380/09) judgment [GC] 28 September 2015
Bramelid and Malmström v. Sweden (8588/79; 8589/79) decision [EComHR] 12 October 1982
Bramelid and Malmström v. Sweden (8588/79; 8589/79) report 12 December 1983
Breisacher v. France (76976/01) decision 26 August 2003
Broniowski v. Poland (31443/96) judgment [GC] 22 June 2004
Brosset-Triboulet and Others v. France (34078/02) judgment [GC] 29 March 2010
Bruncrona v. Finland (41673/98) judgment 16 November 2004
Buffalo S.r.l. in liquidation v. Italy (38746/97) judgment 3 July 2003
Bäck v. Finland (37598/97) judgment 20 July 2004
Cacciato v. Italy (60633/16) decision 16 January 2018

Calvelli and Ciglio v. Italy (32967/96) judgment [GC] 17 January 2002
Capital Bank AD v Bulgaria (49429/99) decision 9 September 2004
Capital Bank AD v. Bulgaria (49429/99) judgment 24 November 2005
Case 'relating to certain aspects of the laws on the use of languages in education in Belgium' v. Belgium (1474/62 et al.) judgment 23 July 1968
Cassar v. Malta (50570/13) judgment 30 January 2018
Centro Europa 7 S.r.l. and Di Stefano v. Italy (38433/09) judgment [GC] 7 June 2012
Chapman v. the United Kingdom (27238/95) judgment [GC] 18 January 2001
Chassagnou and Others v. France (25088/94; 28331/95; 28443/95) judgment [GC] 29 April 1999
Chiragov and Others v. Armenia (13216/05) judgment [GC] 16 June 2015
Comingersoll S.A. v. Portugal (35382/97) judgment [GC] 6 April 2000
Communauté genevoise d'action syndicale (CGAS) v. Switzerland (21881/20) judgment 15 March 2022
Cooperativa La Laurentina v. Italy (23529/94) judgment 2 August 2001
Coopérative des agriculteurs de la Mayenne and Coopérative laitière Maine-Anjou v. France (16931/04) decision 10 October 2006
Cosmos Maritime Trading and Shipping Agency v. Ukraine (53427/09) judgment 27 June 2019
CRASH 2000 OOD and Others v. Bulgaria (49893/07) decision 17 December 2013
Credit and Industrial Bank v. the Czech Republic (29010/95) judgment 21 October 2003
Credit Europe Leasing Ifn S.A. v. Romania (38072/11) judgment 21 July 2020
Danderyds kommun v. Sweden (52559/99) decision 7 June 2001
de Buck v. Belgium (1420/62) decision [EComHR] 18 December 1963
De la Cierva Osorio de Moscoso and Others v. Spain (41127/98 et al.) decision 28 October 1999
Denisov v. Ukraine (76639/11) judgment [GC] 25 September 2018
Depalle v. France (34044/02) judgment [GC] 29 March 2010
Di Marco v. Italy (32521/05) judgment 26 April 2011
Doğan and Others v. Turkey (8803/02 et al.) judgment 29 June 2004
Družstevní záložna Pria and Others v. the Czech Republic (72034/01) judgment 31 July 2008
Dudgeon v. the United Kingdom (7525/76) judgment 22 October 1981
Durini v. Italy (19217/91) decision [EComHR] 12 January 1994
Dzemyuk v. Ukraina (42488/02) judgment 4 September 2014
Edward Zammit Maempel and Cynthia Zammit Maempel v. Malta (3356/15) judgment 15 January 2019
Edwards v. Malta (17647/04) judgment 24 October 2006
EEG-Slachthuis Verbist Izegem v. Belgium (60559/00) decision 10 November 2005

Efstathiou and Michailidis & Co. Motel Amerika v. Greece (55794/00) judgment 10 July 2003
Elia S.r.l. v. Italy (37710/97) judgment 2 August 2001
Engel and Others v. the Netherlands (5100/71 et al.) judgment 8 June 1976
Erbs v. France (23313/94) decision [EComHR] 18 May 1995
Fenech v. Malta (19090/20) judgment 1 March 2022
Ferrazzini v. Italy (44759/98) judgment [GC] 12 July 2001
Ferretti v. Italy (25083/94) decision [EComHR] 26 February 1997
Forminster Enterprises Limited v. the Czech Republic (38238/04) judgment 9 October 2008
Forrer-Niedenthal v. Germany (47316/99) judgment 20 February 2003
Frascino v. Italy (35227/97) judgment 11 December 2003
Fredin v. Sweden (no. 1) (12033/86) judgment 18 February 1991
Frizen v. Russia (58254/00) judgment 24 March 2005
G.J. v. Luxembourg (21156/93) judgment 26 October 2000
G.I.E.M. S.r.l. and Others v. Italy (1828/06; 34163/07; 19029/11) judgment [GC] 28 June 2018
Gasus Dosier – und Fördertechnik GmbH v. the Netherlands (15375/89) judgment 23 February 1995
Gaygusuz v. Austria (17371/90) judgment 16 September 1996
Georgescu and Prodas Holding S.A. v. Romania (25830/03) decision 27 May 2014
Ghigo v. Malta (31122/05) judgment 26 September 2006
Gillow v. the United Kingdom (9063/80) report [EComHR] 3 October 1984
Golder v. the United Kingdom (4451/70) judgment 21 February 1975
Gratzinger and Gratzingerova v. the Czech Republic (39794/98) decision [GC] 10 July 2002
Gubarev and Serdyukov v. Russia (42334/06) decision 18 June 2019
Gudmundsson v. Iceland (511/59) decision [EComHR] Yearbook III (1960)
Guiso-Gallisay v. Italy (58858/00) judgment [GC] 22 December 2009
Handyside v. the United Kingdom (5493/72) judgment 7 December 1976
Hatton and Others v. the United Kingdom (36022/97) judgment [GC] 8 July 2003
Hellborg v. Sweden (47473/99) judgment 28 February 2006
Hentrich v. France (13616/88) judgment 22 September 1994
Hirst v. the United Kingdom (No. 2) (74025/01) judgment [GC] 6 October 2005
Hutten-Czapska v. Poland (35014/97) judgment [GC] 19 June 2006.
Håkansson and Sturesson v. Sweden (11855/85) judgment of 21 February 1990
Ian Edgar (Liverpool) Limited v. the United Kingdom (37683/97) decision 25 January 2000.
Iatridis v. Greece (31107/96) judgment [GC] 25 March 1999
Identoba and Others v. Georgia (73235/12) judgment 12 May 2015

Imbert de Trémiolles v. France (25834/05; 27815/05) decision 4 January 2008
Immobiliare Saffi v. Italy (22774/93) judgment [GC] 28 July 1999
International Bank for Commerce and Development AD and Others v. Bulgaria (7031/05) judgment 2 June 2016
Ireland v. the United Kingdom (5310/71) judgment 18 January 1978
Islamic Republic of Iran Shipping Lines v. Turkey (40998/98) judgment 13 December 2007
J.A. Pye (Oxford) Ltd and J.A. Pye (Oxford) Land Ltd v. the United Kingdom (44302/02) judgment [GC] 30 August 2007
Jahn and Others v. Germany (46720/99; 72203/01; 72552/01) judgment [GC] 30 June 2005
James and Others v. the United Kingdom (8793/79) judgment 21 February 1986
JKP Vodovod Kraljevo v. Serbia (57691/09; 19719/10) decision 16 October 2018
Jokela v. Finland (28856/95) judgment 21 May 2002
Johnston and Others v. Ireland (9697/82) judgment 18 December 1986
Kamoy Radyo Televizyon Yayıncılık ve Organizasyon A.Ş. v. Turkey (19965/06) judgment 16 April 2019
Katikaridis and Others v. Greece (19385/92) judgment 15 November 1996
Katte Klitsche de la Grange v. Italy (12539/86) judgment 27 October 1994
Khoroshenko v. Russia (41418/04) judgment [GC] 30 June 2015
Kind v. Germany (44324/98) decision [EComHR] 30 March 2000
KIPS DOO and Drekalović v. Montenegro (28766/06) judgment 26 June 2018
Kirilova and Others v. Bulgaria (42908/98 et al.) judgment 9 June 2005
Kirovogradoblenergo, PAT v. Ukraine (35088/07) judgment 27 June 2013
Klass and Others v. Germany (5029/71) judgment 6 September 1978
Klaus and Yuri Kiladze v. Georgia (7975/06) judgment 2 February 2010
Koua Poirrez v. France (40892/98) judgment 30 September 2003
Kontakt-Information-Therapie and Hagen v. Austria (11921/86) decision [EComHR] 12 October 1988
Kopecký v. Slovakia (44912/98) judgment [GC] 28 September 2004
Kotov v. Russia (54522/00) judgment [GC] 3 April 2012
Kozacıoğlu v. Turkey (2334/03) judgment [GC] 19 February 2009
Kristiana Ltd. v. Lithuania (36184/13) judgment 6 February 2018
Kurban v. Turkey (75414/10) judgment 24 November 2020
Könkämä and 38 other Saami villages v. Sweden (27033/95) decision [EComHR] 25 November 1996
Könyv-Tár Kft and Others v. Hungary (21623/13) judgment 16 October 2018
Lallement v. France (46044/99) judgment 11 April 2002
Langborger v. Sweden (11179/84) judgment 22 June 1989
Lekić v. Slovenia (36480/07) judgment [GC] 11 December 2018

Lelas v. Croatia (55555/08) judgment 20 May 2010
Lindheim and Others v. Norway (13221/08; 2139/10) judgment 12 June 2012
Lithgow and Others v. the United Kingdom (9006/80 et al.) judgment 8 July 1986
Ljubljanska banka d.d. v. Croatia (29003/07) decision 12 May 2015
Lohuis and Others v. the Netherlands (37265/10) decision 30 April 2013
Loizidou v. Turkey (15318/89) judgment [GC] 18 December 1996
M. & Co. v. Germany (13258/87) decision [EComHR] 9 February 1990
M. v. Austria (9465/81) decision [EComHR] 4 October 1984
M.A. v. Denmark (6697/18) judgment [GC] 9 July 2021
M.S.S. v. Belgium and Greece (30696/09) judgment [GC] 21 January 2011
Maggio and Others v. Italy (46286/09 et al.) judgment 31 May 2011
Magyar Helsinki Bizottság v. Hungary (18030/11) judgment [GC] 8 November 2016
Malhous v. the Czech Republic (33071/96) decision [GC] 13 December 2000
Malhous v. the Czech Republic (33071/96) judgment [GC] 12 July 2001
Malik v. the United Kingdom (23780/08) judgment 13 March 2012
Malone v. the United Kingdom (8691/79) judgment 2 August 1984
Mamatkulov and Askarov v. Turkey (46827/99; 46951/99) judgment [GC] 4 February 2005
Marckx v. Belgium (6833/74) judgment 13 June 1979
Marini v. Albania (3738/02) judgment 18 December 2007
Matczyński v. Poland (32794/07) judgment 15 December 2015
Matos e Silva, Lda., and Others v. Portugal (15777/89) judgment 16 September 1996
Matthews v. the United Kingdom (24833/94) judgment [GC] 18 February 1999
Maurice v. France (11810/03) judgment [GC] 6 October 2005
Megadat.com SRL v. Moldova (21151/04) judgment 8 April 2008
Mellacher and Others v. Austria (10522/83; 11011/84; 11070/84) report [EComHR] 11 July 1988
Mellacher and Others v. Austria (10522/83; 11011/84; 11070/84) judgment 19 December 1989
Melnychuk v. Ukraine (28743/03) decision 5 July 2005
Melo Tadeu v. Portugal (27785/10) judgment 23 October 2014
Michaud v. France (12323/11) judgment 6 December 2012
Microintelect OOD v. Bulgaria (34129/03) judgment 4 March 2014
Mouvement raëlien suisse v. Switzerland (16354/06) judgment [GC] 13 July 2012
Müller v. Austria (5849/72) decision [EComHR] 16 December 1974
N.K.M. v. Hungary (66529/11) judgment 14 May 2013
Nada v. Switzerland (10593/08) judgment [GC] 12 September 2012
Nassau Verzekering Maatschappij N.V. v. Netherlands (57602/09) decision 4 October 2011

National & Provincial Building Society, the Leeds Permanent Building Society and the Yorkshire Building Society v. the United Kingdom (21319/93; 21449/93; 21675/93) judgment 23 October 1997
NIT S.R.L. v. the Republic of Moldova (28470/12) judgment [GC] 5 April 2022
Nobel and Others v. the Netherlands (27126/11 et al.) decision 2 July 2013
Norwegian Confederation of Trade Unions (LO) and Norwegian Transport Workers' Union (NTF) v. Norway (45487/17) judgment 10 June 2021
O.B. Heller, a.s. and Československá obchodní banka, a.s. v. the Czech Republic (55631/00; 55728/00) decision 9 November 2004
O.B. and Others v. Norway (15997/90) decision [EComHR] 8 January 1993
O'Sullivan McCarthy Mussel Development Ltd v. Ireland (44460/16) judgment 7 June 2018
OAO Neftyanaya kompaniya Yukos v. Russia (14902/04) decision 29 January 2009
OAO Neftyanaya Kompaniya Yukos v. Russia (14902/04) judgment 20 September 2011
Offerhaus and Offerhaus v. the Netherlands (35730/97) decision 16 January 2001
OGIS-Institut Stanislas, OGEC St. Pie X and Blanche de Castille and Others v. France (42219/98; 54563/00) judgment 27 May 2004
Olczak v. Poland (30417/96) decision 7 November 2002
Öztürk v. Germany (8544/79) judgment 21 February 1984
Paeffgen GmbH v. Germany (25379/04 et al.) decision 18 September 2007
Panorama Ltd and Miličić v. Bosnia and Herzegovina (69997/10; 74793/11) judgment 25 July 2017
Papachelas v. Greece (31423/96) judgment [GC] 25 March 1999
Papamichalopoulos and Others v. Greece (14556/89) judgment 24 June 1993
Papamichalopoulos and Others v. Greece (14556/89) judgment 31 October 1995
Parrillo v. Italy (46470/11) judgment [GC] 27 August 2015
Paulet v. the United Kingdom (6219/08) judgment 13 May 2014
Phillips v. the United Kingdom (41087/98) judgment 5 July 2001
Pincová and Pinc v. the Czech Republic (36548/97) judgment 5 November 2002
Pine Valley Developments Ltd and Others v. Ireland (12742/87) judgment 29 November 1991
Pinnacle Meat Processors Company and 8 Others v. the United Kingdom (33298/96) decision [EComHR] 21 October 1998
P. Plaisier B.V. and Others v. the Netherlands (46184/16; 47789/16; 19958/17) decision 14 November 2017
Posti and Rahko v. Finland (27824/95) judgment 24 September 2002
Potomska and Potomski v. Poland (33949/05) judgment 29 March 2011
Powell and Rayner v. the United Kingdom (9310/81) report [EComHR] 19 January 1989

Pressos Compania Naviera S.A. and Others v. Belgium (17849/91) judgment 20 November 1995
Pretty v. the United Kingdom (2346/02) judgment 29 April 2002
Prince Hans-Adam II of Liechtenstein v. Germany (42527/98) judgment [GC] 12 July 2001
Project-Trade d.o.o. v. Croatia (1920/14) judgment 19 November 2020
Prötsch v. Austria (15508/89) judgment 15 November 1996
Pudas v. Sweden (10426/83) decision [EComHR] 5 December 1984
Pyrantienė v. Lithuania (45092/07) judgment 12 November 2013
R & L, s.r.o. and Others v. the Czech Republic (37926/05 et al.) judgment 3 July 2014
R.Sz. v. Hungary (41838/11) judgment 2 July 2013
Radio France and Others v. France (53984/00) decision 23 September 2003
Raimondo v. Italy (12954/87) judgment 22 February 1994
Reisner v. Turkey (46815/09) judgment 21 July 2015
Renfe v. Spain (35216/97) decision [EComHR] 8 September 1997
Roman Zakharov v. Russia (47143/06) judgment [GC] 4 December 2015
Rosenzweig and Bonded Warehouses Ltd. v. Poland (51728/99) judgment 28 July 2005
Rozhkov v. Russia (No. 2) (38898/04) judgment 31 January 2017
Ryabykh v. Russia (52854/99) judgment 24 July 2003
S. and Marper v. the United Kingdom (30562/04; 30566/04) judgment [GC] 4 December 2008
S.A. Dangeville v. France (36677/97) judgment 16 April 2002
S.C. Fiercolect Impex S.R.L. v. Romania (26429/07) judgment 13 December 2016
Sakhnovskiy v. Russia (21272/03) judgment [GC] 2 November 2010
Sargsyan v. Azerbaijan (40167/06) judgment [GC] 16 June 2015
SCEA Ferme de Fresnoy v. France (61093/00) decision 1 December 2005
Schembri and Others v. Malta (42583/06) judgment 10 November 2009
Sciortino v. Italy (30127/96) judgment 18 October 2001
Scordino v. Italy (no. 1) (36813/97) judgment [GC] 29 March 2006
Selmouni v. France (25803/94) judgment [GC] 28 July 1999
Shchokin v. Ukraine (23759/03; 37943/06) judgment 14 October 2010
Shesti Mai Engineering OOD and Others v. Bulgaria (17854/04) judgment 20 September 2011
SIA AKKA/LAA v. Latvia (562/05) judgment 12 July 2016
Sigurdur A. Sigurjónsson v. Iceland (16130/90) judgment 30 June 1993
Šilih v. Slovenia (71463/01) judgment [GC] 9 April 2009
Silver and Others v. the United Kingdom (5947/72 et al.) judgment 25 March 1983
Skibińscy v. Poland (52589/99) judgment 14 November 2006
Skubenko v. Ukraine (41152/98) decision 6 April 2004

Slavic University in Bulgaria and Others v. Bulgaria (60781/00) decision 18 November 2004

Slovenia v. Croatia (54155/16) decision [GC] 18 November 2020

Smith Kline and French Laboratories Ltd v. the Netherlands (12633/87) decision [EComHR] 4 October 1990

Smokovitis and Others v. Greece (46356/99) judgment 11 April 2002

Société Colas Est and Others v. France (37971/97) judgment 16 April 2002

Soering v. the United Kingdom (14038/88) judgment 7 July 1989

Sovtransavto Holding v. Ukraine (48553/99) judgment 25 July 2002

Soyuer and Others v. Turkey (49445/07) decision 21 June 2011

Špaček, s.r.o. v. the Czech Republic (26449/95) judgment 9 November 1999

Spadea and Scalabrino v. Italy (12868/87) judgment 28 September 1995

Sporrong and Lönnroth v. Sweden (7151/75; 7152/75) judgment 23 September 1982

State Holding Company Luganksvugillya v. Ukraine (23938/05) decision 27 January 2009

Stec and Others v. the United Kingdom (65731/01; 65900/01) decision [GC] 6 July 2005

Stec and Others v. the United Kingdom (65731/01; 65900/01) judgment [GC] 12 April 2006

Stoll v. Switzerland (69698/01) judgment [GC] 10 December 2007

Stran Greek Refineries and Stratis Andreadis v. Greece (13427/87) judgment 9 December 1994

Stretch v. the United Kingdom (44277/98) judgment 24 June 2003

Svenska Managementgruppen AB v Sweden (11036/84) decision [EComHR] 1 December 1985

Svitlana Ilchenko v. Ukraine (47166/09) judgment 4 July 2019

Terazzi S.r.l. v. Italy (27265/95) judgment 17 October 2002

Terra Woningen B.V. v. the Netherlands (20641/92) judgment 17 December 1996

The Communist Party of Russia and Others v. Russia (29400/05) judgment 19 June 2012

The former King of Greece and Others v. Greece (25701/94) judgment [GC] 23 November 2000

The Holy Monasteries v. Greece (13092/87; 13984/88) judgment 9 December 1994

The Karibu Foundation v. Norway (2317/20) judgment 10 November 2022

The Sunday Times v. the United Kingdom (No. 1) (6538/74) judgment 26 April 1979

Tkachevy v. Russia (35430/05) judgment 14 February 2012

Tre Traktörer Aktiebolag v. Sweden (10873/84) judgment 7 July 1989

Tyrer v. the United Kingdom (5856/72) judgment 25 April 1978

Ukraine-Tyumen v. Ukraine (22603/02) judgment 22 November 2007

United Communist Party of Turkey and Others v. Turkey (19392/92) judgment [GC] 30 January 1998
Urbárska obec Trenčianske Biskupice v. Slovakia (74258/01) judgment 27 November 2007
Uzan and Others v. Turkey (19620/05 et al.) judgment 5 March 2019
Vallianatos and Others v. Greece (29381/09; 32684/09) judgment [GC] 7 November 2013
Van Marle and Others v. the Netherlands (8543/79 et al.) judgment 26 June 1986
Vasileva v. Denmark (52792/99) judgment 25 September 2003
Vékony v. Hungary (65681/13) judgment 13 January 2015
Velikovi and Others v. Bulgaria (43278/98 et al.) judgment 15 March 2007
Verein Klimaseniorinnen Schweiz and Others v. Switzerland (53600/20) judgment [GC] 9 April 2024
Veselá and Loyka v. Slovakia (54811/00) decision 13 December 2005
VgT Verein gegen Tierfabriken v. Switzerland (24699/94) judgment 28 June 2001
Vijatović v. Croatia (50200/13) judgment 16 February 2016
Vinter and Others v. the United Kingdom (66069/09; 130/10; 3896/10) judgment [GC] 9 July 2013
Vistiņš and Perepjolkins v. Latvia (71243/01) judgment [GC] 25 October 2012
Von Hannover v. Germany (no. 2) (40660/08; 60641/08) judgment [GC] 7 February 2012
Vujović and Lipa D.O.O. v. Montenegro (18912/15) judgment 20 February 2018
Västberga Taxi Aktiebolag and Vulic v. Sweden (36985/97) judgment 23 July 2002
Wasa Liv Omsesidigt v. Sweden (13013/87) decision [EComHR] 14 December 1988
Wemhoff v. Germany (2122/64) judgment 27 June 1968
Werra Naturstein GmbH & Co KG v. Germany (32377/12) judgment 19 January 2017
Winterwerp v. the Netherlands (6301/73) judgment 24 October 1979
Wittek v. Germany (37290/97) judgment 12 December 2002
Wouterse, Marpa Zeeland B.V. and Metal Welding Service B.V. v. the Netherlands (46300/99) decision 1 October 2002
X and Church of Scientology v. Sweden (7805/77) decision [EComHR] 5 May 1979
X v. Austria (7830/77) decision [EComHR] 13 July 1978
X v. Federal Republic of Germany (9177/80) decision [EComHR] 6 October 1981
X v. Germany (8410/78) decision [EComHR] 13 December 1979
X v. the United Kingdom (3039/67) decision [EComHR] 26 May 1967
Xenodochiaki S.A. v. Greece (49213/99) decision 15 November 2001
Yarrow and Others v. the United Kingdom (9266/81 et al.) decision [EComHR] 28 January 1983
Young, James and Webster v. the United Kingdom (7601/76; 7806/77) judgment 13 August 1981

Zagrebačka banka d.d. v. Croatia (39544/05) judgment 12 December 2013
Ždanoka v. Latvia (58278/00) judgment [GC] 16 March 2006
Zelenchuk and Tsytsyura v. Ukraine (846/16; 1075/16) judgment 22 May 2018
Zwierzyński v. Poland (34049/96) judgment 19 June 2001
Öneryildiz v. Turkey (48939/99) judgment [GC] 30 November 2004

Other Case Law

Case C-584/10 P, *Commission and Others v. Kadi*, 18 July 2013
Case concerning the Barcelona Traction, Light & Power Co Ltd (Belgium v. Spain) (Merits) [1970] ICJ
Hulley Enterprises Limited (Cyprus) v. The Russian Federation (PCA Case No AA 226)
Pennsylvania Coal Co. v. Mahon 260 U.S. 393 (1922)
Shaughnessy v. Mezei, 345 U.S. 206 (1953)
Starrett Housing Corporation v. Government of the Islamic Republic of Iran, Interlocutory Award 19 December 1983, 4 Iran-US Claims Tribunal
Veteran Petroleum Limited (Cyprus) v. The Russian Federation (PCA Case No AA 228)
Yukos Universal Limited (Isle of Man) v. The Russian Federation (PCA Case No AA 227)

Bibliography

Books

Alexy, R *A Theory of Constitutional Rights* (Oxford University Press 2010).

Allen, T *Property and the Human Rights Act 1998* (Oxford University Press 2005).

Arai-Takahashi, Y *The Margin of Appreciation Doctrine and the Principle of Proportionality in the Jurisprudence of the ECHR* (Intersentia 2002).

Bates, E *The Evolution of the European Convention on Human Rights: From Its Inception to the Creation of a Permanent Court of Human Rights* (Oxford University Press 2010).

Bingham, T *The Rule of Law* (Allen Lane 2010).

Bjørge, E *The Evolutionary Interpretation of Treaties* (Oxford University Press 2014).

Brown, A *A Theory of Legitimate Expectations for Public Administration* (Oxford University Press 2017)

Christoffersen, J *Fair Balance: Proportionality, Subsidiarity and Primarity in the European Convention on Human Rights* (Martinus Nijhoff Publishers 2009).

Çoban, A R *Protection of Private Property Rights Within the European Convention of Human Rights* (Ashgate 2004).

Dolzer, R and Schreuer, C *Principles of International Investment Law* (Oxford University Press 2012).

Dzehtsiarou, K *European Consensus and the Legitimacy of the European Court of Human Rights* (Cambridge University Press 2015).

Ely, J W *The Guardian of Every Other Right: A Constitutional History of Property Rights* (3rd edn, Oxford University Press 2008).

Emberland, M *The Human Rights of Companies. Exploring the Structure of ECHR Protection* (Oxford University Press 2006).

Fernández Esteban, M L *The Rule of Law in the European Constitution* (Kluwer Hague 1999).

Gardiner, A *Treaty Interpretation* (2nd edn, Oxford University Press 2015).

Garnsey, P *Thinking about Property: From Antiquity to the Age of Revolution* (Cambridge University Press 2007).

Glas, L R *The Theory, Potential and Practice of Procedural Dialogue in the European Convention on Human Rights System* (Intersentia 2015).

Gowder, P *The Rule of Law in the Real World* (Cambridge University Press 2016).

Greer, S *The European Convention on Human Rights – Achievements, Problems and Prospects* (Cambridge University Press 2006).

Harris, D J et al., *Law of the European Convention on Human Rights* (4th edn, Oxford University Press 2018).

Harris, J W *Property & Justice* (Oxford University Press 2003).

Kraakman, R and others (eds) *The Anatomy of Corporate Law: A Comparative and Functional Approach* (Oxford University Press 2004).

Lautenbach, G *The Concept of the Rule of Law and the European Court of Human Rights* (Oxford University Press 2013).

Legg, A *The Margin of Appreciation in International Human Rights Law – Deference and Proportionality* (Oxford University Press 2012).

Letsas, G *A Theory of the Interpretation of the European Convention on Human Rights* (Oxford University Press 2007).

Maxwell, D 'The Human Right to Property: A Practical Approach to Article 1 of Protocol No. 1 to the ECHR' (Hart Publishing 2022).

McLachlan, C, Shore, L, and Weiniger, M, *International Investment Arbitration: Substantive Principles* (2nd edn, Oxford University Press 2017).

Merrills, J G *The Development of International Law by the European Court of Human Rights* (2nd ed. Manchester University Press 1988).

Mowbray, A *The Development of Positive Obligations under the European Convention on Human Rights by the European Court of Human Rights* (Hart Publishing 2004).

Nussberger, A *The European Court of Human Rights* (Oxford University Press 2020).

Popović, D *Protecting Property in European Human Rights Law* (Eleven International Publishing 2009).

Rainey, B, McCormick, P and Ovey, C, *Jacobs, White and Ovey: The European Convention on Human Rights* (8th edn, Oxford University Press 2020).

Rook, D *Property Law and Human Rights* (Blackstone 2001).

Schlatter, R *Property – The History of an Idea* (Rutgers University Press 1951).

Schutte, C B *The European Fundamental Right of Property: Article 1 of Protocol No. 1 to the European Convention of Human Rights: Its Origins, Its Workings and Its Impact on National Legal Orders* (Kluwer 2004).

Schwarz, K-A, *Vertrauensschutz als Verfassungsprinzip. Eine Analyse des Nationalen Rechts, des Gemeinschaftsrechts und der Beziehungen zwischen beiden Rechtskreisen* (Nomos 2002).

Shaw, M *International Law* (8th edn, Cambridge University Press 2017).

Sigron, M *Legitimate Expectations under Article 1 of Protocol No. 1 to the European Convention on Human Rights* (Intersentia 2014).

Simpson, A W B *Human Rights and the End of Empire: Britain and the Genesis of the European Convention* (Oxford University Press 2001).

Solheim, S *Eiendomsbegrepet i Den europeiske menneskerettskonvensjon* [The term 'property' in the European Convention on Human Rights] (Gyldendal 2010).

Sprankling, J G *The International Law of Property* (Oxford University Press 2014).

Sumption, J *Trials of the State Law and the Decline of Politics* (Profile Books 2019).

Tamanaha, B Z *On the Rule of Law: History, Politics, Theory* (Cambridge University Press 2004).

Van Banning, T R G *The Human Right to Property* (Intersentia 2002).

Van der Walt, A J *Constitutional Property Clauses* (Kluwer 1999).

Van Dijk, P et al. (eds), *Theory and Practice of the European Convention on Human Rights* (Intersentia 2018).

Waldron, J *The Right to Private Property* (Clarendon Press 1988).

Chapters in Books

Allen, T 'The Human Rights Act (UK) and Property Law' in J McLean (ed), *Property and the Constitution* (Hart Publishing 1999) 147–169.

Arai-Takahashi, Y 'The Margin of Appreciation Doctrine: A Theoretical Analysis of Strasbourg's Variable Geometry' in A Føllesdal, B Peters and G Ulfstein (eds), *Constituting Europe: The European Court of Human Rights in a National, European and Global Context* (Cambridge University Press 2013) 62–105.

Bernhardt, R 'Comparative Law in the Interpretation and Application of the European Convention on Human Rights' in S Busuttil (ed), *Mainly Human Rights – Studies in Honour of J. J. Cremona* (Foundation Internationale Malta 1999) 33–40.

Bernhardt, R 'Thoughts on the Interpretation of Human Rights Treaties' in F Matscher and H Petzold (eds), *Protecting Human Rights: The European Dimension. Studies in Honour of Gérard J Wiarda* (Heymann 1988) 65–72.

Bernhardt, R 'The Convention and Domestic Law' in R St J Macdonald et al. (eds), *The European System for the Protection of Human Rights* (Martinus Nijhoff Publishers 1993) 25–40.

Brems, E 'Procedural Protection – An Examination of Procedural Safeguards Read into Substantive Convention Rights' in J Gerards and E Brems (eds), *Shaping Rights in the ECHR – The Role of the European Court of Human Rights in Determining the Scope of Human Rights* (Cambridge University Press 2013) 137–161.

Christoffersen, J and Rask Madsen, M 'Introduction: The European Court of Human Rights Between Law and Politics' in J Christoffersen and M Rask Madsen (eds), *The European Court of Human Rights Between Law and Politics* (Oxford University Press 2011) 1–13.

Cremona, J J 'The Proportionality Principle in the Jurisprudence of the European Court of Human Rights' in U Beyerlin et al. (eds), *Recht zwischen Umbruch und Bewahrung – Festschrift für Rudolf Bernhardt* (Springer Verlag 1995) 323–330.

De Sena, P 'Economic and Non-Economic Values in the Case Law of the European Court of Human Rights' in Dupuy, P-M et al. (eds), *Human Rights in International Investment Law and Arbitration* (Oxford University Press 2009) 208–218.

Frowein, J 'The Protection of Property' in R St J Macdonald et al. (eds), *The European System for the Protection of Human Rights* (Martinus Nijhoff Publishers 1993) 515–530.

Fura-Sandström, E 'Business and Human Rights – Who Cares?' in L Calflisch et al. (eds), *Liber Amicorum Luzius Wildhaber: Human rights: Strasbourg Views / Droits de l'homme: regards de Strasbourg* (Engel 2007) 159–176.

Gerards, J 'Procedural Review by the ECtHR: A Typology' in J Gerards and E Brems (eds), *Procedural Review in European Fundamental Rights Cases* (Cambridge University Press 2017) 127–160.

Haeck, Y 'The Genesis of the Property Clause under Article 1 of the First Protocol to the European Convention on Human Rights', in H Vandenberghe et al. (eds), *Propriété et droits de l'homme / Property and Human Rights* (Bruylant 2006) 163–194.

Harris, J W 'Is Property a Human Right?' in J McLean (ed), *Property and the Constitution* (Hart Publishing 1997) 64–87.

Herzfeld Olsson, P 'Every Natural or Legal Person is Entitled to the Peaceful Enjoyment of His or Her Possessions: Article 1, Protocol 1 to the European Convention on Human Rights' in F Dorssemont, K Lörcher and I Schömann (eds), *The European Convention on Human Rights and the Employment Relation* (Hart Publishing 2013) 381–416.

Honoré, A M 'Ownership' in A G Guest (ed), *Oxford Essays in Jurisprudence: A Collaborative Work* (Oxford University Press 1961) 107–126.

Kriebaum, U 'Is the European Court of Human Rights an Alternative to Investor-State Arbitration?' in P-M Dupuy et al. (eds) *Human Rights in International Investment Law and Arbitration* (Oxford University Press 2009) 219–245.

Leijten, I 'Defining the Scope of Economic and Social Guarantees in the Case Law of the ECtHR' in E Brems and J Gerards (eds), *Shaping Rights in the ECHR: The Role of the European Court of Human Rights in Shaping the Scope of Human Rights* (Cambridge University Press 2013) 109–136.

Letsas, G 'The ECHR as a Living Instrument: Its Meaning and Legitimacy' in A Føllesdal and B Peters and G Ulfstein (eds), *Constituting Europe: The European Court of Human Rights in a National, European and Global Context* (Cambridge University Press 2013) 106–141.

Macdonald, R St J 'The Margin of Appreciation' in R St J Macdonald et al. (eds), *The European System for the Protection of Human Rights* (Martinus Nijhoff Publishers 1993) 83–124.

Malfliet, K 'Property Rights as Human Rights: A Post-Communist Paradigm?' in F Feldbrugge and W Simons (eds), *Human Rights in Russia and Eastern Europe* (Kluwer 2002) 163–186.

Matscher, F 'Methods of Interpretation of the Convention' in R St J Macdonald et al. (eds), *The European System for the Protection of Human Rights* (Martinus Nijhoff Publishers 1993) 63–82.

Nordtveit, E 'The Changing Role of Property Rights: An Introduction' in E Nordtveit (ed), *The Changing Role of Property Law: Rights, Values and Concepts* (Edward Elgar Publishing 2023).

Nussberger, A 'Procedural Review by the ECHR: View from the Court' in J Gerards and E Brems (eds), *Procedural Review in European Fundamental Rights Cases* (Cambridge University Press 2017) 161–176.

O'Leary, S 'The EU Charter Ten Years On: A View from Strasbourg' in Bobek, M and J Prass (eds), *The EU Charter of Fundamental Rights in the Member States* (Hart Publishing 2020) 37–68.

Pellonpää, M 'The Commission's Case-Law on Article 1 of Protocol No. 1' in M de Salvia and M E Villiger (eds), *The Birth of European Human Rights Law: Liber Amicorum Carl Aage Nørgaard* (Nomos 1998) 165–173.

Pellonpää, M 'Reflections on the Notion of "Deprivation of Possessions" in Article 1 of the First Protocol of the European Convention on Human Rights', in P Mahoney et al. (eds), *Protecting Human Rights: The European Perspective. Studies in Memory of Rolv Ryssdal* (Heymann 2000) 1087–1105.

Pellonpää, M 'Does the European Convention on Human Rights Require "Prompt, Adequate and Effective" Compensation for Deprivation of Possessions?' in M Tupamäki (ed), *Liber Amicorum Bengt Broms* (Finnish Branch of the International Law Association 1999) 374–394.

Popelier, P 'The Court as Regulatory Watchdog: The Procedural Approach in the Case-Law of the European Court of Human Rights' in P Popelier, A Mazmanyan and W Vandenbruwaene (eds), *The Role of Constitutional Courts in Multilevel Governance* (Intersentia 2012) 249–268.

Prebensen, S C 'Evolutive Interpretation of the European Convention on Human Rights' in P Mahoney et al. (eds), *Protecting Human Rights: The European Perspective. Studies in Memory of Rolv Ryssdal* (Heymann 2000) 1123–1137.

Raz, J 'The Rule of Law and Its Virtue' in J Raz, *The Authority of Law: Essays on Law and Morality* (Oxford University Press 1979) 210–229.

Ress, G 'Reflections on the Protection of Property under the European Convention on Human Rights' in S Breitenmoser et al. (eds), *Human Rights, Democracy and the Rule of Law. Liber Amicorum Luzius Wildhaber* (Nomos 2007) 625–645.

Rozakis, C and Voyatzis, P '"Le Droit au Respect de ses Biens" Une Clause Déclaratoire ou une "Omnibus" Norme' in H Vandenberghe et al. (eds), *Propriété et droits de l'homme / Property and Human Rights* (Bruylant 2006) 2–28.

Schermers, H G 'The International Protection of the Right to Property' in F Matscher and H Petzold (eds), *Protecting Human Rights: The European Dimension. Studies in Honour of Gérard J Wiarda* (Heymann 1988) 565–580.

Schreuer, C and Kriebaum, U 'The Concept of Property in Human Rights Law and International Investment Law', in S Breitenmoser et al. (eds), *Human Rights, Democracy and the Rule of Law: Liber Amicorum Luzius Wildhaber* (Nomos 2007) 752–758.

Schwaighofer, C 'Legal Persons, Organisations, Shareholders as Applicants (Article 25 of the Convention)' in M de Salvia and M E Villiger (eds), *The Birth of European Human Rights Law / L'éclosion du Droit Européen des Droits de l'Homme: Liber Amicorum Studies in Honour of Carl Aage Nørgaard – Mélanges en l'honneur de Carl Aage Nørgaard* (Nomos 1998) 321–331.

Storberget, K '17. mai og alle de andre dagene' [Constitution Day and all the other days] in A Føllesdal, M Ruud and G Ulfstein (eds), *Menneskerettighetene og Norge: Rettsutvikling, Rettsliggjøring og Demokrati* [Human Rights and Norway: Legal developments, juridification and democracy] (Universitetsforlaget 2017) 91–111.

Waldock, H 'The Evolution of Human Rights Concepts and the Application of the European Convention on Human Rights' in *Mélanges offerts à Paul Reuter: le droit international, unité et diversité* (Pedone 1981).

Waldron, J 'The Concept and the Rule of Law' in L May and P Morrow (eds), *Procedural Justice* (Routledge 2012) 200–259.

Wildhaber, L 'The Protection of Legitimate Expectations in European Human Rights Law' in M Monti et al. (eds), *Economic Law and Justice in Times of Globalisation / Wirtschaftsrecht und Justiz in Zeiten der Globalisierung, Festschrift for Carl Baudenbacher* (Nomos 2007) 253–264.

Wildhaber, L and Wildhaber, I 'Recent Case Law on the Protection of Property in the European Convention on Human Rights' in C Binder et al. (eds), *International Investment Law for the 21st Century: Essays in Honour of Christoph Schreuer* (Oxford University Press 2009) 657–677.

Articles

Allen, T 'Compensation for Property under the European Convention on Human Rights' (2007) *Michigan Journal of International Law* 287–335.

Allen, T 'Liberalism, Social Democracy and the Value of Property under the European Convention on Human Rights' (2010) 59(4) *International and Comparative Law Quarterly* 1055–1078.

Alvik, I 'Concessions in International Law' (2022) 91 *Nordic Journal of International Law* 568–594.

Anderson, D 'Compensation for Interference with Property' (1999) 6 *European Human Rights Law Review* 543–558.

Arnardóttir, O M 'Rethinking the Two Margins of Appreciation' (2016) 12 *European Constitutional Law Review* 27–53.

Bellamy, R 'The Democratic Legitimacy of International Human Rights Conventions: Political Constitutionalism and the European Convention on Human Rights' (2014) 25(4) *European Journal of International Law* 1019–1042.

Bernhardt, R 'Evolutive Treaty Interpretation, Especially of the European Convention of Human Rights' (1999) *German Yearbook of International Law* 11–25.

Bhasin, A 'Future Income versus Goodwill under A1P1 – A Distinction Without a Difference?' (2012) 17(3) *Judicial Review* 226–235.

Bjørge, E 'The Convention as a Living Instrument Rooted in the Past, Looking to the Future' (2016) *Human Rights Law Review* 243–255.

Brems, E 'The Margin of Appreciation Doctrine in the Case-Law of the European Court of Human Rights' (1996) 56 *Zeitschrift für ausländisches öffentliches Recht und Völkerrecht* 240–275.

Brems, E and Lavrysen, L 'Procedural Justice in Human Rights Adjudication: The European Court of Human Rights' (2013) 35 *Human Rights Quarterly* 176–200.

Brems, E and Lavrysen, L 'Don't Use a Sledgehammer to Crack a Nut: Less Restrictive Means in the Case Law of the European Court of Human Rights' (2015) 15 *Human Rights Law Review* 139–168.

Bårdsen, A 'Reflections on "Fair Trial" in Civil Proceedings According to Article 6 §1 of the European Convention on Human Rights' (2007) 51 *Scandinavian Studies in Law* 99–130.

Costello, C 'The Bosphorus Ruling of the European Court of Human Rights: Fundamental Rights and Blurred Boundaries in Europe' (2006) 6(1) *Human Rights Law Review* 87–130.

Craig, P 'Formal and Substantive Conceptions of the Rule of Law: An Analytical Framework' (1997) *Public Law* 467.

Crema, L 'Disappearance and New Sightings of Restrictive Interpretation(s)' (2010) 21 *European Journal of International Law* 681–700.

Dolzer, R 'Indirect Expropriations: New Developments?' (2003) 11 *NYU Environmental Law Journal* 64–93.

Endresen, C 'Taxation and the European Convention for the Protection of Human Rights: Substantive Issues' (2017) 45(8/9) *InterTax* 508–526.

Fortier, L Y and Drymer, S L 'Indirect Expropriation in the Law of International Investment: I Know It When I See It, or Caveat Investor' (2004) 19 *ICSID Review Foreign Investment Law Journal* 293–327.

Frigo, M 'Peaceful Enjoyment of Possessions, Expropriation and Control of the Use of Property in the System of the European Convention on Human Rights' (2001) 10 *Italian Yearbook of International Law* 45–69.

Frowein, J 'The European Convention on Human Rights as the Public Order of Europe' (1990) vol I *Collected Courses of the Academy of European Law* 267–358.

Gerards, J 'How to Improve the Necessity Test of the European Court of Human Rights?' (2013) 11 *International Journal of Constitutional Law* 466–490.

Gerards, J 'Pluralism, Deference and the Margin of Appreciation Doctrine' (2011) 17(1) *European Law Journal* 80–120.

Gerards, J and Senden, H 'The Structure of Fundamental Rights and the European Court of Human Rights' (2009) 7 *International Journal of Constitutional Law* 619–653.

Giupponi, B O 'Disentangling Human Rights and Investors' Rights in International Adjudication: The Legacy of the Yukos Cases' (2017) 24 *Willamette Journal of International Law and Dispute Resolution* 127.

Gragl, P 'An Olive Branch from Strasbourg? Interpreting the European Court of Human Rights' Resurrection of *Bosphorus* and Reaction to *Opinion 2/13* in the *Avotiņš* Case' (2017) 13 *European Constitutional Law Review* 551–567.

Helgesen, J E 'What Are the Limits of the Evolutive Interpretation of the European Convention on Human Rights?' (2011) 7 *Human Rights Law Journal* 275–281.

Huijbers, L M 'The European Court of Human Rights' Procedural Approach in the Age of Subsidiarity' (2017) 6(2) *Cambridge Journal of International and Comparative Law* 177–201.

Kleinlein, T 'The Procedural Approach of the European Court of Human Rights: Between Subsidiarity and Dynamic Evolution' (2019) 68 *International & Comparative Law Quarterly* 91–110.

Kriebaum, U 'Regulatory Takings: Balancing the Interests of the Investor and the State' (2007) 8 *Journal of World Investment and Trade* 717–744.

Lang, R 'Unlocking the First Protocol: Protection of Property and the European Court of Human Rights' (2008) 29 *Human Rights Law Journal* 205–215.

Lauterpacht, E 'Issues of Compensation and Nationality in the Taking of Energy Investments' (1990) 8 *Journal of Energy & National Resources Law* 241–250.

Leijten, I 'The Right to Minimum Subsistence and Property Protection under the ECHR: Never the Twain Shall Meet?' (2019) 21(4) *European Journal of Social Security* 307–325.

Letsas, G 'Two Concepts of the Margin of Appreciation' (2006) 26(4) *Oxford Journal of Legal Studies* 705–732.

Lowe, L 'Regulation or Expropriation?' (2002) 55 *Current Legal Problems* 447–466.

Mahoney, P 'Judicial Activism and Judicial Self-Restraint in the European Court of Human Rights: Two Sides of the Same Coin' (1990) 11 *Human Rights Law Journal* 57–88.

Mahoney P 'Marvellous Richness of Diversity or Invidious Cultural Relativism?' (1998) 19 *Human Rights Law Journal* 1–8.

Marks, S 'The European Convention on Human Rights and its "Democratic Society"' (1996) 66 *British Yearbook of International Law* 209–238.

Mowbray, A 'The Creativity of the European Court of Human Rights' (2005) 5 *Human Rights Law Review* 57–79.

Mowbray, A 'A Study of the Principle of Fair Balance in the Jurisprudence of the European Court of Human Rights' (2010) 10(2) *Human Rights Law Review* 289–317.

Mowbray, A 'Subsidiarity and the European Convention on Human Rights' (2015) 15 *Human Rights Law Review* 313–341.

Myklebust, I E 'The Protection of Private Ownership Rights in the ECHR and Norwegian Planning and Building Law' (2014) 32(3) *Nordic Journal of Human Rights* 220–237.

Peukert, W 'Protection of Ownership under Article 1 of the First Protocol to the ECHR' (1981) 2 *Human Rights Law Journal* 37–78.

Popelier, P 'Legitimate Expectations and the Law Maker in the Case Law of the European Court of Human Rights' (2006) 1 *European Human Rights Law Review* 10–24.

Popelier, P and Van de Heyning, C 'Procedural Rationality: Giving Teeth to the Proportionality Analysis' (2013) 9(2) *European Constitutional Law Review* 230–262.

Rietiker, D 'The Principle of "Effectiveness" in the Recent Jurisprudence of the European Court of Human Rights: Its Different Dimensions and Its Consistency with Public International Law – No Need for the Concept of Treaty *Sui Generis*' (2010) 79 *Nordic Journal of International Law* 245–277.

Rui, J P 'The Interlaken, Izmir and Brighton Declarations: Towards a Paradigm Shift in the Strasbourg Court's Interpretation of the European Convention on Human Rights' (2013) 31(1) *Nordic Journal of Human Rights* 28–54.

Ruiz Fabri, H 'The Approach Taken by the European Court of Human Rights to the Assessment of Compensation for "Regulatory Expropriations" of the Property of Foreign Investors' (2002) 11 *NYU Environmental Law Journal* 148–173.

Saul, M 'The European Court of Human Rights' Margin of Appreciation and the Processes of National Parliaments' (2015) 15 *Human Rights Law Review* 745–774.

Spano, R 'Universality or Diversity of Human Rights? Strasbourg in the Age of Subsidiarity' (2014) 14 *Human Rights Law Review* 487–502.

Spano, R 'The Future of the European Court of Human Rights – Subsidiarity, Process-based Review and the Rule of Law' (2018) *Human Rights Law Review* 1–22.

Spano, R 'The Rule of Law as the Lodestar of the European Convention on Human Rights: The Strasbourg Court and the Independence of the Judiciary' (2021) *European Law Journal* 1–17.

Spielmann, D 'Allowing the Right Margin: The European Court of Human Rights and The National Margin of Appreciation Doctrine: Waiver or Subsidiarity of

European Review?' (2012) 14 *Cambridge Yearbook of European Legal Studies* 381–418.

Steininger, S 'What's Human Rights Got To Do With It? An Empirical Analysis of Human Rights References in Investment Arbitration' (2018) 31 (1) *Leiden Journal of International Law* 33–58.

Sudre, F '"Le Droit au Respect de ses Biens" au Sens de la Convention Européenne des Droits de l'Homme' (2005) 3 *Cahiers du GRIDAUH* 67–80.

van den Broek, P 'The Protection of Property Rights under the European Convention on Human Rights' (1986) 13(1) *Legal Issues of Economic Integration* 52–90.

Underkuffler, L 'Property and Change: The Constitutional Conundrum' (2015) 91 *Texas Law Review* 2015–2037.

Winisdoerffer, Y 'Margin of Appreciation and Article 1 of Protocol No. 1' (1998) *Human Rights Law Journal* 18–20.

Other Sources

Council of Europe, *Collected Edition of the 'Travaux Préparatoires' of the European Convention on Human Rights / Recueil des Travaux Préparatoires de la Convention Européenne des Droits de l'Homme* (Martinus Nijhoff 1975–1985) vol 1–8.

Council of Europe, *Collected Edition of the Travaux Préparatoires*, Doc H(61)4.

Council of Europe, *The Right to Property under the European Convention on Human Rights: A Guide to the Implementation of the European Convention on Human Rights and Its Protocols* (Human Rights Handbook Series no. 10 2007).

Council of Europe, *Explanatory Report to Protocol No. 14 to the Convention for the Protection of Human Rights and Fundamental Freedoms, amending the control system of the Convention* (Council of Europe Treaty Series no. 194 2004).

Gauksdóttir, G *The Right to Property and the European Convention on Human Rights: A Nordic Approach* (PhD thesis, Lund University 2004).

Merriam-Webster Online Dictionary <www.merriam-webster.com/dictionary/> accessed 30 May 2025.

Sermet, L 'The European Convention on Human Rights and Property Rights' 11 *Human Rights Files* (Council of Europe Publishing 1998).

Spano, R 'The Democratic Virtues of Human Rights Law – A Response to Lord Sumption's Reith Lectures' Inaugural Bonavero Institute Annual Human Rights Lecture, London, 20 February 2020. <https://echr.coe.int/Documents/Speech_20200220_Spano_Lecture_London_ENG.pdf≥ accessed 30 May 2025.

Åhman, K *Egendomsskyddet. Äganderätten enligt artikel 1 första tilläggsprotokollet till den europeiska konventionen om de mänskliga fri- och rättigheterna* (PhD thesis, Uppsala University 2000).

Index

www.ingramcontent.com/pod-product-compliance
Lightning Source LLC
Chambersburg PA
CBHW051401240926
51852CB00002B/85